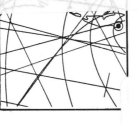

D0732425

The Loran-C
Users Guide

by Bonnie Dahl

RICHARDSONS' MARINE PUBLISHING
600 Hartrey Ave. Evanston, IL 60202

1-800-873-4057
(708) 491-0991
Fax (708) 491-0014

Library of Congress catalog card number 85-62189
ISBN 0-932647-09-X

ACKNOWLEDGEMENTS

In the writing of this book there are a number of individuals and agencies who have made important contributions. I would like to thank the *United States Coast Guard, The Institute of Navigation, The Wild Goose Association* and those manufacturers (*Digital Marine Electronics, King Marine Electronics, Micrologic, Newmar, Sitex* and *Trimble*) who provided photos and other materials to help illustrate this text. A special thank you also goes to those consultants *at Micrologic, Magnovox* and the *Coast Guard*, who gave technical assistance on different aspects of radio navigation systems.

I would like to thank Dave Brown of *Lakeland Boating* for his advice and encouragement on many aspects of the project. I would also like to thank the staff at *Cruising World* for their assistance in the publication of a two part article from this material. I want to thank the fellow boaters who allowed pictures to be taken of their receiver and antenna installations, and who shared their experiences in using the Loran system.

A very special note of appreciation goes to Hal Sherman, retired Commander of the United States Coast Guard, who read the text for technical accuracy. Commander Sherman has been involved with the development of Loran-C since 1963 in such areas as; engineering, system design, implementation and operational management. He has also assisted with the implementation of the Loran-C chains in Saudi Arabia, and has authored and co-authored several papers on Loran-C. It was a distinct honor to receive his input on the technical aspects of the material in this text.

I would also like to thank Wally Haskins who took on the formidable task of editing the manuscript.

Finally I would like to thank my husband and family who have given me encouragement and support in all phases of this project.

Bonnie Dahl

CONTENTS

To Peter and Kristin,
who have shared in many
navigation adventures.

FORWARD

The manuals which Loran manufacturers now include with their receivers are a far cry from those few pages of stapled mimeographed copy owners struggled with in the early days of Loran-C use. Most manuals seen in recent years have been excellent, giving some basic Loran information and good clear instructions on operating that particular receiver. However, it is not their purpose to present a lengthy dissertation on all aspects of Loran-C, so there is often a lot that is left out. Thus, there has arisen a need in the field for a book which will provide the Loran user with more than just the basic mechanics of operating a particular Loran receiver - a book which will fill the gap between the manufacturer's manuals and the occasional article one finds in marine literature.

Since the potential readership of this book varies from those who are already experienced Loran users and those who are just beginning, there are sections which will be important to both. To those who are experienced, those sections which take a deeper look into various aspects of Loran theory or suggest alternative ways of using Loran will be of interest. For those who are just beginning to use Loran, those sections which concentrate on the basics and simple mechanics will be important so they can better use and understand the system. This book should help alleviate those feelings of inadequacy and lack of self-confidence which are often experienced with any new venture. A beginner may even send his set in for repairs, when a few computerized tricks learned here may well have overridden his problem. Knowing the *why* of something can lead to a better understanding of the *how*, and help identify or adjust to system limitations.

Although this book is often directed towards those who use Loran-C for cruising, it should be pointed out that the information contained herein will be useful to the racer and the sports fisherman as well. Knowing what the windward ability is, how to calculate set and drift, and how to return to a good fishing reef, are just as important as knowing that one is on course to a favorite anchorage. The additional information presented in theory and techniques should enable all users, regardless of special interests, to better understand some of the intracacies of the system and thus expand their use and application of Loran-C in daily navigation.

Within the text there are a number of charts and diagrams which are provided to illustrate various aspects of the concept discussed. While every effort has been made to make these as accurate as possible, it should be noted that the charts are not intended to be, nor should they be, used for actual navigation.

It has been one of the goals of this book to present all aspects of Loran - the bad along with the good. It is important to know system limitations as well as its advantages and strong points. Thus, there may be some sections (the chapter on accuracy in particular) where one may wonder how the system works at all with all the possible problems which could affect it. Yet, the overall picture of Loran-C is far from being negative. For example: The bad news is that Loran-C skywaves do occur and could really play havoc in reception and reading of signals. The good news is that the receiver tracks early on the pulse so that the possibility of skywave contamination is extremely remote. The bad news is that the earth's conductivity (ASF) does affect the TD readings. The good news is that receiver manufacturers have developed microprocessor programming and calibration to enable highly sophisticated built-in corrections for ASF. Even within the possibilities of system limitations, the presence of interfering factors rarely produces results which are less than the original intents of the system, which are ¼ mile accuracy, 95% of the time. Loran-C not only works, but it has far exceeded original expectations.

In this book there are a number of references to satellite navigation. At the time of this writing there are two different systems in use: Transit (also know as Nav Sat or Sat Nav) and GPS (Global Positioning System). The Transit system which provides intermittent worldwide coverage with 4 or 5 satellites is primarily an interim system which, according to the Federal Navigation Plan, will be replaced by GPS by the mid 1990's. GPS is still in its embryonic stages and, when completed by 1989, will consist of 18 satellites which will provide continuous world wide coverage. Unless otherwise specified, all references in this text to satellite navigation, and using it in conjunction with Loran-C, will relate to the Transit system.

When the past 50 years are contrasted with those of the last 500 (whether it is in reference to navigation or otherwise), it is apparent that the 20th century has produced a technological revolution which has been unsurpassed by any other time in history. In the area of navigational aids, the key element in this revolution has, of course, been in the development of radionavigation systems. Recent decades have seen, in addition to Loran-C, the emerging of a variety of systems: radiobeacons, OMEGA, VOR/DME, Transit, and GPS to name a few. As a result, there is presently a very heavy battle going on virtually around the world regarding the future navigation standard.

To some, the ultimate answer may appear to be GPS. But that system still is years away from being available to the **little guy** - the average consumer. There is also some uncertainty of the degree of accuracy which will be provided to the non-military community with this system. As currently proposed, civilian capabilities with GPS will be better than the predictable or absolute accuracy of Loran-C, but they will not equal those of Loran-C in repeatable mode. There will also be some areas where GPS cannot provide the same accuracy as Loran-C. So until some enhanced form of GPS is developed to provide accuracies that are equal to existing systems for harbor and harbor approaches, Loran-C and other nav-aids will still remain an important part of coastal navigation. The question must be asked if a single radionavigation aid can really serve the needs all of users, and it would appear that some sort of navigational mix might be the solution.

To address these problems, the Department of Defense and Transportation has developed the Federal Radionavigation Plan (FRP) to determine the most cost effective method of reducing the overlap of federally funded radionavigation systems. A key element in this plan is the establishment of GPS by the military and withdrawal of military support and use in other systems. This does not mean, however, that all the other systems are going to be discontinued simply because the military isn't using them. According to the plan many of the existing systems will remain in use until well in to the next century and Loran-C is one of these. To quote from the FRP: The Department of Defense "will phase out military use of overseas Loran-C by 1992. The United States will discontinue Loran-C transmitting stations established for military use that do not serve the North American continent, as military Loran-C users become GPS equipped. The Loran-C system serving the continental United States and its coastal areas will remain a part of the navigation system mix into the next century." The future of Loran-C use for the average consumer, at least in those waters surrounding the continental US, appears to be very bright, if not assured for many decades.

The Little Box
with Magic Numbers

It was hard to tell which was worse: the inky black of the night, or the pea-soup fog which had been our companion for most of the trip.

The day had been long - a 100 mile run from the Apostle Islands in Western Lake Superior to the Upper Entry of the Keweenaw Waterway. Just after clearing the islands, the fog had descended and for the past 12 hours we had seen nothing beyond our small cocoon of existence. Along this stretch of the lake, the shoreline was bold and foreboding, yielding few harbors of refuge, so with no place left where we could tuck in and get off the lake, we were committed to making our destination. Now, because of a late start and a dying wind, we were reluctantly making a harbor approach at night - something we rarely do even in well known areas. With the added presence of dense fog, our situation was tenuous at best and now, as our landfall closed, everyone came out on watch as our anxiety heightened with the prospect of making the narrow entrance.

In spite of a well marked breakwater, complete with a fog horn and radio beacon, we had good cause for concern. Years of cruising on fog-prone Lake Superior had taught us that even when navigational aids are present, navigating in fog can still be uncertain. Quickly, we had learned to use every aid available, and to use one system to check another. Thus, on this trip as usual, we had kept an updated running fix with our dead reckoning, the RDF was tuned to home in on the beacon, and we now all listened for that first faint summons from the fog horn. But this time something was different - in addition to our usual navigational aids we were armed with a secret weapon: a little box with magic numbers.

The RDF gave us a null, but it varied 15-20 degrees. The fog horn produced a vague position somewhere off in the distance - and certainly these were helpful aids which would become clearer the closer we got to our destination. But now, at the touch of a finger, we knew our exact position, how far out we were from the breakwater entrance, its bearing from us, our true course, how much off track we were, which direction to correct, our ground speed, and our time to go at that speed. We even had an alarm set to go off when we were a half mile from the entrance. With fine tuning that made us think of the space shuttle coming in for a landing, we made the final adjustments that homed us in on our target - the entrance to the waterway. The little box of course was our new Loran-C receiver and, like many others, we were discovering the confidence of knowing our exact position and marvelling at all the little extras that came with our full function navigator. To say the least, we were impressed when we slipped into the entrance arm of the harbor.

Even with just TDs (time difference readings) alone, we found that the capabilities of Loran-C are fantastic. We had many occasions to experience this later on in the same cruise, when a malfunction in our receiver threw out our Lat/Lon capabilities and all the resulting computer functions. All we were left with were TDs.

After weeks of working with Lat/Lon and waypoint naviga-tion, it took a bit for us to regain confidence in just simple position fixing. The situation was also complicated by the fact that, at that time, the only chart available with Loran overlay lines for our area, was a small scale (1:600,000) chart. With a distance equivalent to 50 microseconds between the lines, on this chart it wouldn't take much of an error in plotting to throw us off by as much as half a mile. Another disadvantage with the small scale chart was that detailed representations of harbor entrances were lacking, so use of Loran in entering the anchorage was severely curtailed. Still, in using just TDs, the system worked nicely for us, giving position fixes which were well within the limits of these parameters.

An example of navigating with just TDs alone comes to mind when on this same trip we were making a run from the Slate Islands in Northeast Lake Superior to a small group of islands, Les Petits Ecrits, which lie up against the mainland shore. These islands are so small that, on the small scale Loran chart which we were using, they appeared as mere specks of dust. Our approach was further complicated because the entrance to the anchorage was particularly tricky in that we had to pass through a narrow 300 foot opening between two of the larger islands, to each side of which were a number of rocks and shoal areas. Even in fair wea-ther, these islands were difficult to spot as they would blend into the massive bold shoreline of Superior's North shore. So when fog closed in again, as it does so often on this section of the lake, and because we had only TDs to work with, we began to think of alternative anchorages. But, as the alternatives were quite a bit further, it was decided to give this one a fair shot.

We began to navigate constantly using every tool we had, again using one technique to check on the other. A compass course was laid, kept accurate with the use of the autopilot; the log ticked off the miles as we kept advancing our fix - and of course we had the Loran. Without previous TD readings to home in on, we were on straight position fixing, relying on only absolute accuracy (See Chap. 7). But even with just TDs, we were able to tell when we were deviating from our rhumb line and make the needed compass corrections. Still, I can remember thinking as we closed on the mainland - "We have to be out of our minds to be doing this - if we get this one, it will be more than just luck." And it must have been; for when our navigation and the Loran showed us to be a mile from the islands, we slowed down to a crawl and crept in with all hands on deck watching for those first faint shadows which announce the presence of land. A final correction was made as indicated by the Loran, the depth sounder began to move up and we heard the cry of gulls who sensed our presence. Then there it was - the opening passage between the islands, right where it should be. On just TDs alone and the small scale chart, we were just 100 feet off! As we slipped in through that small entrance, we came upon a couple of fishermen in a small boat. I don't know who was more suprised, those men hugging the security of the shoreline or us when we ghosted in out of the thick mist into the safety of the anchorage.

These stories are not unusual, and each year we are hearing more fantastic tales than these from sailors all around the Great Lakes and in areas of coastal and offshore cruising who are using the Loran system in navigation. As individual confidence grows and the inherent capabilities of Loran are explored, skippers everywhere are discovering what a boon the magic numbers are to everyday navigation. Next to the fiberglass hulls, aluminum masts and dacron sails, Loran may very well become one of the more important advances in the enjoyment of recreational boating.

However, there are always those who are ready to discount a new product or system. I am reminded of a fellow boater we heard remark a while back: "I don't know what all this fuss concerning Loran-C is all about. It seems to me that if you know where you start from and where you are going, dead reckoning should be able to take you there." And in theory this is correct.

Yet, many of us have become unsure of our position because of tacking, and have had our hands full because of rough weather so that an accurate running fix has been hours behind. Many of us have been cruising in the North country near concentrated iron deposits and have seen our compass needle slowly drift off or swing erratically. How many times have we experienced the added anxiety when fog closes in or visibility is reduced by rain? At times such as these, in foul weather or fair, it comes down to this: it is nice to know your position - exactly.

CHAPTER ONE

Loran-C: Past, Present and Future

Ever since man has taken to water in the most basic of craft, there has been the need to navigate from one point to another. Be it the ancient dhow which plied the waters of the Nile, the Polynesian canoes used in eastward exploration, the Viking ships which roamed the North Sea, or the mammoth supertankers which now prowl the oceans, a common denominator in any navigation has been and still is, to know one's position. Without knowing position, it is impossible to know what direction to take or what distance needs to be traveled to reach a specified destination. In fact, it is on this single point of information that all navigating techniques and systems depend.

Early Tools and Techniques for Establishing Position

Even in the very beginning of early exploration, familiar landmarks were used to establish position. Called "coasting," this type of navigating involved primarily piloting by the use of "eyeball" navigation in coastal waters. Then, as man ventured further and further from the security of known waters, dead reckoning came into use. Knowledge of position was the most important factor and it was estimated on direction and distance traveled from a given point.

As man's ability to navigate successfully from one place to another developed, so did the tools which assisted him in accomplishing the task. Many of these were either dependent on knowing one's approximate position or used in establishing it. For example, use of the lodestone, which later developed into direction finding with the magnetic compass, depended on knowing approximate position before venturing out on a specific bearing to a destination. Even the log and sundial, which were forerunners of contemporary knotmeters and quartz chronometers, were important instruments in establishing position, as running fixes were updated with dead reckoning in distance run by multiplying speed by lapsed time. The leadline was used to determine position from shore as its modern day counterpart, the depth sounder, is used to determine relative position by following contour lines on a chart. And of course the importance of position fixing was primary in the use and development of the astrolabe and then the sextant. Even today, the sextant remains one of the more important instruments used on the high seas, especially with small non-commercial vessels. However, its use is dependent on good visibility, and it is often noted in contemporary boating magazines how days may pass on a particular voyage before the weather will clear enough to give an accurate sun or star sight.

Contemporary Tools for Position Fixing

To meet the demands of navigating in conditions of reduced visibility and in coastal cruising, modern technology has produced a number of options. Heading the list of course, has been radar, which is but a sophisticated extension of eyeball navigation where position is established in relation to known land masses. Aside from its advantage of being a major asset in conditions of reduced visibility, its disadvantages are that there is a bit of art involved in interpreting some signals, and its range is limited, so its use in navigation is diminished the further one heads off shore.

The use of other transmitted radio signals to establish position has produced a number of different aids to navigation. Probably the most basic of these aids is RDF (radio direction finder) which uses the same principles employed by a hand bearing compass with which bearings are taken from objects of known position - in this case a radio transmitting station. In coastal navigation, this system certainly has its place, but all too often its use is limited because of short range or lack of stations in good geometric positions to produce accurate fixes by triangulation. More often than not, these stations are best used for single point bearings or as homing devices - as long as they are in the right position. Accuracy is also subject to criticism, for often a null can vary by many degrees, which, depending on distance from the source, can fix a vessel's position as being in an uncomfortably large area.

Fortunately, the 20th century has produced a number of other navigation systems which also utilize the reception of transmitted radio signals of specific frequencies. Under the general heading of hyperbolic systems, these systems are different from the RDF, which establishes position only by direction. Instead, they depend on the fact that radio signals travel at a specific speed and distance traveled, i.e., position of reception, is directly proportional to lapsed time between transmission and reception of the signal. The word "hyperbolic" comes from the fact that, as signals are received from two different sources, position is established between the sources along a line that is in the form of a hyperbola. (See Chapter Two on basic theory and Fig. 2.3). Systems which fall under this classification are LORAN, DECCA, and OMEGA. The Loran system differs from the other two in that its signals are propagated as pulses, whereas DECCA and OMEGA, which operate with longer wavelengths and very low frequency, use continuous transmission instead of pulses. For years it was DECCA that rivaled the use of Loran in coastal waters, but then it was phased out when Loran was chosen as the national radionavigation aid in the 1970's. The OMEGA system (along with differential OMEGA) is gaining in popularity and usefulness in that, with just eight stations, it provides continuous worldwide position fixing capabilities of 2-4 miles. At present, one of its greatest disadvantages for the average boater is the cost factor which, for most receivers, is upward of many thousands of dollars.

Another type of radionavigation system utilizes transmitted signals beamed from satellites as opposed to land based stations such as the above. Here the principle utilized is that of the Doppler shift. An onboard receiver measures the slight change of the signal frequency which is caused by the orbital motion of the satellite. This system differs from the other ones in that it is non-hyperbolic because receivers utilize signals from a single source. For the most part, it can be considered a world wide system with satellite acquisition available in most areas of the world. Accuracy of fixes and recent cost reduction of receivers have made the system appealing to many in recreational boating. However, at present its main disadvantage is that position fixing is not continuous, and is dependent on satellite passes which can result in the time between accurate fixes being anywhere from 30 to 90 minutes. If ship's position is mid-ocean this doesn't present a problem, and the system certainly is an improvement over a daily sunsight. But, if one is trying to make a tricky harbor entrance in reduced visibility, the time needed for an accurate update may be crucial. Onboard computers will adjust for this by electronic dead reckoning, but accurate fixes are still only available with each satellite pass.

The future of position fixing via satellite however is bright. This is because of a national committment through the Department of Defense and a joint service program to establish the NAVSTAR Global Positioning System (GPS). When completed, the GPS will consist of 18 satellites and 3 in-orbit spares positioned in 6 evenly spaced orbital planes so that world wide coverage is assured. With 12 hour orbits, 4-7 satellites will be available for position fixing at any given point and any given time. Accuracy levels are predicted in the range of 100 meters (328 feet) for civilians and 25 meters for the military. Initially, use will be primarily by the military and receivers will be very expensive - as they were with Loran-C. It is projected that it won't be until the mid 1990's or later that the cost will be sufficiently reduced so that GPS will be available for general public use.

With each of the above systems having its advantages and disadvantages - whether it is cost, range, accuracy etc., use will depend greatly on individual requirements and area of use. On the great expanses of the open oceans, out of range of some land based (Loran) stations, OMEGA and satellite navigation appear to hold the most promise. However, in continental and coastal cruising, Loran has clearly become the preferred navigational system in the past decade. This is due to two factors, one of which has been the commitment of the US Coast Guard in the establishment of Loran chains which provide excellent coverage for both coasts, the Great Lakes, and the Gulf of Mexico. Even for offshore cruising, particularly in the Northern Hemisphere, Loran is now a valuable asset. (See Fig. 1.3).

The other factor, and probably the most important for putting Loran into the hands of the recreational boater, is that of cost reduction. Along with the development of the microprocessor and mini-computers, in just the past few years, sets which used to cost in excess of $3000 can now be purchased for $1000 - and even less. If the RDF were a commonplace piece of equipment on boats in the '70s, today the Loran is quickly becoming the navigational instrument of choice in the '80s and into the '90s.

The First Loran: Loran-A

The word "loran" is an acronym which stands for LOng RAnge Navigation. The system was first developed in the early 1940's by the Radiation Laboratory of the Massachusetts Institute of Technology. It operated with a much higher frequency than the present day Loran-C (in the 1.7 to 2.0 mHz band) and had an average fix error of 1 to 2 miles. It had a moderate range of 600-800 miles over water, but over land this range was considerably reduced. Then in 1974, when it was decided to implement Loran-C as the official aid in radionavigation, a phase-out period was initiated for Loran-A.

Domestic Loran-C

The development of modern Loran-C for commercial and domestic use came in the 1970's and was a product of many factors. Without question the most important of these was the commitment of the U.S. government to an official radio aid-to

-navigation system for the navigable waters of the United States. This decision was brought about as shipping increased and vessels became larger. These needs demanded an ability to navigate accurately far out to seaward beyond normal visual and piloting navigation aids.

In response to this problem, the Secretary of Transportation commissioned the U.S. Coast Guard in 1972 to conduct a study on the feasibility of establishing one of the known radionavigation systems as the official aid for navigating in coastal waters. The area under concern was the Coastal Confluence Zone (CCZ), which was defined as extending seaward from a harbor entrance to 50 nautical miles (nm) offshore, or the edge of the continental shelf (100 fathom curve), whichever was greater. Note: the CCZ did not include the harbors themselves.

The study consisted of roughly 3 different parts:

- **Identification of the accuracy parameters of various user groups (i.e. commercial fishermen, recreational boaters, commercial shippers/deep draft mariners) and the ranges of accuracy required in various parts of the CCZ.**

- **The benefits and limitations of all existing radionavigation system in meeting these requirements.**

- **Recommendation of a selected system which was cost effective.**

The accuracy parameters which were arrived at in the study were impressive: the system chosen would have to provide "95% assurance that a vessel could fix its position to an accuracy of ¼ nm." After more research and discussion, the final recommendation came in July, 1972 - in favor of Loran-C. Finally, after lengthy debate between various groups, the recommendation became official, and on May 16th, 1974, the Secretary of Transportation publicly announced that Loran-C was to be established as the official radionavigation system for the coastal waters of the United States.

The areas to be included in the CCZ, were the East Coast and the Gulf of Mexico, and the West Coast from California to Alaska.

To meet the commitment for a national system of radionavigation, 16 new stations were built in the Great Lakes Region, the Gulf of Mexico and the West Coast - with the West Coast receiving first priority because of poor Loran-A coverage and increased tanker shipping. Many of the existing stations had their functions redefined. Coverage also extended well into Canadian waters, and through close coordination with the Canadian govern-

9940	US West Coast Chain	Apr 77
7960	Gulf of Alaska Chain	Jun 77
5990	Canadian West Coast Chain (partial: X & Y)	Sep 77
9960	Northeast US Chain (partial: X & Y)	Sep 77
7980	Southeast US Chain	Dec 79
9960	Northeast US Chain (completed: added Z)	May 79
9930	Old US East Coast Chain (terminated)	Sep 79
7980	Southeast US Chain (completed: added Z)	Oct 79
8970	Great Lakes Chain	Mar 80
5930	Canadian East Coast Chain (partial: X & Y)	Apr 80
5990	Canadian West Coast Chain (completed: added Z)	Nov 80
5930	Canadian East Coast Chain (completed: added Z)	Jul 83
7930	Labrador Sea Chain (commissioned)	Dec 83

Fig. 1.1   Development Of Coastal Coverage For United States and Canada

ment, two new stations were built which were jointly funded by both countries.

A summary of the development of coastal coverage for both countries is found in Fig. 1.1. A graphic representation of the individual chains and their areas of coverage is found in Fig. 1.2. With the results of domestic expansion, by 1981 there were 41 high-power Loran-C stations around the world.   (See Fig. 1.3).

Another factor which cannot be discounted in contributing to the increased use of Loran-C is the revolutionary advances of high technology equipment in the field of electronics. With the utilization of micro-processors, integrated circuits and semi-conductors, Loran receivers have evolved from the large cumbersome units of the 40's and 50's to the compact, easy to use receivers of today. Not only are the sets smaller, but they are now far more

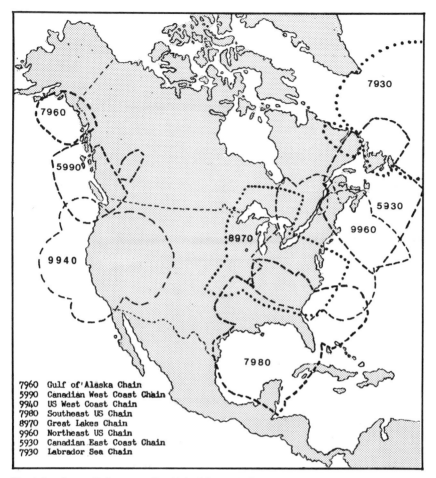

7930

7960

5990

9940

8970

5930

9960

7980

7960	Gulf of Alaska Chain
5990	Canadian West Coast Chain
9940	US West Coast Chain
7980	Southeast US Chain
8970	Great Lakes Chain
9960	Northeast US Chain
5930	Canadian East Coast Chain
7930	Labrador Sea Chain

Fig. 1.2   Loran-C Coverage For United States & Canada

sophisticated in what they can do. Where coordinate conversion used to be done separately, now internal micro-computers perform the calculations with split second accuracy. The utilization of microprocessor counter/timer chips has improved the time keeping qualities of the receivers and advanced the accuracy and reliability of data readouts. Cost reduction of electronic components is another facet of the revolution: chips which a few years ago cost hundreds of dollars are now available for a small fraction of that. Combined with the lack of Loran-C patent restrictions and the competition of the open market (there are approximately 25 commercial receiver manufacturers) a wide variety of receivers are now available and at costs that put them within the reach of the average customer.

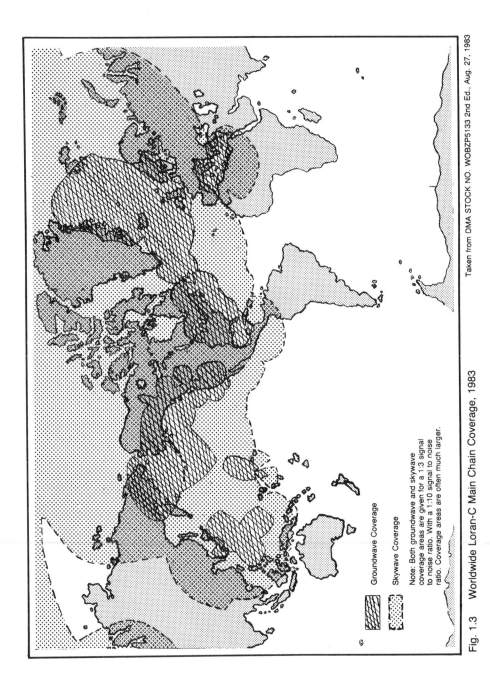

Groundwave Coverage

Skywave Coverage

Note: Both groundwave and skywave coverage areas are given for a 1:3 signal to noise ratio. With a 1:10 signal to noise ratio. Coverage areas are often much larger.

Taken from DMA STOCK NO. WOBZP5133 2nd Ed., Aug. 27, 1983

Fig. 1.3   Worldwide Loran-C Main Chain Coverage, 1983

Similar advances in electronic technology have taken place at the transmitter sites. Originally, the transmitters were all vacuum-tube design. Parts of the equipment such as the timing control and synchronizing circuits were changed over to transistor or micro-circuit construction. Semi-conductor based transmitters made possible utilizing larger antennas. Individual power modules provided transmitters of varying sizes. These allowed a building block design which enabled transmitters to tailor signal coverage to specific area requirements. For more recent high power transmitters, solid state construction was used, a trend which is continuing in present day upgrading of sites.

Mini-Loran

A spin-off from Loran-C has been the use of low power, often portable, transmitters to establish chains with correspondingly reduced areas of coverage. These short range systems do not fall under the general classification of Loran-C (which stands for long range navigation), but because they use the same basic principles and carrier frequency as Loran-C are called "mini-Loran."

Low power means transmitters which generate signals in the order of hundreds of watts in contrast to the high power main chain transmitters which put out signals that are hundreds of kilowatts or even megawatts. The resultant range is usually that of a few hundred miles as opposed to the often better than thousand mile range for main chain Loran. Because of this reduced range, advantages are increased accuracy due to reduced propagation errors (See ASF factor, Chap. 7) and considerably less skywave contamination. Absolute accuracies are often better than 30 meters with repeatable accuracies of 10 meters common.

Aside from transmitted power, signal characteristics for mini Loran are like the regular Loran-C in every respect except one, and that is in the phase coding. (See Chap. 2) This is because it is important to keep these signals from interfering with the signals of the regular chains which are usually present in the same area. By changing the pattern of the pulse groups for mini-Loran regular receivers are no longer able to pick up the signals, so not only does the Mini-Loran not interfere with regular Loran, but it means that specially designed receivers must be used. Because of this, Mini-Loran has become, in most areas, a user paid service.

The advantages of reduced interference, increased accuracies and flexibility with smaller portable transmitters have provided a system capable of numerous applications. For example, narrow channel navigation by large ships has been used in a number of areas. One of these was the experimental chain located in the St. Mary's river, an area of conjested shipping between Lake Huron and Lake Superior. Operating with 4 stations, this chain functioned from 1975 to 1980, and demonstrated that Loran could be used successfully in restricted areas.

Other uses for the Mini- chains have been for offshore survey work, oil rig movement and positioning, and pipe/cable laying and maintenance. Locations have been literally world wide, ranging from the permanent stations around the British Isles to the flexible systems in the Yellow Sea, Java Sea, and South China Sea. Other Mini- stations have been used in Alaska, Australia, Brazil, the Ivory Coast, Japan, Newfoundland, and New Zealand. The use of Mini-Loran has been so great throughout the world that, at times, there have been as many as 15 separate chains with 40-50 transmitters.

For a number of years this adapatation of Loran was used to manage traffic in the Suez Canal. This system consisted of three stations strategically positioned to give optimal crossing angles of lines of position. It differed from ordinary Loran use in that the receiver position was relayed back to a central control station via a portable unit, the Cort (Carry-On Receiver/Transmitter) so that traffic was monitored and controlled as vessels passed through the canal. This elaborate communication network, along with radar and computer data banks on thousands of vessels, coordinated one of the most advanced techniques for handling high density traffic in the world.

Other Uses for Loran-C

Along with the national comittment of utilizing Loran-C as the official coastal radionavigational aid, comes the possibilities of employing Loran-C for land use. Signal propagation does not stop at the land-water boundaries, but naturally extends well into the interior of the contiguous 48 states. In fact, with the present existing chains, 2/3 of this area is now already covered by Loran signals. (See Fig. 1.2) Because of population distribution, this area represents an even larger portion of the nation's population, 92%. To get 100% land coverage, 3-5 additional Loran-C stations would need to be established in the mid-continental region.

It doesn't take much imagination to visualize that even with present signal coverage, land applications for Loran-C are a distinct possibility. Various government and private agencies have been well aware of this fact, and in recent years a number of studies have been conducted in the areas of mass transit, truck and rail transportation, vehicle monitoring and vehicle dispatching. Particularly with those agencies which respond to emergencies, such as fire fighting, law enforcement, ambulance and paramedic units, exact position fixing can provide invaluable time saving, if not life saving, advantages.

A key to utilizing Loran in these situations is Automatic Vehicle Monitoring (AVM) which consists of using a transceiver along with Loran positioning equipment on the mobile unit to transmit position back to a base station much in the same way that the CORT was used in the Suez Canal. Time difference readings along with other valuable information, are then transmitted back to the central control where fleet control, especially in reducing response time in dispatching, is greatly enhanced.

One of the main disadvantages to this system, is that in highly populated areas (where these systems would be most apt to operate) there is often interference in the form of power lines, traffic lights, etc., which may reduce accuracy and reception of signals. Even large metal objects, such as buildings and bridges, are known to cause warpage of the hyperbolic lines of position and reduce accuracy. To get around these problems, dead reckoning instruments can be added to allow the vehicle to coast through the area of disturbance much in the same way the dead reckoning equipment in some Sat Navs establishes position between satellite passes.

Another area where Loran has been used is in airborne navigation. In the years which followed WWII, the air force used the automatic aircraft guidance system which evolved into the present Loran-C. Recent years have seen interest from the FAA (Federal Aviation Administration) in the use of Loran-C as an approach guidance system as well as for airborne navigation. Particularly in the state of Vermont, along with the Coast Guard and other agencies, preliminary tests have been conducted on the feasibility for using Loran-C for enroute and non-precision approaches of aircraft in general aviation. Use of Loran-C navigation in air traffic control and other special navigational requirements has also been explored.

In the past few years there has been a tremendous growth of LORAN-C usage by the general aviation community. Part of the reason for this is that, until recently, use of Loran receivers required considerable manual processing of data (which was undesirable for aircraft navigation) or the use of complex computers which were very expensive. Now, as a spin-off from the computer revolution, highly automatic receivers are available at a fraction of the cost of early models. To meet the demand in airborne use, many manufacturers are now producing aircraft Loran-C receivers along with their marine models.

Although airborne use of Loran-C today is primarily in the private, non-commercial sector of the user community, it does continue to expand in other areas as well. For example, the U.S. Coast Guard is now using Loran-C on aircraft which are used for search and rescue missions.

At present, most domestic use of Loran in aviation is concentrated in coastal and adjacent areas. The reason is that these areas are within the Coastal Confluence Zone (CCZ) and receive prime Loran coverage. This points out that one of the biggest disadvantages in using Loran in aviation is that coverage is not world wide. Even here in the U.S., there are large areas in mid-continent where it may be difficult to acquire and lock on to Loran signals. However the FAA now officially has embraced Loran as a nav-aid and has embarked on a program to enhance overland coverage.

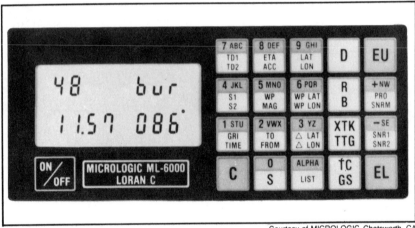

Courtesy of MICROLOGIC Chatsworth, CA

Fig. 1.4   Faceplate For An Airborn Loran-C.

Maintaining and Improving Loran-C

To keep Loran-C operating at its present capabilities, the first priority is to upgrade existing stations and then continue maintenance so they can keep abreast with current demands of the system. Through the Loran-C Improvement Plan, a schedule for replacing old equipment and improving existing facilities has been established. Many of the transmitter stations have been operating in the original buildings, and some with even original equipment which dates back nearly 30 years. To improve service new transmitters, generators etc. have been added at various sites. Many of these new transmitters are contemporary solid state units which will function with minimum supervision.

USCG Loran-C Transmitter Station at Malone, FL. Note the exhaust stacks for the emergency stand-by diesel generators. These generators assure uninterrupted operation of the Loran chain even during severe weather and blackouts.

USCG Loran-C Transmitter Room at Malone, Fl. These are state of the art, solid state transmitters.

To assist in reducing manpower at transmitting sites, the Coast Guard initiated the Remote Operating System (ROS). The ROS provides for the operation of a transmitting station to be controlled from a remotely located station. This concept was initially tested in 1980 with the Canadian transmitting station at Port Hardy, British Columbia, and a remote controlling station at Alert Bay, British Columbia. The results of the test demonstrated that transmitter sites could be operated with a minimum of four people as long as the station did not have chain control responsibility, and there was a backup off duty technician which could be summoned for emergency repair and maintenance work. (Four people represents quite a difference from the 32 men that Hal and Margaret Roth found at the Attu Loran station in the Aleutian Islands in their 1967-68 Pacific circumnavigation.) The main advantage to the ROS is that a given remote station does not control just one transmitter site - but many, thus reducing manpower even more. For example, the X secondary at Middletown, California, in the West Coast Chain 9940 now controls all the other transmitters in that chain.

Another area in which a number of different agencies have been working is in updating and correcting the hyperbolic lattice grids of Loran-C charts. Because radio waves travel at different speeds over land as opposed to over water, these grids on the original charts usually did not reflect this error (known as ASF - the Additional Secondary Factor) especially in areas close to land. Even with calculated predictions made by the Defense Mapping Agency, it has remained for the Coast Guard to conduct field surveys for verification of data. These surveys were completed in 1982 for the Great Lakes and CCZ and have increased the accuracy of Loran charts for continued use of Loran-C in these areas.

Expansion of Loran-C

Aside from the considerations of maintenance and updating the present system, there are always questions about future expansion. Here the concerns fall into roughly two areas:

1. Extending the CCZ to include harbor approaches, the harbors themselves, and inland waterways.

2. Extending coverage into areas not presently serviced by Loran-C.

When the Coast Guard made its decisive study in 1972 which favored utilization of Loran-C, it is important to note that the definition of the CCZ did not include the harbors themselves, but only the area from the harbor entrance extending seaward. It was felt then that existing visual aids, short-range audio beacons and radar would remain the primary aids for navigating in these areas. However, utilization of these aids is often reduced by poor visibility, ice cover, removal during winter, etc. Thus, there appears to be a need for a precise all-weather navigation aid in these areas too.

For a radionavigation aid to be utilized in restricted waters, it must be extremely accurate and provide position fixes at very close intervals. This information must also be integrated with split second accuracy with data from other onboard instruments so that precise position and projected guidance information are readily available. Even with the sophistication of contemporary receivers, present capabilities fall below these parameters for congested shipping in restricted waters.

It is not, however, beyond the Loran system to provide these capabilities. Areas which would need improvement in the present system are the stability of signals and accuracy of readouts. One way to accomplish this would be the use of mini-chains in strategic highly congested areas. Errors which result because of poor station geometry or propagation over long distances could then be alleviated. Another way would be to have monitoring stations at given sites which would then pass corrections on to users - Differential Loran-C. Chart errors could be essentially eliminated by precise charting of key areas and publishing electronic coordinates for known geographic positions, i.e., key buoys, channel boundaries, harbor entrances etc. Actually, the Coast Guard has already been doing this and publication of some of these listings such as waypoints for New York Harbor, Delaware Bay and the St. Mary's River are found in issues of the **Radionavigation Bulletin**, which is published by the Department of Transportation.

The inland waterways are other areas where it has been demonstrated that the need for precise navigation is a growing concern. But because waterways are strung out over large expanses of land, the solution by using mini-chains doesn't seem to be a viable option as it does for large congested harbor areas. Even publishing electronic coordinates at known points may not be feasible because many waterway systems are unstable, and often channels are known to change. Finally, there appears to be less risk for consequences due to grounding in the waterways as opposed to those which occur in the congested areas of harbor approaches. When all these factors are taken together, it appears that the utilization of Loran-C for precision waterway navigation undoubtably remains a low priority item.

With an eye to the future, many are looking to NAVSTAR GPS to provide the answers to all coastal and world wide navigation problems. Current projections are that the system will be operational by 1989, and the military will phase out its use of Loran-C by 1992 in favor of GPS. However, it must be noted that, because of military and security reasons, it is believed that it will be some time beyond that date before the accuracy which is required in restricted waters will be made available for civilian use.

A look at the chart of world wide coverage for Loran-C (See Fig. 1.3) shows that there are large areas, particularly in the Southern Hemisphere which receive little or no coverage. Countries such as Australia, Mexico, Venezuela, and other South American countries have looked to Loran as a means for improving coastal and offshore navigation, particularly in those areas which support oil exploration activities. Even in the Far East, it appears that Loran use will continue and probably expand as a coastal, and even offshore aid to navigation.

Without a doubt, the cruising sailor is benefiting from the spin-off of military and commercial use of Loran-C in these areas of the world. There is one area, however, which remains foremost in mind because it is a favorite cruising ground in the Western Hemisphere - and that is, of course, the Caribbean.

A quick look at Fig. 1.3 will show that the Eastern Caribbean is devoid of Loran coverage, and favorite cruising spots, such as the Virgin Islands, the Lesser Antilles, and even much of the Bahamas, are outside of primary Loran coverage, or, at best, in fringe areas. This fact has not gone unnoticed by the U.S. government, and in 1980 a cost/benefit study was conducted by the Department of Transportation to determine if it were financially feasible to establish coverage in these areas. In this study, the possibility of utilizing differential OMEGA or some other electronic navigation aid was also investigated. Unfortunately, from the standpoint of Loran-C users, when all the checks and balances were in and tabulated, the decision of the study was that the costs of several possible Loran systems far outweighed the possible benefits that could be achieved. As a result, a system of differential OMEGA has since been implemented in the Eastern Caribbean as an alternative radio navigation aid.

The Future of Loran-C

With the many different systems of electronic navigation which are available today, or just waiting around the corner for tomorrow, one can well wonder what the future for any single system will be. Certainly the capabilities of position fixing via satellite cannot be denied for the near or distant future. It is dependent on many factors, and the system will probably go through a development and evolution that is very similar to that which brought Loran-C to the average civilian consumer.

At present, use of Loran for establishing position in between satellite passes is a valuable asset. Satellite fixes then can be used to determine a more exact position devoid of errors from ASF factors or skywave contamination in fringe areas. These corrections can then be fed into the Loran receiver, and by putting the two together, one system can compensate for the limitations of the other. Even with the ensuing development of GPS, Loran-C still is the official navigation aid for the coastal waters of the United States. With the millions of dollars which have been invested to establish the Loran-C system in the U.S. it is doubtful that the service will be terminated soon. And, although the military will be turning to GPS in the early 1990's, the Coast Guard has acknowledged comittment to sustaining the Loran-C system until the year 2000.

With continued use of Loran-C gaining momentum through the 1980's, projections are for a user community well in excess of 270,000 by the year 1990. New uses for Loran along with the possibilities of extended and improved coverage will of course serve only to increase these numbers. Until such a user community can be provided with an alternative which at least meets present radionavigation standards, it would seem highly unlikely that non-military users would be left without some electronic aid to navigation. When such an alternative is available there will probably be a phase-out, or transition period similar to that which was allowed for the changeover from Loran-A to Loran-C so that even with the satellite GPS alternative it is expected that for some time the two systems will be used simultaneously. Thus, the future for Loran-C does indeed look bright for the non-military user - at least until the year 2000.

CHAPTER TWO

Loran-C Theory

Section I Basic Theory

Chain Configuration

The word 'loran' is an acronym taken from the words LOng RAnge Navigation, because it utilizes the reception of radio signals from stations which are often quite distant from the position of the receiver. The Loran system is made up of sets of these transmitting stations which are positioned in groups of 3 - 5 stations which are called chains. A chain is established with the stations in specific geometric positions, which are called triads, stars, or wyes. In each chain, one of the stations is designated as a master (M), while the others are called secondaries, which are specified as Whisky, X-ray, Yankee, or Zulu, (W,X,Y, or Z). In the old Loran-A system, the secondary stations were called slaves because their transmissions were dependent on, and initiated by, reception of the master signal. The term "secondary" is a Loran-C term because with the newer system, which uses more accurate time and frequency controls, these stations can operate independently from the master, even though they are synchronized to it. (See Fig. 2.1).

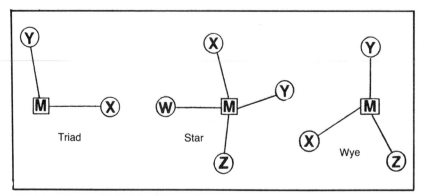

Fig. 2.1   Geometric Position of Loran Stations

Where Distance is Time

Each station emits a series of coded pulses, with the signals from the secondaries synchronized to the master signal. These radio waves travel at a specific speed, so the time it takes a radio signal to travel a given distance is directly proportional to that distance. An understanding of how this works can be gained by looking at the reception of signals from a single transmitter.

A diagram showing a transmitting station in the center and each 100 miles out from the center represented by a circle can serve as a simplified example. (See Fig. 2.2) Thus circle A is 100 miles from the transmitter; circle B is 200 miles; circle C is 300 miles, etc. A transmitted radio signal is omni-directional, that is, it travels outward in all directions from the source. If the signal is presumed to travel, in this particular example, at one second per 100 miles, and it is picked up five seconds after transmission, it can be assumed that the receiver is located somewhere on circle E.

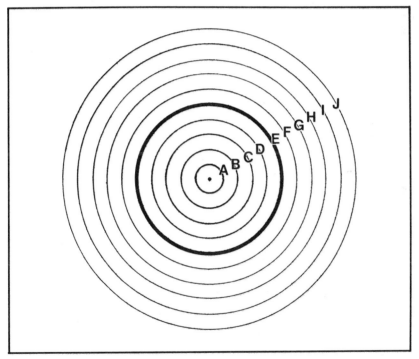

Fig. 2.2   Signal Propagation From A Single Source

Hyperbolic Reception

When radio signals are received from two transmitting sources and the time between the reception of these signals is compared, something interesting happens. No longer is position

27

established as being somewhere along a circular pathway around a single source, but instead position is found in relation to the two stations. Once again position is not an absolute or fixed spot, but it is found along a line between the two stations. The shape of this line is a hyperbola. A reference to the diagram, Fig. 2.3 will show how this can be.

Again, for simplicity, the assumption will be made that each circle represents an increase of 100 miles from the transmitting source, and the time for a signal to travel this distance is an additional one second. If a receiver were exactly the same distance from the two stations, it would receive signals exactly at the same time from each and its position would be established as being somewhere between the two on line AB. However, if the position is 100 miles closer to one of the transmitting sources, perhaps M, the receiver would be 100 miles further away from S and it would take one second longer to receive its signal. This would then establish position as being somewhere along the line CD. If the receiver were 200 miles closer to M it would take two seconds longer to receive the signal from S so position would be somewhere along EF etc. The closer the receiver is to a given station, the more acute the hyperbola becomes and favors that station. The importance of this will be noted in chapter seven, on checking the accuracy in using received signals.

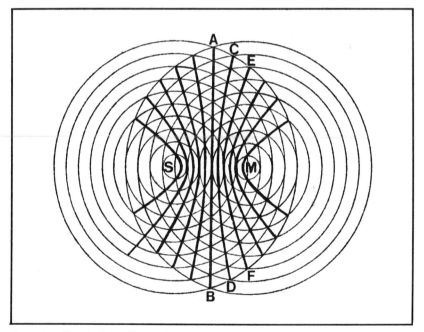

Fig. 2.3   Hyperbolic positions of lines of reception between two transmitting sources.

Time Differences

In navigating with Loran, an onboard receiver picks up the signals from a given set of stations and its computer measures the slight difference in time in receiving the two signals. This time delay (TD) is incredibly small and measured in microseconds. (In space, radio waves, which are a part of the electromagnetic spectrum, travel at 186,000 miles per second, the same as their cousins, infrared waves, visible light, and x-rays. So, with the finite distance traveled here on earth, a very small unit of time measurement is needed). A microsecond is one millionth of a second. It is these TDs, in microseconds which are displayed on the Loran receiver read-out.

Establishing a Line of Position

A TD reading is the same as one of the hyperbolas in the example, and it places the receiver position as being somewhere along a line in relation to the two stations. In navigation this is called a line of position or LOP. An LOP is plotted by using a navigational chart to which Loran overlay lines have been added. These overlay lines are actually the TD hyperbolas between the stations.

In receiving signals from a master and one of its secondaries, S-1 or X, the difference in time in receiving the signals might be displayed as 25730.8 microseconds. This would establish position as being somewhere along the TD 25730.8 line as shown in Fig. 2.4A. At this point the question of the value of this information may occur since Loran is supposed to be exact position fixing. But before going on to exact position fixing it should be noted that even

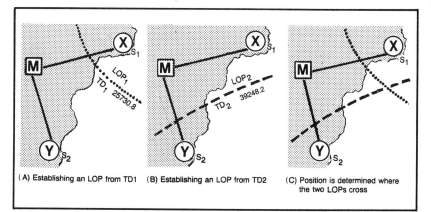

(A) Establishing an LOP from TD1   (B) Establishing an LOP from TD2   (C) Position is determined where the two LOPs cross

Fig. 2.4   Plotting A Fix With TDs

a single TD reading gives valuable information. This information is just as important as establishing a single point bearing from a hand bearing compass which can then be used with other navigational aids to establish position. (See chapter 8). Even if only one station pair is tracked, a single reading will give important information as to where the receiver is, and maybe even more important, where it is not.

Establishing a Fix

For obtaining that exact position a second LOP obtained by receiving signals from the master and another secondary is necessary. Again, the time difference in receiving the signals is given in microseconds and plotted on the charts using the overlay lines. (Fig. 2.4B) Where the two lines cross is the ship's position, or fix. (Fig. 2.4C).

Obtaining a third LOP from a third secondary in the chain, if it is available, will supply a really accurate fix. This may turn out to be surprising, however, as 'pinpoint' trust in a fix where the lines cross may not be as exact as expected. One may get the familiar "cocked hat" produced in triangulation from three different bearings such as that found in using a RDF (radio direction finder). Position within the triangulated area is highly accurate as long as there is good reception from the stations, and other factors which affect accuracy have been checked. (See chapter 7). It may be less misleading than the cross between two LOPs which may not be as exact as many like to believe.

Section II: Not So Basic Theory

The following section is a more detailed description of the Loran system and signal transmission which will expand the user's understanding of system characteristics. It really is not necessary to understand this background information for the use of the Loran under favorable conditions. To get the most out of the Loran, even where some say it won't work, requires a little more understanding of Loran-C theory. This section will prove helpful for those who are operating in fringe areas, or who have difficulty in tracking signals. For, in spite of the limitations of the system, there are often little tricks that a knowledgeable operator can use to squeeze out a few hundred extra miles or improve on the accuracy of an unreliable signal. This ability could be a god-send in conditions of reduced visibility.

Carrier Frequency

Radio signals travel in the form of electromagnetic energy that can be best described as waves. Each wave consists of continuous reversing lines of force which are represented as peaks and troughs in the wave. The distance from one part of the wave to the corresponding part in the next wave is called a wavelength, or one cycle. The frequency of a radio signal is the number of cycles which occur in one second.

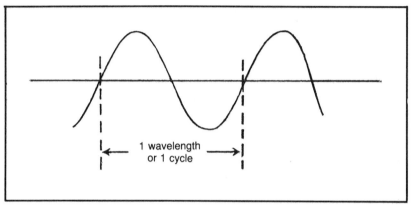

1 wavelength
or 1 cycle

Fig. 2.5   A Typical Wave-form

Loran-C is called a low frequency radio aid to navigation because it operates in the band of 90 to 110 kHz with a carrier frequency of 100 kHz. (A Hertz is a radio signal that has one cycle per second. A kiloHertz is a radio signal of 1000 cycles per second). The Loran-A system operated with a frequency that was 10 times higher than the Loran-C frequency. Other types of radio transmissions, such as amateur radio and FM transmitters operate with frequencies that are 100, 1000 or even millions of times greater. Because of this low frequency, Loran-C radio waves are very long - on the order of 3000 meters (almost two miles). (See Fig. 2.6).

Because radio energy travels so fast, it is important that the frequency which is used for a radio-navigation system is such that it lends itself to an accurate measurement of time. At the same time it should be able to provide a large area of coverage. Not all frequencies will provide both.

The 100 kHz frequency for Loran-C was chosen because it meets both the requirements of accurate time measurement and longer range due to stable propagation characteristics, i.e., the ability to predict groundwave propagation. Unfortunately, no fre-

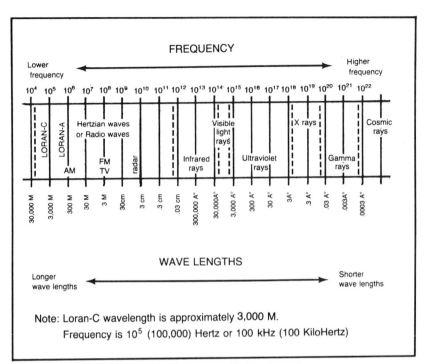

Fig. 2.6   Position of Loran-C in Electromagnetic Spectrum

quency is perfect and the 100 kHz band suffers from the possibilities of skywave contamination at long ranges. Even more important is the fact that the 100 kHz frequency is close to frequencies used by other types of transmitters and often, in areas of urban congestion and coastal cruising, transmissions of similar frequencies cause interference with receiving the Loran signal. It is because of this interference, called 'noise', that Loran receivers are equipped with notch filters which screen out the effects of interfering radio signals.

Groundwaves Vs. Skywaves

When a radio wave leaves a transmitter, it has two general pathways it can take. It can follow along the curvature of the earth, or it can travel in all directions away from the earth as skywaves. A groundwave will gradually lose its strength until it is completely diminished. Distance travelled is dependent on signal strength and the nature of the intervening terrain. Some skywaves will keep on traveling away from the earth, never to be heard from again, but many are reflected to the earth by the ionosphere and can be received often thousands of miles away from the transmitting source. (See Fig. 2.7).

32

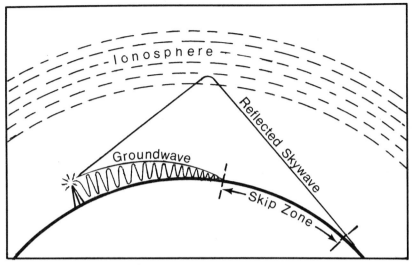

Fig. 2.7   Groundwave Vs. Skywave

The ionosphere is made up of many gaseous layers which are located in the earth's upper atmosphere approximately 30 to 300 miles above the surface of the earth. The ionization of gas particles in these areas is caused by the particles being bombarded by cosmic rays and the sun's ultraviolet rays which turn them into charged particles or ions. The amount of this ionization in the various layers will vary between night and day, as well as seasonally, and with the amount of sunspot activity. For example, those areas closest to the earth will contain more ionized particles at high noon because there are more gaseous particles located closer to the earth. However, towards nightfall, this layer disappears as sunlight ceases and the charged particles, because of their close proximity to each other (as opposed to being further out in space and further apart), recombine and become neutral gaseous particles again. In those layers which are further away from the earth, ionization will last far through the night because the further spaced particles don't have as much chance to recombine and become neutral. This, in effect, moves the ionization layer out even further from the earth during the night, often by as much as two hundred miles. (See Fig. 2.8)

Increased sunspot activity will also affect the outer extremities of the ionosphere, and these layers will then become highly ionized for long periods of time.

When radio waves strike the layers in the ionosphere they are reflected, or more technically accurate, refracted a number of times

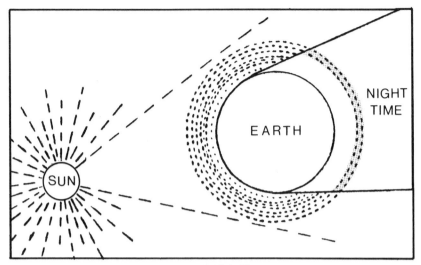

Fig. 2.8   Ionization Layers in Day Time & Night Time

until they are bent back to earth. The amount of this bending is dependent on the angle at which the wave strikes the ionosphere, the wavelength and frequency of the signal and the conditions of the ionosphere. For example, longer wavelengths/lower frequencies will bend more for a given ionization layer. Ionospheric conditions refer to both the density, i.e., the number or ions produced, and the distance of the various layers from the earth. The further the ionized layer is from the earth, the greater is the corresponding surface distance for receiving the signals. (See Fig. 2.9) This ex-

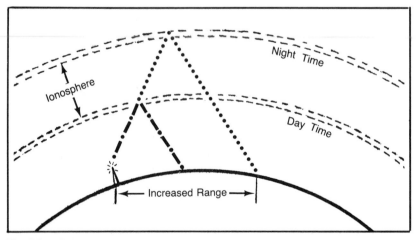

Fig. 2.9   Relation of Range to Ionosphere Height

34

plains why often skywave propagation has greater range at night (or in periods of increased sunspot activity) than during the regular daylight hours. To cite but one familiar example of this phenomenon, AM radio stations can be received at night hundreds of miles further than their daytime range.

The overall effect of skywave propagation, by bouncing signals off the ionosphere, is that of increasing the range of Loran reception. The question then arises, "Why not use just skywaves and have a really long range system for navigation?" The answer to this lies in the fact that utilization of skywaves does not meet the accurate time measurement requirement. This is because the conditions in the ionosphere are not stable, but are continually changing. Propagation characteristics can change not only from day to day, but even every few hours. It is impossible to predict ionospheric conditions; thus it is also impossible to predict arrival times for the reflected skywave signals. Loran, of course, depends on the ability to predict arrival time of signals so that accurate distances can be determined.

Because skywaves use the same signal characteristics, i.e., frequency, as groundwaves, they too will be picked up by a Loran receiver. However, because the skywave has traveled a longer distance, to the ionosphere and back, the arrival of the skywave signal will be slightly later, (35 to 1000 microseconds) than that of the groundwave signal. Because time is distance with the Loran system, these time delays, if read by the receiver could produce errors anywhere from 5 miles to well over 100 miles. Thus it is important that the receiver can distinguish between the two types of signals. This has been accomplished in two different ways, and is discussed later in this chapter.

Aside from contaminating the regular Loran groundwave signal and, in spite of different time measurements, skywaves are often used for extending range and coverage in fringe areas. Fig. 1.3 shows areas of primary coverage, and then those areas of fringe coverage which occupy much of the Northern hemisphere. Reception of the skywave signal is still an accurate measurement of time lapsed versus distance traveled - even though this distance is not an accurate representation of the actual distance of the receiver from the transmitting source. If the exact position can be verified through some other source, a buoy or anchorage, etc., this can be compared to the Loran read-out. The error can then be programmed into the set, which will add or subtract it as the need may be, and the Loran can be used for continued navigation in the area. This correction may be valid for an area of fifty or sixty miles.

However because of the often changing conditions in the ionosphere it should be updated whenever possible by verifying the vessel's known position from other navigational aids. Particular care is needed when one is navigating with skywaves both day and night. An excellent way to verify position and update a skywave correction is to use satellite navigation and then use the Loran for navigating between satellite passes. At the time of this writing, there is even a manufacturer which interfaces the two for just this purpose. A final note on using skywaves for navigation is that they can't be expected to always be present or readily tracked. A look at Fig. 2.7 will show that there is sometimes a "skip zone" which lies between groundwave and skywave reception. The diagram is oversimplified in that it shows the reflection of only one skywave. Certainly there are countless other waves which strike the ionosphere at varying angles and fill in the gap. But because reception of the signal is now dependent on a number of varying factors, it is possible in these fringe areas to experience periods when no signal is received at all, or the signal received may be so erratic that reliability is uncertain.

Absolute Vs. Relative Time

When radio signals are received there are two different ways of measuring time. Absolute time is the direct measurement of the actual time it took the signal to travel from a single source to the receiver. Relative time is a comparison between the absolute times of signal transmission from two different sources to the receiver. On most Loran receivers, the readout given is in relative time or time differences (TDs) between two stations.

Some very sophisticated and expensive receivers may be equipped with highly accurate timing devices (Cesium Beam Clocks) so that they can measure the actual or absolute time delay between signal transmission and reception. When absolute time is used it puts receiver position as somewhere on a circle with the transmitter in the center as in Fig. 2.2. Exact position is then determined by using the absolute propagation time from another transmitter. This sounds almost like hyperbolic position fixing, but it isn't because the time measurements are actual and not a comparison between transmitting sources. A disadvantage to using absolute time is that every variance in propagation time, no matter how small, must be noted and accounted for. For example, the addition of notch filters to screen out noise will delay the signal ever so slightly, which must be measured and compensated for with absolute time. Not so however with relative time, for these delays will affect the reception of all signals equally and the errors are cancelled out as one time delay is compared with the other. Whichever measurement is used, the most common unit of measurement is the microsecond, one millionth of a second.

Other Units of Time Measurement

Sometimes other small time measurements are used in describing various aspects of Loran-C. A millisecond (msec) is the next unit larger than a microsecond and represents one thousandth of a second. There are a thousand microseconds in a millisecond. Unbelievable as it may seem, there is even a unit of measurement that is smaller than a microsecond - the nanosecond.

Unit	Abbreviation	Size
millisecond	msec	1/1,000 sec
*microsecond	μsec	1/1,000,000 sec
nanosecond	ηsec	1/1,000,000,000 sec

* TDs are displayed on Loran receivers and charts as microseconds.

Fig. 2.10   Small Units For Measuring Time

A nanosecond (nsec) is the next unit smaller than a microsecond and represents one billionth of a second. There are a thousand nanoseconds in a microsecond.

Noise

Like other radio receivers, loran receivers are subject to interference from other electrical signals. Falling under the broad category of noise, this interference can be anything which inhibits or reduces reception of the Loran-C signal. Noise originates from a number of different sources.

One type of noise occurs naturally as charged particles in the lower atmosphere are formed during thunderstorms and periods of high electrical activity in a manner similar to forming ions in the atmosphere. The result is the familiar static and crackling noise which is often heard on the radio. This noise can overpower a Loran-C signal, particularly if the signal is weak, or if the operation is in fringe areas a thousand miles or more from a transmitter. This is why Loran-C coverage will often be reduced by as much as

200 - 300 miles in those areas when there are intervening cold fronts or thunderstorms.

Other sources of noise are man-made and fall into two categories; those which are external to, or outside, the boat, and those which are produced on the boat itself. External noise results from large power generators and nearby transmitters which broadcast in frequencies which are close to the 100 kHz Loran-C band in the range of 70 to 150 kHz. To screen out this type of interference, Loran-C receivers are equipped with notch filters. A more thorough discussion of notch filters and their use is found in Chapter Three.

The other source of man-made noise is found within the ship's environment itself, and is probably the greatest cause of noise, or Radio Frequency Interference (RFI), as it is often called. This noise can reach the Loran-C receiver through two pathways, radiated or conducted, or a combination of the two. Radiated noise is usually picked up though the Loran-C antenna and comes from: engines, (gasoline), generators, alternators, inverters, power control circuits, switching regulators, etc. The brushes on electric motors of any kind cause random sparking which is especially conducive to producing this type of noise. Conducted noise usually enters the receiver through its own power supply and originates from wiring which runs parallel to the Loran receiver power supply line. With all the operating gear, (VHF radios, antennas, power cables, and other shipboard electrical equipment), and wiring found on today's boats, it doesn't take much extraneous noise to interfere with Loran-C signals - even in areas where there is strong signal reception.

The amount of noise interference is measured by comparing it with the strength of the Loran-C signal. This is called the Signal to Noise Ratio or SNR. The higher the SNR, the better: a high SNR means strong signal reception in comparison to the amount of noise that is present. A low SNR means that there is more noise in relation to the strength of the signal. In remote or weak signal areas even a small amount of noise can overwhelm the signal. (See Chap. 3 for noise reduction techniques).

Land Propagation Errors

In space, radio waves travel at the speed of light or 186,000 miles per second. But when radio waves travel through different media, this velocity (along with the strength of the signal) is attenuated or reduced. This attenuation varies according to the type of medium the signals are passing over, with minimum attenuation occurring over sea water and maximum attenuation found over rocky, mountainous and ice covered terrains. The effect is similar to that of refraction or bending of light as it passes from air into water, and with Loran it means that the signals travel slower over land than over water. Since the basic principle of Loran is the timing of signal transmission, this retardation as radio waves pass from water to land may have a considerable effect on position fixing.

The phenomenon is called the Additional Secondary Factor (ASF) because this land retardation is in addition to the normal retardation found over an all sea water path. Time differences which are calculated in the Loran system as though the signals traveled over only sea water will thus be in error when the signal passes over land. Often these differences are so slight that they really don't make that much difference in position. There are times however that position is affected considerably by the error and then it must be taken into account. Even when the receiver is many miles out to sea, the signals may still be affected by ASF as transmitters are often located many miles inland. Fortunately the ASF error is fairly consistent for a given area (even though it will change from place to place), so there are a number of ways in which this error can be dealt with. This topic is explored in depth in chapter 7.

Crossing Angles

A fix is determined by crossing two lines of position (LOP). A LOP can be a TD line or a LOP determined with another navigational technique, such as a bearing taken from a radio beacon with a RDF. Position may not be exactly where the two LOPs cross, but instead it will be within an "area of uncertainty" determined by the error of the system in use. This degree of error is affected by the angle at which the two LOPs cross. Those fixes determined from LOPs with larger crossing angles will be more accurate than those with smaller crossing angles. Those with crossing angles closest to 90 degrees will be most accurate.

Two examples of the crossing angles in two sets of LOPs will show how this works.

In the first set of LOPs (Fig. 2.11A), the angle between the lines is 85 degrees. With the hypothetical navigation technique being used in this example to derive those LOPs one might expect a legitimate working error of 0.1 nautical mile to either side of the line. The probable position in regard to the fix is now determined by that error. Marking off 0.1 nautical mile to either side of each LOP will show the area of uncertainty or area of expected position is somewhere within a circle formed by these "error lines." Doing the same thing with two LOPs that cross at a much smaller angle, perhaps 25 degrees, and putting the possible deviation error lines of 0.1 to either side of each LOP and the area of expected position will become much larger, even though the deviation error is still 0.1 nautical mile. (See Fig. 2.11 B)

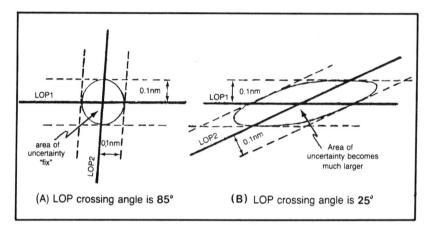

(A) LOP crossing angle is 85°   (B) LOP crossing angle is 25°

Fig. 2.11   Effect of Crossing Angle Size on Accuracy of Plotted Position

This concept applies to crossing any set of LOPs from any navigational aid or technique - not just TD LOPs. Generally speaking, LOPs should be used that have a crossing angle of 60 degrees or better. With TDs because of the inherent accuracy of the system it is possible to use lines that cross at less than 60 degrees, but then the probability of reduced accuracy should be noted. Although a 15 degree minimum crossing angle is assumed in the Loran system design to achieve quarter mile accuracy, general practice is to disregard TDs that cross with less than 30 degrees as their fixes may be unreliable.

Group Repetition Interval

Since all chains operate on the same frequency, 100 kHz, identification of a single Loran chain must be done by some means other than channel selection, i.e., tuning in to different frequencies. Instead, individual stations, and even whole chains, are identified by the timing and certain characteristics of the signals as they are received. For a single Loran chain, which consists of a master and at least two secondaries, identification is provided by a four digit number, the Group Repetition Interval, or GRI.

The GRI for a given chain is actually a measure in microseconds of the transmission time between two consecutive master signals. (See Fig. 2.12).

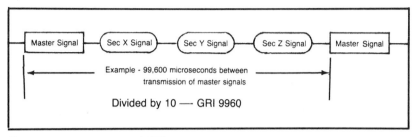

Fig. 2.12   Determination of GRI

Since this time interval must also include the transmissions from the secondaries, it is dependent on the number of secondaries in the chain and the number of microseconds between secondary transmissions. For each chain, a GRI is selected that allows adequate time for the transmission of the master signal and its secondaries before the master signal transmits again. The range assigned for these GRIs is between 40,000 and 99,990 microseconds. The designation, or identifier, of each chain then becomes the first four digits of the designated GRI, or the GRI divided by 10. For example, the assigned code for the Northeast U.S. Chain is 9960, as there are 99,600 microseconds between the transmission of master signals in that chain.

Propagation Characteristics of the Pulse Group

The transmitted signals from the stations within a chain, whether they are secondaries or a master, consist of groups of pulses. The reason for using pulses as opposed to continuous transmission is that pulses permit highly accurate measurement of time differences, and also the means to distinguish between ground and skywave reception. Pulsed transmissions along with specific time separations also prevent interference from one transmitter to another. The reason for having multiple pulses instead of a single pulse, (as was the case with Loran-A) is so that more signal energy is available at the receiver which improves the signal to noise ratio without having to increase the transmitter power.

A pulse group for each secondary is made up of a series of 8 (eight) pulses. The master pulse group also has 8 pulses, but it has an additional ninth pulse which identifies it as the master. Each pulse is spaced 1000 microseconds apart, with the ninth pulse in

the master signal 2000 microseconds after the eighth.
(See Fig. 2.13).

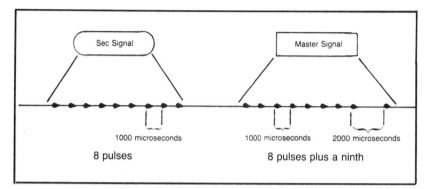

Fig. 2.13   Characteristics of the Pulse Group

In normal operation, the pulses of each pulse group are transmitted for a designated amount of time, 200 - 300 microseconds. But sometimes the transmissions may not be up to tolerance; then certain pulses in the secondary pulse group are blinked to warn receivers that the navigation information displayed may be in error. When compared with the short time span of the normal pulse, a few hundred microseconds, these blinks are of fairly long duration - ranging from 0.2 - 0.8 seconds.

In the past, both the master and secondary pulse groups were utilized for blink purposes. With the master it was the ninth pulse (which also identifies the station as a master) that was used for blink. However, the system was changed and master blink is no longer used to notify users of system abnormalities. Instead, notification will be by means of secondary blink.

Secondary blink utilizes the first two pulses of the secondary pulse group. Here the blink is a simple "on/off" signal with the "on" being transmitted for 0.2 - 0.35 seconds and then repeated every 4 seconds. When a blink signal is received, the receiver will give some sort of warning (alarm/light/flashing numbers) to indicate that the data is in error and should not be used.

Pulse Characteristics

A single Loran pulse consists of 20 to 30 cycles or wavelengths. An individual cycle has a duration of 10 microseconds. For example:

The Loran-C frequency is 100 kHz

or

100 X 1,000 cycles = 100,000 cycles/second

There are 1,000,000 microseconds in a second.

Therefore when divided:

$$\frac{1,000,000 \ \mu\text{seconds/second}}{100,000 \ \text{cycles/second}} = 10 \ \mu\text{seconds/cycle}$$

     The shape of the pulse is roughly teardrop (Fig. 2.14) with the waves or cycles extending above and below an imaginary horizontal centerline. Since radio waves are reversing forces of

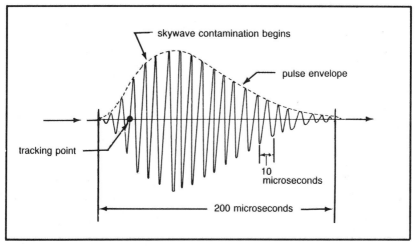

Fig. 2.14 The Loran-C Pulse

electromagnetic energy, it may be helpful to think of those portions of the cycles which are above the line as being in the positive (+) phase of the cycle, and those parts which are below the line as being in the negative (-) phase of the cycle. The amplitude (height above or below the imaginary centerline) of the individual cycles varies and it is this which gives the pulse its distinctive shape. This shape even has a name - it's called the pulse envelope. The envelope is not a physical entity as such, but just represents a curve that could be drawn by connecting the peaks of the individual cycles. The characteristic pulse envelope for the Loran signal is such that it begins with cycles quickly rising in amplitude to a peak and then slowly tapering off in decreasing height until the pulse is ended. All this occurs very quickly - within 200-300 microseconds.

Because the Loran-C system depends on exact timing of arrival of signals, it is important that the same reference point in the pulse be used for timing each signal. With a pulse of 200 microseconds it would make quite a difference if this point were at the beginning or end of the pulse. The very beginning of the pulse isn't a good place to track because interference from extraneous noise has a greater effect at this point where there is less power. Ideally, the easiest reference point to identify on the pulse is at peak amplitude. However, the skywaves which are being transmitted at the same time as the groundwaves must be taken into consideration. Because they travel a longer distance, (to the ionosphere and back), they will be coming in slightly later than the groundwave signals: 35 to 1,000 microseconds later. A look at the beginning of the pulse and a measurement of 35 microseconds into it (or 3 and one-half cycles) will show that this is where skywave contamination may begin, and of course the peak of the pulse is included in this area. Thus, a tracking point must be chosen which is far enough into the pulse to avoid interference from noise, but not so far in, that the tracking will be contaminated with erroneous skywaves. This tracking point, or measuring "mark" as it is sometimes called, is at the zero crossing point of the 3rd cycle - just ahead of possible skywave contamination.

To "synchronize" the signals of a master pulse and secondary pulse emission times, the times the pulses are transmitted, are established by superimposing the two pulses until their envelopes are exactly matched. The zero crossing points of the third cycle are further matched, which provides time differences accurate to better than 0.1 microseconds. On the other end, the receiver must use this tracking point in each pulse to measure the time difference in signal arrival. It is the characteristic shape of the pulse with its specific amplitude of individual cycles or "leading edge" in the first part of the pulse that helps the receiver to identify this cycle.

At this point it might be questioned, what does all this technical jargon have to do with using the Loran-C? Sometimes when signals fade or get too weak, this tracking point may slip or jump a cycle or more. The phenomenon is aptly named cycle slip or envelope shift, and it may produce errors of 10 microseconds or more. Most receivers issue some type of warning, flashing numbers etc. when this happens, but actually the error isn't too difficult to spot if position can be verified by some other means and then plotted on a chart with Loran overlay lines. A quick comparison between chart co-ordinates and receiver co-ordinates will show an error that is in distinctive multiples of 10 - a sure tip-off for cycle slip. For example, the reading may be 10 or 20 microseconds too large or too small depending on whether the receiver is tracking further into the pulse or closer to the beginning. Fortunately, many contemporary receivers are equipped to compensate for this problem with a manual "cycle stepping" procedure whereby the operator can step up or step down the cycle tracking point to get the receiver back on the correct measuring mark. Another technique is to prevent cycle slipping from occurring in the first place so that operation in a fringe, or known cycle slip area can be done accurately by putting the receiver in a "lock" or "track" mode. Correct tracking then, of course, must be verified.

Finally, there may be times when the receiver is tracking the correct cycle, but, because of distance, the signal is so weak that the readouts are intermittent. The cycle step procedure can then be used to move deeper into the pulse by 1 or 2 cycles where there is more power. The disadvantage here of course is the danger of skywave contamination along with the introduced error of + or - 10 or 20 microseconds which must be accounted for with each reading. Moving deeper into just the secondary pulse will increase the time differences while moving deeper into just the master pulse will decrease the time differences. Moving deeper into both the master and secondary pulses the same number of cycles will cause the errors to cancel each other out, and the time differences will be the same as if the tracking were done at a regular mark. (A further explanation of this is in the section: The Overall Picture). With some sets the error can be programmed in and the receiver will automatically make the correction for each readout. Thus, with a little understanding of signal propagation characteristics, most receivers can be tailor - made to operate successfully far beyond those areas designated as areas of primary coverage. This is but one of the ways that those who are cruising as far away as Venezuela have been able to send back reports of using Loran in those remote waters - thousands of miles away from nearest transmitters.

There is one other characteristic of the Loran pulse that needs to be examined, phase coding. There are two different ways that the receiver has of distinguishing between groundwaves and skywaves; one of which is the previously discussed utilization of a tracking point or measuring mark at the zero crossing point of the third cycle. Choosing this particular point to track can help effectively avoid all those skywaves coming in 35 microseconds behind the groundwaves. But, there are those really latecomers, the skywaves that are tagging along 1000 microseconds behind their groundwave counterparts. A check on Fig. 2.13 will show that there are 1000 microseconds between pulses, and these later skywaves could possibly interfere with the next groundwave pulse in the group. So that the receiver can distinguish between a ground-wave pulse and the skywave from the previous pulse, the system uses another propagation trick: phase coding.

Phase coding can best be understood by checking with the basic wave form again such as Fig. 2.15A. In this diagram it can be noted that the first phase of the wave goes above the imaginary centerline. If the wave form in A were inverted it would have a wave form that would now look like that in B. It is still the same wave form; it has the same amplitude, the same frequency (cycles/second), but the positive peaks that were above the line are now below the line.

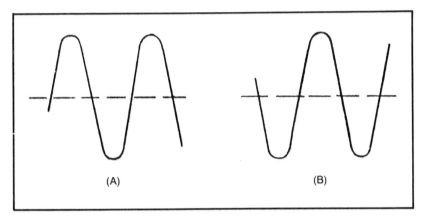

Fig. 2.15   Changing Phase In A Waveform

This is what is done in phase coding. The regular Loran-C pulse is "flipped" when transmitted, or inverted, so that the positive peaks become negative and vice versa. The pulse shape is still the same, the number of cycles is still the same, the tracking point is still the same. The only difference is that the Loran receiver can detect if the pulse has been inverted or not.

Not all the pulses in a Loran pulse group have their phases reversed; some do and some do not. Those that are transmitted in their normal phase (usually identified as being "in phase") are given the designation " + ". Those which are inverted, or are 180 degrees "out of phase" are identified by a "-". It is important to remember that there are 8 pulses in a pulse group with the master signal having an additional 9th. These pulses are then transmitted either in regular phase or out of phase - according to a pre-determined code.

46

	A	B
Master	+ + − − + − + − +	+ − − + + + + + −
Secondary	+ + + + + − − +	+ − + − + + − −

Fig. 2.16   Phase Coding Of The Pulse Group

All the secondaries are coded alike, but the master is coded differently so the receiver can tell which is the master signal and which is a secondary. Actually, there are two different codes (A and B) for the master and two different codes for the secondaries. As the signal pulse groups are transmitted, the phase coding is alternated between the two different codes: first the master and secondaries will be transmitted in the "A" code, then the next sequence will be in the "B" code. This is done to aid the receiver in distinguishing one Group Repetition Interval from the next.

The pulse groups, which are now transmitted in a recognizable pattern, enable the Loran receiver to distinguish between groundwave signals and the longer delayed skywave signals. When these skywaves of a given groundwave arrive 1000 microseconds late, they will be 1 pulse late. Although they carry the same phase code as their groundwave counterparts, they will not be "read" by the receiver because they are 1 pulse off the code sequence.

By phase coding the pulse groups, a number of objectives are achieved: 1. Differentiation between master and secondary signals. 2. Assistance in GRI identification. 3. Elimination of late skywave contamination. 4. Some protection from other (non-Loran) transmission.

The Overall Picture

When everything is put together, a diagrammatic representation of Loran chain propagation characteristics can be seen as in Fig. 2.17. Here the relationship of each secondary to the master in the group can be seen. All the Loran signals are transmitted on the 100 kHz carrier frequency. Individual chain identification is achieved through the Group Repetition Interval which is a measurement in microseconds of the emission time between two successive master pulse groups. Each station within the chain transmits signals in the form of a pulse group at a specific time within the GRI.

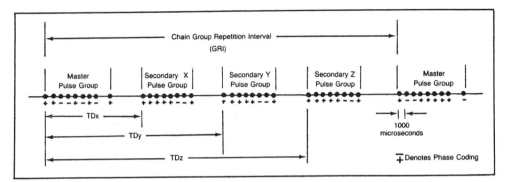

Fig. 2.17　Chain Propagation Characteristics

Each pulse group contains 8 pulses with the master pulse having an additional 9th pulse which is used for master identification. The pulse groups are further identified by phase coding which also enables the receiver to screen out late skywave contamination. Within each pulse, a specific cycle is identified as a tracking mark. This enables the receiver to screen out other skywave contamination and provides a highly accurate measuring point to measure time differences from one signal to another. It is these differences in arrival time of the signals that are the TD readouts on a Loran receiver. For example, TDx is the difference in microseconds between the arrival of the signal from the master and secondary X.

This diagram is also very helpful in explaining what happens when one or more of the signals is cycle stepped and the tracking mark is changed. When just the master is cycle stepped by moving the tracking point into the master pulse by 1 or 2 cycles, it can be seen from the diagram that one is moving closer to a given secondary (X) and thus reducing or decreasing the gap between the master and the secondary signal reception. This results in a decrease of the time difference between the signals (TD-X) by 10 or 20 microseconds, depending on how many cycles were stepped (or moved) into the master. If just the secondary is cycle stepped the diagram shows that one is moving away from the master, and the differences will increase, 10 or 20 microseconds. If both the master and the secondary are cycle stepped the same number of cycles, these variances will cancel each other out and the result will be the same time differences as if tracking at the regular mark in the pulses.

When viewed in its entirety, Loran signal propagation emerges as a highly sophisticated system which is capable of transmitting predetermined radio signals whose arrival time can be measured to a fine degree of accuracy. By utilizing system characteristics such as phase coding and blink, these signals can also transmit valuable information for signal identification and quality control. At the other end of the system is the Loran receiver, which, through the use of contemporary electronic engineering, not only tracks and records the time differences of received signals, but also performs a variety of other functions from computed data.

CHAPTER THREE

Hardware

Section I: The Loran-C Receiver

The basic functions of the Loran receiver are to acquire and track transmitted signals and measure their arrival time. Arrival times between a master and at least two of its secondaries are then compared, and it's these differences that are given as readouts on the receiver and then used to plot position. But this is not all. Through the use of microcomputers, many receivers also will process this data into an unbelievable array of useful navigational information. With a wide variety of functions, along with the numerous accessories that are now available, the choices are many for the potential Loran consumer to make.

Size, Shape, Power Consumption

Preliminary considerations in choosing a Loran are: overall size, shape of the housing, and power consumption. Modern technology has reduced the size of receivers (along with cost) from the large cumbersome units of the '60s into compact attractive units which fit nicely into most nav-stations. Some are small enough to be held in the palm of the hand. Although the external housing is usually rectangular in shape, this will vary as the larger dimension may be either horizontal or vertical. So this may be a factor in choosing what type of receiver will fit best into a specific area. The power drain for most receivers is quite small, 0.5 - 1.5 amps, but it does vary, and if the unit is to be used on a sailboat this may also be an important factor.

The Keyboard

The most important part of the receiver for the operator is the front panel, which is divided into two main parts: the keyboard and the display screen. Sometimes there is a third part - the power on/off switch. This switch may also contain a brightness control, or there may be a separate switch which adjusts the intensity of the screen readout for night vs. daytime use. On some receivers the on/off switch is part of the keyboard.

The keyboard (sometimes called the keypad) usually consists of two types of keys: those which are numbered 0 - 9, and those which are lettered. The numbered keys are used to enter data such as manual control for group repetition interval (GRI), station selection and waypoint information. On some receivers they can also be

Fig. 3.1   Loran Receivers May Vary In Size And Shape.

used to enter information for utilizing the computer functions of the receiver. Calculating the range and bearing between two waypoints, or converting a set of Lat/Lon coordinates to their corresponding TDs are examples of the computer functions.

Fig. 3.2 A Typical Display Screen & Keypad of a Loran Receiver. Courtesy of MICROLOGIC Chatsworth, CA

The lettered keys usually represent abbreviations for various functions of the receiver. Some examples of these are given in Fig. 3.3.

Ent,E	Enter
CLR,CL,C	Clear
TD	Time Difference
LAT	Latitude
LON	Longitude
L/L	Latitude, Longitude
R/B	Range & Bearing
COG	Course Over Ground
SOG	Speed Over Ground
TTG	Time To Go
XTK/XTE	Cross Track
WPT	Waypoint
C/D	Course To Destination
D/D	Distance To Destination
GRI	Group Repetition Interval

Fig. 3.3   Some Common Abbreviations Used On Loran Receivers

Time differences can be represented a number of different ways: TD-1, TD-2, or by the station designation X, Y, etc. Sometimes the various functions are not controlled by keys as such, but instead are controlled by switches with a knob which may switch to five or six different functions. The trend, however, seems to be towards keys, with most receivers having keys that utilize more than one function. For example, in one mode the key may serve as a number key, while in another mode it will work as a specific func-

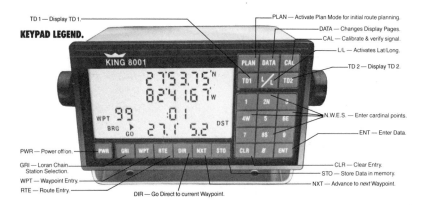

Typical of modern Loran-C design this King 8001 receiver has many standarized keypad entry functions, and a large display.

tion key. Another trend is towards completely enclosed front panels with touch control instead of actual keys. These units are sealed to prevent corrosion from the salt air. Some front panels will also be equipped with different lights which will indicate the specific mode or function that is in use. Without a doubt, it is in this area of the keyboard and front panel display that the greatest diversity in receivers occurs. This, then, brings up another consideration when choosing a Loran - it must be easy to use and not require a course in computer programming to operate.

Data Characteristics

Loran receivers also differ in the manner in which the data is displayed on the screen. Some receivers use red-light figures (LED), while others use pencil-black (LCD). There is a trend toward the more energy efficient liquid crystal displays (LCD), as opposed to the light emitting diodes (LED), which consume 100 times as much power. Whatever type is used, it is important that the receiver provide a good clear readout with good number size and easy to read characterizations.

Single Vs. Dual Readouts

Probably one of the biggest differences in display screens is whether they have single or dual readouts. With a dual readout, both TDs for a fix or both the latitude and longitude are given at the same time. With a single readout, only one is given. Single readouts often have the option of switching automatically between the two, or displaying the last four digits of each so that both TDs, or both latitude and longitude can be squeezed into the display area at the same time. While it may be argued that only one coordinate can be plotted at a time, the trend does seem to be toward larger display areas, even greater thàn dual readouts, on which large amounts of information can be presented. Finally, some screens will have functions permanently printed on them, while others will flash the functions as part of the information given - just another of the many choices which are available to the Loran user.

Data Precision

Another area of concern with the display is the degree of precision with which the data is presented. Again, not all receivers are the same: some will present TDs to the nearest 0.1 microsecond, while others will give the reading to the nearest 0.01 microseconds. There are two considerations in determining the importance of that 1/100 of a microsecond.

One is that it depends on the area of use. In an area in which the Loran-C charts being used have particularly small gradients, (it will be helpful to think of the gradient as being the distance the signal travels in a microsecond) it isn't too important to have that additional digit. For example, an area with a small gradient might mean that 0.1 microsecond equals 60 feet. Since there is already a high degree of accuracy, that extra six feet gained by using 0.01 microsecond really isn't needed. But the distance between hyperbolic lines changes, and if the cruising area has charts with large gradients (for example: 0.1 microseconds = 720 feet), then it probably is desirable to have that extra 0.01 microsecond.

Another factor in making this decision is how the Loran-C is going to be used. If the traveling is to be from one spot to another and the TDs are being used primarily to plot on a chart, the need for the extra digit is questionable, because on most charts the scale is such that 0.01 microseconds won't even register. But, if the TDs are going to be used to home in on, and come back to the same spot, the need is for repeatable accuracy, and to have the readout expressed to the nearest 0.01 microsecond may be helpful.

Data precision also affects those receivers which provide Lat/Lon coordinates. Most receivers display these as degrees, minutes and tenths and hundredths of minutes. (Some receivers also have the option of displaying Lat/Lon data as degrees, minutes, seconds.) A few receivers, however, will display this information only to 0.1 minute. Here the extra digit, or 0.01 minute is important when it is realized that 0.1 minute, which is also 0.1 nautical mile, equals roughly 200 yards, or 600 feet. The 0.01 minute puts the accuracy back into the 60 foot range, which is possible with Loran-C when using the system for homing techniques.

Number of Tracking Secondaries

The number of secondaries which are tracked at a given time often will vary with different Loran receivers. All receivers will track at least two, which are what is needed to obtain a fix by crossing two LOPs. But some receivers will track up to five secondaries or all the secondaries in a chain. This may be desirable in order to confirm a fix. Some receivers will even make the choice as to which secondaries are the best station pairs and provide the most reliable data. Chains and stations can be selected either automatically by the receiver or manually by the operator. It is important to have both features, because sometimes it may be necessary to override the automatic selection by the receiver by using the manual control. (See chapter 6 on selection of chains and station pairs.)

Notch Filters

Notch filters are used to screen out or "notch out" those signals from other transmitters which broadcast with frequencies that are close to the 100 kHz Loran band. There are two kinds of notch filters: internal and external. All sets have internal notch filters - and again there are two different kinds- those which are tuned and pre-set for specific frequencies at the factory, and those which will tune automatically inside the receiver as conditions change.

The number of pre-set internal filters will vary, with at least two being standard, and the more the better. The problem with pre-set filters is that they are good for only a certain area. A move to another area requires them to be tuned to the new area by a technician. Fortunately, these areas are quite large, so if all cruising is confined to a certain area, i.e., a certain section of the West Coast, there should be no problem. But, should the cruise pass through the Panama Canal and then continue up the Eastern Seaboard, these internal filters would have to be re-set.

On some receivers this isn't a problem because the internal filters will adjust spontaneously to any area, without the aid of a technician. Automatically, they will scan the frequency range, adjusting themselves to knock out any problem noise. Naturally, the cost of a receiver will increase proportionately with the sophistication of the set, and this automatic function of filters is one of the characteristics of higher priced receivers.

Another way of dealing with the notch filter problem is through the use of external, or tunable, notch filters. Some sets come with these in addition to the pre-set internal filters. A common arrangement is to have two internal pre-set filters and two external tunable ones. With some other receivers the addition of external notch filters is an accessory which can be adjusted right on the spot for given conditions. This is done by using a tuning knob, a variable RF (radio frequency) filter and some kind of an indicator. The danger with these manual controls is that they are user dependent; trouble may be caused by their not being tuned accurately. For example, one difficulty lies in making sure not to set the notch filters within the Loran band itself. That may result in tuning out the very signal which should be received. This can be difficult when the interfering signal is quite close to the Loran band.

Adjusting for ASF

Because radio waves travel at different speeds over land than over water, often there are discrepancies in received data and a plotted position may be in error from the vessel's actual position. This error, which is known as the Additional Secondary Factor (ASF) must be accounted for in some way. There are a number of ways to do this, (see chapter 4 on updating charts and chapter 7 on ASF.) One of these ways is through the receiver.

With a high degree of sophistication, some receivers are equipped with a micro-processor chip which will automatically make these corrections internally to the data as it is received. This is an important feature for a Loran receiver to have because ASF is one of the most important factors which affects the accuracy of readouts, hence plotted positions. Initially there were only a few manufacturers who offered the ability to make this correction, but the as price of microelectronics has continued to drop, more receivers are being made which provide this useful feature. Again, it is but one of those qualities that separates the more costly sets from their less expensive competitors.

Although the inclusion of automatic adjustment for ASF is on the rise, many receivers are still being manufactured without this ability. On these receivers there still is a way to make this correction on the data. The correction can be entered into the receiver memory manually. Because the ASF error is fairly constant for a coastal area of 20-25 miles, all that is needed is some other means to verify the vessel's position, and then to compare this position with the position indicated by the Loran receiver. Once the difference is known, it can be fed into the Loran and used for continued navigation in the area. However, it is important that the set has the capabilities to receive such manual input as some do not. Therefore, another important feature to look for in any Loran receiver is that it can correct for ASF, either automatically or from manual inputs.

Waypoints

One of the most useful applications of using Loran is in waypoint navigation. This is the method in which coordinates from a chart or previous fix are entered into the Loran and the receiver responds to the ship's position in relation to the waypoint with such vital information as distance and bearing to the waypoint, which way to steer etc. The reason the number of waypoints is important is that they are remembered by many of the better receivers when the power is off and can be recalled at another time, a convenience as opposed to re-entering waypoints each time they are needed.

The number of waypoints offered on various receivers differs immensely. The number of waypoints needed depends on where the receiver is used and in what manner. Certainly, for the lobster fisherman, who may be setting out a string of thirty or forty pots, having a large number of waypoints to identify each location is a considerable asset. Those who cruise for pleasure will often use the Loran in a similar manner by navigating through a string of waypoints (sometimes called waypoint rolling) to a given location. In this case, having more available waypoints can be helpful, especially if there is a string that is commonly used, (i.e., down a particular channel etc.), it can save a lot of time to have this string stored in the Loran's memory. If there is a large number of anchorages that are consistently visited, again it is convenient to have the extra waypoints so that these coordinates are ready for instant recall. (With a large number of waypoints available, skippers will often organize them into categories - see chapter 6 on mechanics).

For many Loran users however, having a large number of waypoints may not really be a concern. This is because it is relatively easy to program in the waypoints as they are needed. Particularly, if the cruising is done in the same general area with a few favorite spots, and no waypoint rolling is used, having one-hundred waypoints is not an important feature. Contemporary receivers reflect this fact, as many of the more popular sets on the market today offer 8-10 waypoints which certainly are adequate for most types of Loran navigation.

Another feature to look for in using waypoints is whether the receiver is able to switch automatically from one waypoint to the next when one is navigating through a string. With some receivers this changing from one waypoint to the next has to be done manually by the operator. The manual feature, of course, is necessary when using waypoints that are not in sequence, but the automatic option can be very helpful when conditions are rough or the operator is busy just handling the boat.

TD Vs. Lat/Lon Readouts

One of the biggest questions that the navigator faces when he is considering a Loran receiver is whether or not he needs a more expensive set which reads in Lat/Lon also, or is a set with just TD readouts good enough. This may be a difficult decision to make, and the following illustration will help.

A few years ago three boats were cruising together on Lake Superior's remote East Shore where there are few, if any, navigational aids present. In this particular situation they had been traveling in fog so thick for most of the trip that it was difficult to keep three boats together. They were confident, however, as among the three boats were two Loran receivers. One of the sets had only TD readouts, and as the boats approached the shore and their wilderness anchorage, the difference between the single TD readings versus Lat/Lon conversions quickly became apparent. The reason was that they were cruising in an area where there were no large scale charts with Loran overlay lines available. On the small scale chart (1:600,000), which was the only one available with Loran overlays, there was no detail of the entrance to the anchorage. In fact, it's exact position was so vague that all which showed on this chart was a name along a bold area of shoreline. Without prior TDs to home in on, the TD function of the receivers was next to useless.

Those, however, with Lat/Lon capabilities had switched to a much larger scale chart. This was particularly important because the approach to this remote harbor was unusually tricky, with outlying rocks and shoal areas to each side, through which there was only a narrow slot to make the entrance between a number of small islets. Now, with this chart, as with any chart, they were able to find their position with Lat/Lon coordinates. An update on position before leaving the previous anchorage had allowed them to correct for land propagation errors in the area so they were reasonably confident in the accuracy of their readings. They also programmed in the chart Lat/Lon coordinates for just outside the entrance as a waypoint on which to home in on so they had the added functions of range, bearing, time to go etc. But more importantly, they could then determine their position on that large scale chart which showed the entrance detail and those outlying rocks and shoals. Once again, without deviating, they slowly closed in on the entrance, slipped between the rocks and rounded the entrance islets into the safety of the anchorage - all in very poor visibility.

Whether it is important to have the Lat/Lon function depends on where the cruising is to be done, and how the receiver will be used. If position fixing is all that is of importance, and if there are adequately detailed, large scale Loran charts available for the area, a receiver which displays only TDs will probably do just fine. Though it takes a little more time, there are a number of things that can be done with TDs alone. For example, one can get range and bearing to a certain point; the only difference is that the operator instead of the receiver calculates these from the readout position. Cross track errors can be calculated by plotting a series of fixes. (See chapter 8 on Practical Applications). It must be noted that often a fix established with TDs is more accurate than one with Lat/Lon because of land propagation errors (ASF).

A deciding factor, however, in favor of the Lat/Lon receiver is that with many receivers which provide Lat/Lon capabilities, there usually is also included a whole battery of additional navigational information. Once the initial investment for a receiver is made, for just a few hundred dollars more, one can get not only the Lat/Lon function, but all the other functions which come along with the set and make it such an important tool in everyday navigation.

The Full Function Navigator

Many Loran receivers on the market today offer a degree of sophistication which is equalled by few other navigation instruments. Initially designed to just establish position, receivers now can dead reckon, steer the boat, announce arrival at a destination, keep anchor watch, and even self diagnose internal ills and signal reception. See Fig. 3.4. The different navigational functions which a Loran may provide can be roughly divided into 4 separate categories:

1. Position Functions.
2. Dead Reckoning Functions.
3. Steering Functions.
4. Computer Functions.

Position Functions	Dead Reckoning Functions	Steering Functions	Computer Functions
TDs	Speed over bottom	Waypoint navigation	TDs to Lat/Lon
Lat/Lon	Velocity over bottom	Course to steer	co-ordinates
Storage of present	Course over bottom	(true)	Lat/Lon to TDs
position	Distance to waypoint	Course to steer	Two point range
Arrival warning	Distance run	(mag)	& bearing
Anchor watch	Time to go	Crosstrack error	Convert TDs from
Position offsets-	Elapsed time	Course correction	one pair to
ASF correction	ETA	(steer right or	another in the
	Time enroute	left)	same chain
	Adjusting for dynamic	On course meter	Convert TDs from
	lag	Rhumbline steering	one chain to
		Autopilot output	another
			Calculate ASF

Fig. 3.4   The Full Function Navigator: Possible Navigation Functions

Position Functions

Basic position functions are, of course, the TD and Lat/Lon readouts which are used to establish position on a chart. One nice feature with many receivers is that a given set of TDs or Lat/Lon at a "present position" can be stored and thus saved with the touch of a single key. For example, the skipper may not have time to write down TDs he may want to keep when he is passing through a narrow channel entrance and doing some tricky maneuvering. Pressing a particular key will cause the receiver to lock in the coordinates to its memory to be recalled at a later time. This could be extremely useful in a man-overboard search.

On many receivers there is an alarm which will announce arrival at a certain waypoint when position is established as being at that waypoint or a certain distance from it. An anchor watch alarm is but another application of this principle in which arrival at the "waypoint" is indicated by a change in position outside a given range from an initial position.

An additional function which is quite important in establishing position is the use of an offset which measures and adjusts for the ASF error in readings which is due to land propagation errors. In order to use this function, the exact geographic position must be known by other means and then compared to the Loran position. Use of this function will often enhance the accuracy of readings and, once calibrated, the error can be used for further navigation in a given area.

Dead Reckoning Functions

In the area of dead reckoning the Loran receiver really comes into its own. It is almost unbelievable the amount of navigational data that the receiver can compute from just establishing position. Yet, the theory behind these conversions is similar to what is used in making calculations in other navigation. For example, it is easy to see that, since the Loran can establish position so accurately, all it has to do is take the elapsed time and determine the distance between readings to calculate the speed of travel. Likewise, direction can be measured between two consecutive fixes to establish the course traveled. With present position known by the receiver, distance to a given waypoint can be calculated as well as distance run from a previous waypoint. Even in areas known for large land propagation errors, these functions will still provide highly accurate information. For the calculations are based on establishing consecutive position fixes and, if the error is present, it will be the same for each fix in a given area. It will then be cancelled out as it is the differences between fixes which are used in these determinations.

Of course, the Loran is also an excellent time keeping device. Not only will it keep track of elapsed time and the time it will take to reach a particular destination, but some receivers will also give an ETA (estimated time of arrival) on the basis of present speed versus distance left to be traveled.

A word of caution should be made here on using these last two functions: "time to go" and ETA. Because they are computed on the basis of present speed, these values will change if the speed changes. Thus, on long runs, it is not uncommon to see these values jump around, especially if used on a sailboat where speed fluctuates with wind strength. For example, at 100 miles out from the destination, the time readings may be 13.5 hours to go, then 15, then back to 14, etc. As the distance to the destination decreases, these differences in time will lessen and become more reliable.

Many Loran receivers will also keep a very accurate accounting of time while enroute and thus become a vital tool in normal dead reckoning. To use this function, the time must be initially programed into the receiver and it will then keep track of the time internally, even when the function is not displayed. A disadvantage of this function is that it is lost when the power is off and the time will have to be reset whenever there is an interruption of power.

Another important point to note about the speed readout given by the Loran is that it may differ from the speed given by an onboard knotmeter. This is because the Loran speed is based on actual geographic position and gives the true speed over the bottom. The knotmeter tells only how fast the water is going by the keel, and it will be influenced by currents, rough seas etc., so that it may not be an accurate representation of actual speed.

Finally, when using dead reckoning functions such as true course and ground speed, it should be pointed out that a "dynamic lag" occurs whenever these values are changed. In other words, it will take the Loran a few minutes to "catch up" with the indicated position - and those functions which are dependent on it will be slightly behind the true values. This is because these readouts represent an average of the true course and ground speed taken over a specific span of time, which is sometimes called "filtering." The filtering time will usually vary between 1 and 2 minutes, so this is how long it will take before these readings are again reliable.

Receivers are usually set with a nominal time lag which will produce both steady and reliable data. But some receivers offer the option of changing the filtering time. If it is shortened, the displayed readings will respond quickly to course changes, but they will jump around, and over the long run may not be reliable. If the filtering time is lengthened, readings will become quite smooth and accurate, but then it will take a much longer time before they are updated after course changes. If this option is available, the length of filtering time used will depend on whether runs are long with few course changes or frequent tight maneuvers within a given area.

Steering Functions

A full function Loran receiver offers another package of navigational extras - those which pertain to steering directions. Once the receiver knows the position and the desired waypoint, it will tell what course to take to get there, and, if off course, what corrections need to be taken to get back on course. The key element in doing this is, of course, knowing the destination. In order to gain from this package, it is necessary to be able to program at least one waypoint.

A waypoint is a destination. It may be either the coordinates at the end of a run, such as those for a harbor entrance, or a specific point along the way. A waypoint does not have to mark a geographic entity as such - it can by anywhere. Common waypoints are often those at entrances to channels or anchorages, or whenever a change in course is required. But a waypoint can also be out in the middle of nowhere on a straight run so that it can be used to determine arrival time after so much distance is covered. The important thing to remember about waypoints is that, without them, many of the steering functions of the Loran would not be possible.

The ability to employ a number of pre-programmed waypoints is important when utilizing the steering functions of the receiver. Here a whole trip can be planned in advance, with the waypoints entered in for each course change. If the receiver can automatically "roll" from one waypoint to the next, a new steering course will be given upon the arrival at each waypoint.

The course to steer (often called the bearing to the waypoint) may be given as either true or magnetic. Many Loran skippers are finding out how easy it is to do all their chart work and subsequent steering by working with only true course and not going through the hassle of adding or subtracting for magnetic variation. To do this the Loran is not only used for chart work, but the actual steering of the boat itself. An accessory which makes this especially easy is a remote Loran readout in the cockpit or next to the steering station. As long as both the chart work and steering are done with true readings, the errors due to magnetic variation will cancel out. If the preference is to steer a magnetic course with the ship's compass, then magnetic variation can be entered into the Loran and all subsequent chart work can be done with magnetic courses. Should the preference be to use magnetic variation, and for some reason it is not known, the dead reckoning function of the Loran "course over bottom" can be used to compare with the magnetic course and additions or subtractions made as needed.

When off course (usually called cross track error), there are a number of ways in which a Loran receiver can let that be known. Again, there are almost as many variations in displaying this information as there are different types of keyboards. One is a simple readout which is given in nautical miles, along with an indicator which tells if the error is to the right or left of the track. This information may be displayed along with the "time to go" to the destination as in Fig. 3.5.

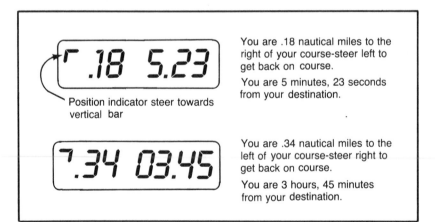

Fig. 3.5   Displaying Crosstrack Error & Time To Go

Sometimes the actual position of the readout on the screen will indicate whether the error is to the right or left of the course. This function may also be displayed with other functions, such as "distance to go," "speed over the bottom," "true course," etc., depending on the mode in operation. (See Fig. 3.6).

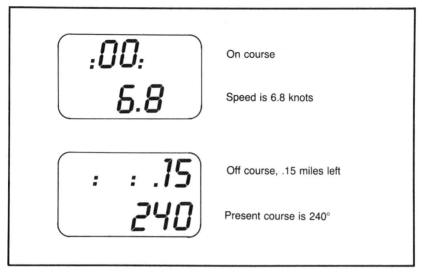

Fig. 3.6   Displaying Cross Track Error & Other Functions

On some receivers there may be the option of turning the display area into an "on course meter" similar to those used on airplanes where positions of vertical and horizontal bars are assigned numerical values to tell how far off course one is and how far to the next waypoint. (See Fig. 3.7) This option is carried even

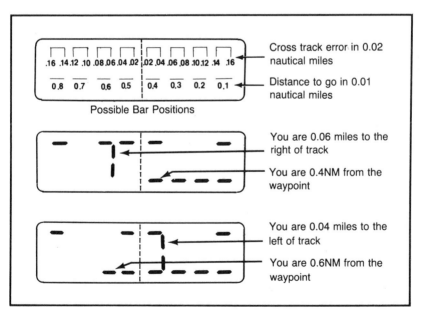

Fig. 3.7   Using An On-Course Meter

further with a remote Course Deviation Indicator which is offered by some manufacturers. And, as if these are not enough devices to indicate being off course, some will sound an alarm when the position is too far off the track.

One of the more useful steering functions for those who are planning long trips is the ability of the receiver to plot a course along a great-circle path as opposed to the rhumb line, thus resulting in a considerable saving of distance traveled. Receivers which can perform this function will automatically compute a series of rhumb line waypoints equally spaced along a great-circle route between two given sets of Lat/Lon coordinates. The Loran then steers accordingly, going from one way point to the next, as in a string, but the course is actually following the chords of a great-circle route. (See Fig. 3.8).

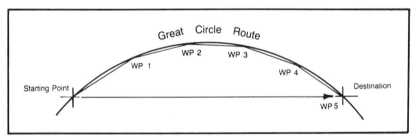

Fig. 3.8   Using The Loran To Plot A Great Circle Route

For example, if a trip is planned from Bermuda to the Azores, the distance between them is large enough to warrant using a great circle route as opposed to a rhumb line, which is much longer. However, plotting the curved great circle line on a Mercator chart is more difficult to calculate and plot. With a Loran receiver it is possible to enter in the departure Lat/Lon at Bermuda and the destination Lat/Lon at the Azores. At this point, range and bearing will be calculated as on a rhumb line. However, in some receivers a special program can compute the route as a great circle path instead. This can then be divided into 7 or 8 smaller segments, each of which is represented by waypoints. A two point range and bearing can then be calculated by the receiver between each set of successive waypoints and recorded. The advantage of this option is that it can be done as a part of cruise planning before leaving Bermuda and the information can be used to guide the vessel's course even when the receiver is well outside the area of signal reception. Another advantage is that, by using the rhumb line segments of the great circle route, it is possible to shave days off the intended voyage.

The ultimate application of the steering functions of a Loran is, of course, to interface it with an autopilot. This can be especially useful when cruising in an area with cross currents. On autopilot alone the steering is done with just an accurate compass course oblivious to set and drift from currents. But with the Loran, which is homing in on a waypoint, the destination is reached no matter what the set is from wind and water, as the Loran will dictate to the autopilot to make whatever corrections are necessary to reach that waypoint.

For example, a vessel on autopilot is trying to make the entrance of a small harbor of refuge on a course of 40°True at 6 knots. (See Fig. 3.9). A fix is established at point A. From this it is determined that the range and bearing to the entrance is 12 nm and 40°T. However, at this point a wind comes up producing a set (direction) of 130°; and a drift (speed) of 2 knots. If these are not corrected for and the autopilot is left on the same setting, at the end of one hour the vessel will be clearly off course ;and not make the entrance on the set course of 40°T. To make the needed corrections, it is necessary to know the actual set and drift and use complicated vector diagrams to calculate the course needed to make good a course of 40°T. Or, if Loran is used, the coordinates of the entrance can be programmed in as a waypoint and the cross track error will indicate the course deviation and the amount of

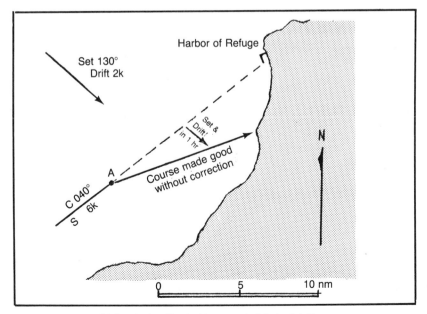

Fig. 3.9   Effects Of Continuing On An Un-corrected Autopilot Course

correction which can then be manually adjusted to the autopilot. But, if the Loran is interfaced with the autopilot, these corrections will be made automatically and the autopilot will home in on the harbor entrance coordinates regardless of any set or drift by wind or current.

Computer Functions

With many receivers it is possible to use their computer functions to perform certain calculations and solve some navigational problems. In most cases the receiver doesn't even have to be tracking. In fact these operations can be done without even having the antenna hooked up, but by just having the Loran connected up to a power source.

One of the more common calculations is to convert TDs to their respective Lat/Lon coordinates. This may be helpful if the previous TDs for a specific location are known, but a Loran chart with overlays is unavailable. The plan is to then navigate with only Lat/Lon coordinates on regular charts. Another reason for converting to Lat/Lon is that waypoints are usually entered as these coordinates instead of TDs. With some receivers it is possible to enter TDs as waypoints, but then the computer functions of the receiver are being used anyway, as it will convert the TDs to Lat/Lon equivalents, and then these are entered in for the waypoints.

It is also possible to do the reverse, or convert Lat/Lon coordinates to their respective TDs. It may be that the area being cruised is one known to have a high ASF error, so the accuracy of the Lat/Lon coordinates is questionable. If an updated chart, with the corrected chart lattice is available, the navigation will be more accurate if the work is done in TDs. So, using the computer functions of the receiver, conversion of any Lat/Lon readings to their corresponding TDs is possible.

These conversions (TD to Lat/Lon: Lat/Lon to TD) can be made with coordinates which are not even in the chain being presently worked. In fact, this can be done with any location in the world. The Loran does, however, have to be helped a bit by programming in the GRI and approximate Lat/Lon to within a few degrees of the desired location.

Probably one of the most valuable uses of Loran receiver computer functions is the ability to determine the range and bearing between any two given waypoints - even when the present location is not one of them. This is particularly helpful in cruise planning when it is desirable to know ahead of time the distance between two anchorages, which destination is further from a given point etc. Again, this can be done with positions outside the working chain - as long as the GRI chain they are in is known, and their approximate latitude and longitude.

The computer functions may also be used to convert TDs from one secondary pair to another in a given chain. This could be useful if there are prior TDs to be used from a particular station pair, but for some reason or other that particular secondary cannot be tracked.

Another function is to be able to change TDs to those of different station pairs in another chain. This is useful when operating in an area in which there is an overlap of chains. Switching to another chain may be useful because of better station geometry for reception of signals, but the input from prior TDs of the first chain is necessary.

The computer functions of the receiver can even be used to calculate the ASF error for a given area. To use this function, however, tracking signals are needed so that position can be established with the receiver. Actual position is determined by being at a known location (dock, buoy, etc.) and this is then lifted from the chart and entered into the receiver. The receiver will compare the two positions and calculate the ASF error for that area. This error can be entered into the receiver and used for further navigation or, if written down, it can be recalled and entered at a future date to be used when returning to that area.

Diagnostic Functions

In addition to the above functions which are primarily navigational, there are a number of receiver functions which usually are not used directly by the operator. These involve a series of self checks and tests of receiver performance. Many of these are geared for the technician who is troubleshooting a malfunctioning receiver. But some of these functions can be useful to the operator as they will indicate via alarms, flashing numbers etc., that either the receiver is having difficulty in tracking signals or the data is in error.

Probably the most important diagnostic function to the operator is the Signal to Noise Ratio (SNR). This is a number value which compares the strength of the incoming signal to the amount of interfering noise. A high SNR means a strong signal in comparison to incoming noise. A low SNR means that there will be a problem with reliability of data because of noise interference. How these numbers are represented on the receiver varies with the manufacturer, so this is another case where the owner's manual needs to be checked.

Other indicators of problems are those which tell if there is a memory failure in the unit or if it is having difficulty in tracking a particular signal. The receiver may indicate if it is experiencing cycle slip so that readings are off in multiples of 10 microseconds or if it is receiving a blink signal indicating a defective secondary signal. Some receivers even have a way of warning the operator that received data is from skywaves as opposed to being from ground-waves. How these warnings are displayed will vary according to the individual unit.

More Options

A check of the options possible to get with a Loran receiver shows that many units are, in fact, extremely sophisticated pieces of equipment. But this is not all. There are some Lorans which are so small, and waterproof, that they are portable and can be taken on a dinghy. Whether diving or fishing off the reefs, this handy little receiver is a real asset in returning to previous locations. (See Fig. 3.10)

Some units are designed so that the face panel is separate from the electronics assembly. The face panel is mounted in the nav-station, and then the electronics box can be hidden away in some locker - up to six feet away. This is an especially useful option on smaller boats on which space is at a premium. Another unit which helps conserve space is actually housed in the same box with a VHF radio. In this case they even share the same antenna!

And, of course, there is the "talking Loran" which actually spews out vital information in verbal language. Not a bad idea when considering those times when the operator's hands are full because of rough weather or involvement in a particularly tricky maneuver.

Where to Buy A Loran Receiver

One of the key factors in recent price reduction of Loran receivers has been the fierce competition in the market, particularly with the increase of marine discount houses. Often a savings of many hundreds of dollars can be realized if the unit is bought through a discount catalogue as opposed to purchasing one through a regular dealer. This then raises an important question:

should the Loran receiver be purchased through a marine dealer or through a mail order discount house?

The purchase of a Loran through a marine dealer usually includes a number of extras that come along with the additional price tag. These are in the form of expertise, installation assistance, and service. As part of the package, many dealers will give useful information and assistance (if not complete installation) in installing the receiver and antenna system. Because he has done it

Fig. 3.10 The Portable Loran Receiver With Battery Pack & Antenna Attachment

Courtesy of MICROLOGIC Chatsworth, CA

so often his experience is beneficial. Particularly if the consumer is not too sure about various aspects of the installation, it may be best to purchase the unit through a marine dealer and have him install it and make sure it is working properly. Even the most sophisticated equipment will not function properly, and signal reception will be poor or erratic if the antenna is not installed correctly or if the unit is not grounded adequately.

Another reason for buying through a local dealer is that, if problems arise, he will be able to diagnose these better than the inexperienced operator. Since many of the receiver's internal diagnostic tests are geared for a technician's background and understanding, it is important to determine if the dealer has an inhouse trained technician. It may be that simply by running these tests he can spot the problem, and then pull out just the erring component, as opposed to taking out the whole receiver to be sent in. If the dealer does not have his own technician, but simply sells the units, the purchaser is no better off than buying from a discount house.

Further, working through such a dealer isn't a viable option for many because of distance. If the purchaser's location is such that he can't make use of these dealer's services, he may do well to consider ordering the receiver through a catalogue. If he is going to have to do the installation himself anyway, he might as well take advantage of those price differences and do some comparison shopping.

To assist the customer, most discount houses have toll free numbers and accept major credit cards. In just a short time, by using the telephone, a half dozen of these outlets can be called and the best buy found. These people have been found to be most helpful and willing to answer questions. Even after the purchase is made they will continue to give assistance over the phone, whether it is with advice on installation or trouble shooting a particular problem. The caller should always get the name of the person he is talking with. This way, if he does have to call back, he can get the same person and not have to explain the problem again to someone new.

The main disadvantage, of course, with ordering from a discount house, is that if the receiver should start to malfunction, the only recourse may be to send the whole unit in for repairs. But, whether it is bought from a dealer or a discount house, the warranty is still the same. It may also be that, even working through a dealer, he may not be able to spot the problem either, and the unit would have to be sent in anyway.

Autopilot Interface

Perhaps the most commonly purchased accessory for a Loran receiver is the autopilot interface. Not only can it save time in distance run and fuel, but it even makes the autopilot steer better - a true course to the destination without deviation from winds or currents. The combination of these two systems is so good that there is a danger of becoming overly reliant on them. Certainly the Loran will direct the autopilot to take the boat through a complicated sequence of turns and maneuvers. But, unless it is so programed, it will not automatically skirt shoals, and of course, it will not maneuver to avoid oncoming traffic. Even though the Loran has taken charge in directing the boat, there still remains the need for keeping a good watch.

The possibility of losing a Loran signal may produce additional problems. What happens then? Some Lorans will warn the autopilot that it is no longer tracking. The autopilot may respond by maintaining a crabbed heading which could reflect a serious error, or it may return to a direct magnetic compass heading. Either way, there must be some means that the operator has of noting that he may no longer be on the track he thinks. In any case, the Loran/autopilot combination is not fool proof, even though it is one of the best adaptations of the system yet.

Remote Readout

Next to the autopilot interface, the most common Loran accessory is the remote readout. This is especially useful for bringing Loran information to an area of the boat where it isn't readily available otherwise. Without a remote readout, it is almost impossible to use the Loran for navigation in tight situations when cruising single handed. The remote unit saves having to have a crewman down below calling out instructions to the helmsman.

On sailboats, on which the main receiver is usually below decks at the nav-station, a remote readout placed near the helmsman in the cockpit is a valuable asset. On powerboats there usually is room for the main receiver in the wheelhouse or main steering station. Then the remote unit is often run to the flying bridge where it can be used to guide exterior course work.The remote readout usually does not display all the functions of the main receiver but primarily gives distance and steering instructions to the next waypoint. Remarkably, these are displayed independently of what the main receiver is reading out down below.

Another useful adaptation of the remote readout is a remote course deviation indicator. This unit, which is placed next to the steering station gives a continuous readout of cross track error. With a meter and indicator needle, or other displays, it tells if the boat is on course (steer left, steer right, on track) or off to either side. A deviation scale will tell the distance off course. It will also indicate arrival at a certain distance out from a pre-selected waypoint.

Additional Notch Filters

Many manufacturers offer the option of purchasing a kit of external tunable notch filters. When leaving the normal area of operation this may be a preferred way of screening out other transmitter signals as opposed to having the internal notch filters tuned by a technician to each cruising area.

Track Plotters

A track plotter is an accessory unit into which a chart or sheet of plain paper is inserted. Through an interface to the Loran receiver, coordinates are transferred to the chart and plotted via pen movement as position changes according to time differences. Accuracy will vary depending on the scale which is used. The advantage of a track plotter is that not only is the ship's position recorded, but also it's actual movement through a given course. This can then be saved and recalled at a future date to guide the ship through the same course.

Track plotters are especially useful for those who have to repeat the same course over and over, such as dragging over oyster beds, or if a good run is found for setting lobster pots. An excellent non-commercial use is in conducting a man-overboard search when a graphic display of ground covered would be produced.

Sat-Nav Interface

Currently there is at least one manufacturer who provides an interface between a Loran receiver and a satellite navigator. For long distance cruisers, this combination is an exceptionally good idea because it brings together the best of both worlds.

The advantage of navigating with Loran is that it provides continuous data. Its disadvantage is that, once outside of primary coverage areas, readings become inaccurate because of skywave signals. With Sat-Nav, accurate position fixes are possible any-where in the world, but the disadvantage is that signals are re-ceived only intermittently as satellites pass overhead. Putting the two systems together capitalizes on the advantage of each. An accurate position is determined by each satellite pass. This is then compared to Loran position which contains the skywave error. Once the error is measured, the Loran compensates for it and continues to navigate until the next satellite pass and position update.

Navigational Computers

More than one manufacturer offers the option of interfacing a Loran with a complete navigational computer. These come with video display and print-out capabilities. One model can call up full-color microfiche reproductions of charts. Ship's position as determined by Loran is placed in the center of the chart in a compass rose. The computer moves the chart as position changes. Normal Loran information (distance and course to waypoints etc.) is numerically displayed. Some units will store up to 500 waypoints and 20 different trip plans. The cost of these units is proportional to their capabilities, putting them out of reach for most of those who cruise for pleasure or sport.

For use in commercial shipping, these units have achieved a level of sophistication that is difficult to believe. One package which consists of just three modules (keyboard, display screen, computer), along with various shipboard sensors will give naviga-tional information from Loran, Sat-Nav, and Omega, in addition to a digital compass and knotmeter. It will measure such things as freshwater level, electrical power, sea state, propeller pitch, rudder angle, and various engine running parameters - all of which are kept on a log which can be retrieved via cassette. Charts are again displayed on the screen to assist in determining position or lines can be drawn in electronically to add individual features. The units are literally tailor-made to fit individual ship's requirements. It is difficult to imagine anything these integrated systems can't do.

Section III: General Tips

LORAN-C SYSTEM INSTALLATION

The following are some basic guidelines for installing a Loran receiver. Because the various connectors, brackets, etc. will vary with different makes of Loran receivers, this section is not intended to provide complete instructions for receiver installation. A purchaser doing his own installation should consult his owner's manual, which gives specific instructions for that unit.

The Antenna

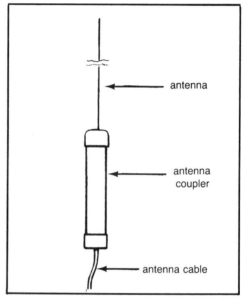

Fig. 3.11   The Antenna System

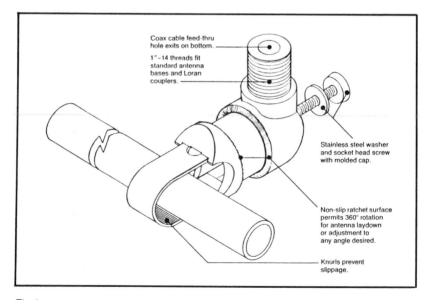

Fig 3.12A   The Railfast™ is a good example of commercially available antenna mounts

courtsey of the Newmar Corp.

The Loran signal is received by an onboard antenna and then passed through an antenna coupler and a cable to the Loran receiver. Antennas are usually stainless steel wire or fiber glass whip. Many receivers are sold with their own antennas which have been especially "tuned" to those receivers.

Choosing the best antenna site is one of the most critical factors in determining receiver performance. The highest quality Loran with a poor antenna installation will perform worse than a low quality receiver with a superb antenna installation. Since most antenna systems contain an integral preamplifier (pre-amp or pre-amp and coupler) excessive height is not a critical factor. However, as a rule of thumb the antenna should be mounted as high above the water as practical, a minimum of 5 to 7 feet. It is also important that it be mounted in a vertical position. It should be positioned away from standing rigging (shrouds and stays) as these will absorb incoming Loran signals. Other transmitting and receiving antenna, along with radar and radio direction finding equipment can also cause interference, so it is important to place a Loran antenna away from these - at least four to six feet.

Large hose clamps are often used to secure the Loran-C antenna coupler to the stern pulpit.

Photo by Bonnie Dahl

On a power boat, the antenna is often mounted on the after part of the cabin top or aft of the bridge structure. On a sail boat, it can be mounted on top of the mast, but this spot has usually been pre-empted by the VHF marine radio antenna which needs height for maximum line of sight range. The main advantage of a Loran masthead mount is to get the antenna up and away from the standing rigging. This, however, is outweighed by the dis-advantage of reduced signal reception on the VHF marine radio. On a ketch, the mizzen masthead may sometimes be used, but on a sloop a Loran antenna is usually mounted on the stern rail (wher-ever the antenna is located it should be noted that the signal reception is reduced the closer one approaches a heeling angle of 40°.) If there are other antennas (VHF,CB) located here, the an-tennas should be placed in separate corners of the stern rail with a separation of at least four feet. Another trick to offset interference from nearby antennas is to tilt one of the antennas slightly so that the two antennas are exactly not parallel to each other.

The Antenna Coupler

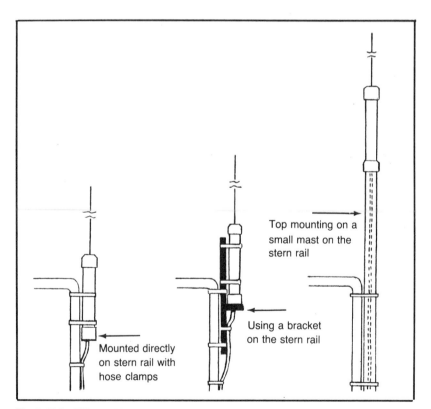

Fig. 3.12 B   Different Ways of Mounting The Antenna & Antenna Coupler

At the base of the antenna, there is a pre-amplifier and antenna coupler which have the function of interfacing the antenna to the cable which carries the signal to the receiver. To perform this function, the coupler must amplify the signal and filter out any additional contaminating noise. It is also designed to discharge any large electrical fields which are caused by lightning or high voltage transmission lines.

It is at the antenna coupler that the antenna system is attached to the boat. Quite often this is done by merely attaching the coupler unit directly to a sturdy structure, such as the stern pulpit with a commercially made bracket or perhaps simply two hose clamps. (See Fig. 3.12A & 3.12B). Often a separate supporting bracket or "mast" will be used. In any case, it is important that the coupler unit is attached securely enough so that it will not move or slip around with the motion of the boat.

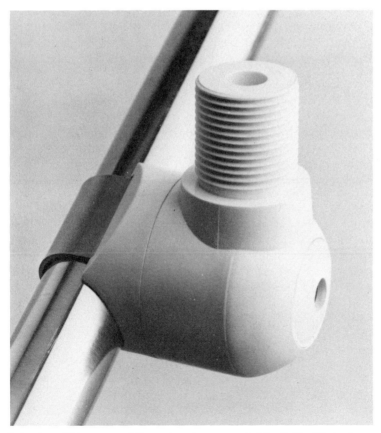

A drawing of this commercially made antenna mount, (The Railfast™), is shown on page 76.

courtsey of the Newmar Corp.

Some antenna couplers need to be grounded; others are grounded through the cable that connects to the receiver, and then the receiver is grounded. This point should be carefully checked in the owner's manual. If the coupler needs to be grounded separately, this should be done with the largest wire possible, at least a no.8 or larger - or a copper strap. The ground should be run independently from other grounds and run to a main hull ground point such as a keel bolt, underwater ballast or ground plate.

The Antenna Cable

The antenna cable connects the antenna and coupler unit to the Loran receiver. When the cable is routed from the coupler to the receiver, it should be kept well away from other transmitters and associated antenna feeders. Running the cable parallel to other wiring should be avoided, and a little slack should be provided to allow a little "give" when the hull "works" or flexes. To avoid breaking or damaging the cable's protective insulation, it should not be run around sharp turns or near heat radiating objects such as manifolds, steam pipes, heaters and other hot objects.

Sometimes there is too much cable and the excess can be wound in a loose coil and taped close to the coupler, away from all other wires. Such a coil should not be placed near the receiver because it may pick up noise and thus produce low SNR numbers. If the cable is too short, it is usually possible to obtain a cable extension kit from the manufacturer.

Cable that is exposed topside should be secured to the stern pulpit or other structure by stainless steel cable clamps or hose clamps so that it will not be whipped about by the motion of the boat. Likewise, below decks it should be held in place by clamps at frequent intervals, but the clamps should not be over tightened as they can cut or crush the cable. The antenna cable should not be allowed to come into contact or become submerged in water standing in the bilge. If water is able to enter the cable the Lorans performance would be seriously degraded.

A final note concerning installation of the antenna system is that it may be wise to install the antenna temporarily, so that the signal to noise ratio can be checked. This is also a good time to check other shipboard equipment against receiver operation. It may be that the antenna site will have to be moved, or that the interference from that equipment will have to be suppressed. Sometimes moving the antenna just two or three feet may make a significant difference in reception of the signal.

Location

The most common place to install a Loran receiver is in the nav-station or, if there is room, at the main steering station on a power boat. Common sense dictates that it be placed in a dry area away from moisture or salt spray. A Loran receiver should not be located beneath ports or near hatches, or other locations which will expose the unit to heat or direct sunlight. The Loran set, along with associated cabling should also be kept away from transmitters, radar, and other antennas and feeders. Finally, it is most important to keep the receiver and associated wiring well away from a magnetic compass. The Loran, or any other electronic equipment or wiring will interfere with the magnetic field which affects the vessels compass. This field varies when the receiver is on or off, resulting in interference for which it is difficult to compensate. Thus it is important that the receiver and wiring be placed at least three feet from any magnetic compass.

Mounting

The receiver should be attached securely enough to wherever it is positioned so that there is no danger of its being vibrated by the motion of the boat. Most receivers come with mounting brackets. These are usually quite versatile so that the unit can be positioned either as an overhead mount, bulkhead mount, or table mount. Whichever mounting type is used, it is important that the receiver be allowed to "breathe" and there is an airflow of at least a few inches of space above and behind the unit. (See Fig. 3.13).

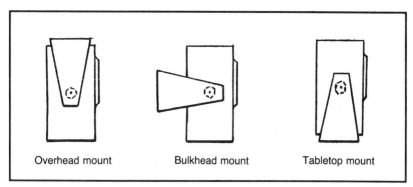

Overhead mount   Bulkhead mount   Tabletop mount

Fig. 3.13   Different Ways of Mounting a Loran Receiver

In positioning the receiver, it is important that it is accessible for inputting data - and that the screen can be easily read. One operator mounted his Loran so high with an overhead mount that he had to stand up at the chart table each time he wanted to read information from the receiver.

This sailboat has a Northstar Loran-C designed for use in exposed locations. This unit features a waterproof control head; the electronics "black box" can be located up to ten feet away in a protected location.

Many will try to mount the receiver in such a way that it can be read from the cockpit. The disadvantage to this location is that often the bright sunlight makes the data fade away to almost nothing, particularly if the unit has an LED display, and makes it difficult to read. Using the tilt or swivel function of the bracket can be very helpful in eliminating this effect. The swing of the receiver must be provided for in the installation along with an allowance for sufficient cable length so there is no strain when the unit is tilted.

A final concern when mounting a Loran is ease of removal. This consideration has two aspects. If the boat is in an area where the threat of theft exists, provisions should be made (hidden locks etc.) to make it difficult for the unit to be slipped out easily. Yet, if the boat is laid up each year through the winter months, the unit should be removable without a major undertaking to be taken home to a warm dry spot for out-of-season storage.

Power Connections

The receiver can be hooked up directly to the ship's battery or the power line can be run through a master control panel. If the power line is run through a panel, it should not be shared with other equipment which can draw high currents.

Excess power cable should be cut off. If it is necessary to add more cable, it may be necessary to have a technician solder the connections inside the power plug. With a direct hookup to the battery, the lead-in wires should be soldered directly to the proper terminal lugs: red wires-positive; black wires-negative.

Grounding the Receiver

Selection of the proper ground for a Loran is one of the most important parts of its installation. Both the antenna coupler (See antenna section in this chapter) and the Loran receiver need to be adequately grounded to insure good signal tracking and accurate receiver performance. A Loran receiver must have its own ground wire; that is, it should not tie into a common ground wire linking together many pieces of equipment. The Loran ground wire should then be lead to the boat's common ground point

On metal boats the ground should be as close to the receiver as practical. The ground strap can be attached to the mast or a section of the hull. Wood and fiberglass boats present more of a problem. The best place to attach a ground on a sailboat is on a keel bolt. If this can't be reached, it may be possible to tap into the underwater ballast. Other good grounding sites are underwater through-hulls. If already grounded, metal tanks or the life-line system provide convenient ground locations. The engine block or drive shaft can also be used, but preferably in fresh water. In salt water, severe electrolysis problems can develop when electricity flows though either of these. Some boats have a grounding plate which is attached to the outside of the hull. It may be made of copper or stainless steel and should be mounted where it is kept under water at all times. It is important to note that this isn't a separate grounding plate just for the Loran. Two ground plates underwater can set up a "potential", a field of electric current, which could cause corrosion of shafts, outdrives etc.

Whatever material is used for the ground wire, it should be heavy. A little bit of overkill here will only help. Ordinary household wire or the wire used for the power line feed are not acceptable. If copper is used, it should be a solid copper wire or a 1-2 inch strap as opposed to copper braid which will corrode and can generate electrical interference. The ground wire should be at least 8 gauge or heavier. Some even use a no. 00 battery cable. Whatever is used it is important that the cable is used just for the Loran receiver and is not shared with any other equipment.

Checking the Installation

Before the unit is turned on for the first time it should be run through a list of final checks. Most manuals will provide a list, and this should be followed closely or there will be risk of causing damage to the receiver. In particular, the polarity of the input power line should be rechecked to make sure it is not reversed. If it is, and the receiver is turned on, it may blow a fuse in the unit. It is also a good precaution to check any soldered connections which have been made, and that all connectors are firmly engaged. The antenna cable should be checked to see that it is not strung too tightly, and ground connections both at the receiver and the grounding unit should be secured. The antenna and its coupler probably won't be installed permanently at this point, but they should be held securely in place.

When the receiver is turned on for the first time all other equipment should be turned off so that performance can be evaluated on the basis of the Loran alone. After it is determined that the receiver is functioning properly, other items of equipment should be turned on one at a time to check for interference noise. After it is assured that the system is working correctly, the antenna and coupler can be permanently mounted.

A case in point occurred on the author's own boat when a forced air ducted furnace heater which was driven by a small motor was installed. After that installation there would be intermittent wild, erratic Loran readings (blinking numbers/low signal to noise ratio) so that sending the set away for repairs was considered. A little trial and error checking showed that this erratic behavior occurred only when the heater was on. A simple capacitor filter added to the heater motor cleared up the problem completely. The low SNR indicated that the Loran receiver was experiencing radio frequency interference from from the heater.

RFI- Noise Reduction Techniques

Once the Skipper has determined that the vessel is experiencing RFI (radio frequency interference), he may want to attempt to solve the problem himself rather than call an experienced technician. To gain an understanding of noise reduction techniques, the user will find *The Radio Amateurs Handbook* to be an excellent source of information. The chapter which deals with mobile communications has an extremely detailed discuission of RFI noise and various possible solutions. Most of these solutions apply to the marine Loran-C environment. The handbook can be checked out from most public libraries or purchased from the:

American Radio Relay League
Newington, CT
06111

If the Loran receiver has been properly installed, yet reception is poor and user tests have verified that the problem is indeed electrical noise caused by the vessel, the following solutions should be useful. The first step is to turn on an AM broadcast radio, or if possible an RDF, and adjust it to the lowest frequency receivable with no station heard, and volume up. If an RDF is used, tune it to the low end of the marine beacon band (about 150 kHz). Static should be heard on the radio. Next, the engine should be started with all electrical circuits turned off. If the engine is gasoline, a series of popping noises will be heard that increase in speed as the throttle is advanced. In this case, the source of the RFI is ignition noise caused by electrical discharges in the ignition system. This noise can be greatly reduced by using interference suppressing spark plug wires. As an alternative to the wire, a set of resistor spark plugs can be installed. Either of these can be purchased at any automotive supply store.

If the source of the noise is a magneto on an outboard motor, reducing noise is a bit more complex. Magnetos generate a great amount of RFI. After the installation of resistor sparkplugs, the noise may still be excessive. To further reduce the RFI noise from outboards, some skippers have lined the inside of the engine shroud with heavy aluminum foil (freezer foil) using contact cement to hold the foil in place. When the outboard shroud is in place, the foil shields and contains the electrical noise created by the outboard's magneto and prevents it from reaching the Loran antenna.

Should the noise (gas or diesel engines) that is heard be a singing sound that varies in pitch as the engine throttle is advanced, the chief suspect is the alternator. A do-it-yourself filter can be installed. Connect the positive side of a 20,000 micro-farad 50 volt D.C. capacitor to the alternator output. Then connect the negative side of the capacitor to the alternator frame. The leads should be kept as short as possible. Other sources of noise are the vessel's instruments (fuel gauges, masthead wind instruments, tachometers). There are a number of user installable filters to cure these problems, available at electronic supply stores and at dealers of two way radio equipment.

While the major source of RFI on yachts is the engine, considerable noise is produced from other equipment which uses electricity. The chief villains are motors, fluorescent lights, TV receivers, radar sets and inverters.

Although many users could make their own filters, commerically made filters such as this one are easily installed even by novices.   Photo by Newmar

Anything which uses electricity should be suspect. With an AM or RDF radio tuned to as low a frequency as possible (or a watch kept on the SNR on the Loran), each piece of equipment should be turned on, one at at time. When the noise heard on the radio increases (or the SNR drops on the Loran-C) a filter should be installed on the offending electrical equipment. Most filters are installed at the source of the noise, whether it be a motor or an alternator. The key to success is to stop the noise at the source so it will not be radiated to the Loran antenna or conducted through the ship's wiring to the Loran receiver. Additional filters can be installed at the Loran set power input to clean up any noise which is being conducted by the ship's wiring.

Photo by Newmar

Many technicians have the knowledge to make all their own filters, but most skippers will want to buy off-the-shelf filters because they work well and take little or no knowledge to install. A chart showing commercially made off-the-shelf filters and their applications is found in Fig. 3.14. Despite the ability to filter out most interference, there are a few items which simply may defy an economical solution to suppressing their interference. TV sets may generate such strong interference signals in their horizontal sweep circuits that there is no practical suppression solution to that noise. Flourescent lights powered by low voltage DC commonly found on board pleasure craft also may defy noise suppression. If all efforts at noise suppression fail, the only cure is to locate the Loran antenna as far as possible from the offending electrical device, or simply turn these items off when the Loran is in use.

FILTER APPLICATION GUIDE

Noise Characteristic	Probable Source	NEWMAR Filter	Filtered Frequency Range	Installation Location
Loran C - Skip Depth sounder-hash Receivers - tone varying with speed of engine	Alternator	NEWMAR -80A NEWMAR -150A	70 KHZ — 100 MHZ	In battery lead from alternator, as close to the alternator as possible
Noise on radio receiver that sounds like electrical motor	Bilge pump motor Bait pump motor Wiper motor	NEWMAR - MTR	50 KHZ — 25 MHZ	On positive power lead at motor causing noise
Ignition noise leakage into various receivers such as Loran C, depth sounders	Electronic Tachometers	NEWMAR - TAC	70 KHZ — 25 MHZ	At ignition coil on tachometer wires
Alternator whine or engine noise on AM/FM/Tape equipment Loran C interference from DC sources	Residual noise in vessels wiring system. Fluorescent lights	NEWMAR - PC10 NEWMAR - PC25	Audio thru 200 MHZ	In the positive and negative power leads close to the receiver/sounder/tape deck
Audio and radio frequency interference in Loran C, RDF's, radio telephones, HF-VHF, SSB, VHF, depth sounders, PA, HiFi systems	DC motors: Refrigeration, Winches, Radar. Chargers, Converters	NEWMAR - 25A	Audio — 25 MHZ	In positive lead at source of offending accessory or close to affected equipment
Radio interference in Loran C, LF Beacon, Broadcast, MF marine, SSB, VHF, HF Marine, CB, FM/TV Band	Gas engine ignition, electronic ignition, fluorescent lights, autopilot, small DC motors	NEWMAR - 10A	70 KHZ — 100 MHZ	In positive lead at source of offending accessory or close to affected equipment
Noise in Loran C, Loss of sync, cycle slip	Residual interference flowing in Loran power system and antenna ground system	NEWMAR - LC (set of 2 filters)	Audio thru 200 MHZ	LC/1: in the positive and negative power leads, close to the receiver LC/2: in ground lead to antenna coupler
Audio and R.F. noise on HF-VHF-SSB transceivers	Motors, chargers, inverters, fluorescent lights; noise in antenna ground system	NEWMAR - SSB (set of 2 filters)	Audio thru 200 MHZ	SSB-1: in the positive and negative power leads close to the receiver SSB-2: in R.F. ground lead

Filter application guide courtesy of the Newmar Corp.

Fig 3.14 These user installable filters by Newmar are designed to solve specific interference problems in Loran-C, SSB Marine Radio and Marine Audio.

CHAPTER FOUR

Charts and Other Resource Materials

Section I: Charts

Nautical charts with Loran overlay lines are an important part of using Loran-C for navigation. Even though many skippers are now using latitude/longitude (Lat/Lon) coordinate readouts from the Loran receiver as opposed to time delays (TDs) for plotting fixes, the charts with Loran overlay lines still remain an integral part of the system. For instance, there may be times in which it is not feasible to navigate with Lat/Lon because the area is one known for ASF error, or there is a loss of Lat/Lon functions of the receiver. Then the only way to continue navigating with Loran is by using the TD readouts and plotting them on charts specially prepared by the chart publisher (usually NOS) which have been superimposed with a grid of predicted time differences.

Charts which have been printed with Loran overlay lines fall into roughly two categories: those which are in the US Coastal Waters (CCZ) and adjacent areas and those which cover areas outside the CCZ.

Loran charts for the CCZ are prepared through the efforts and interaction of three government agencies. These are: The Defense Mapping Agency Hydrographic/Topographic Center (DMAHTC); The National Ocean Survey (NOS); and The United States Coast Guard (USCG). A loose analogy would have the DMAHTC as the writer, the NOS as the publisher, and the USCG as the field tester.

How Loran-C Charts Are Made

The DMAHTC, which is a subdivision of the Department of Defense is the central clearing house for all Loran information. Both the USCG and the NOS help contribute to this collection through surveys and field testing. The Defense Mapping Agency converts raw data to a proper format by processing it with computers. The computers subject the data to various equations, which transform it into the Loran information which is ultimately plotted on the charts.

Because the radio waves are traveling over varying surface terrain, the resulting lines or grid are not exactly the same as if the distances involved were in free space. What results instead is a grid warpage which is caused by the attenuation (slowing down) of the radio signals as they pass over different surfaces. It is this warpage that is predicted by the DMAHTC computers using various mathematical formulas.

The first edition Loran chart of an area grid will display lines that reflect only Secondary Factor (SF) warpage which is due to attenuation of the radio signals traveling over sea water. After field testing by the Coast Guard, the DMAHTC corrects the grids to reflect the added warpage due to Additional Secondary Factors (ASF) or the additional attenuation as the radio signals pass over land; therefore, first edition charts are not as accurate as later editions.

To assist the DMAHTC in the Electronic Navigation Division's Loran verification program, a chart calibration questionaire is available for interested mariners. To provide useful information for this purpose, position must be known by some other means, such as satellite, etc. Loran readouts for each secondary are then given along with actual Lat/Lon position, date and time of day. This information is entered into the DMAHTC data base to assist in verifying theoretically predicted time differences.

Another function of the DMAHTC is to produce, update and distribute ASF tables for the coastal waters of the United States. Again, these computations are performed with data (land conductivity constants) which is supplied by the Coast Guard from field testing. Using a special formula called Millington's Method, these thousands of calculations are again made with a computer and the tables are thus derived in a matrix form. It is this matrix which is used to provide the ASF correction for a given location. (See section on correction tables.)

National Ocean Survey

The National Ocean Survey prepares and publishes the charts with the grid calculations which are received from the DMAHTC.

The updating of charts is an ongoing process with reprint cycles which vary from one to five years. Charts are updated when geographic or hydrographic changes occur or when navigational aids are changed. Updates also occur when the LOP or TD lines need to be updated.

VESSEL NAME _____

LORAN-C RECEIVER MAKE AND MODEL _____

OBSERVER _____

GMT		LORAN-C TIME DELAY (TD) READINGS (XXXXX.XX Usec) Rate Designations				REFERENCE POSITION (Ref. Posit. must coincide with time of TD Reading)		REFERENCE POSITION SOURCE DESCRIPTION (i.e., Visual Bearings, Radar, SATNAV, etc., or pier location or berth designations)
DAY OF YR. YEAR		(xxx)-W	(xxx-X)	(xxx-Y)	(xxx-Z)	LATITUDE XX°-XX.X'N/S	LONGITUDE XXX°-XX.X'E/W	

Fig. 4.1 Loran-C Chart Calibration Questionaire

Factors which affect when a chart is to be printed are:

- If chart features, such as water depths, land masses, navigational aids etc., have changed.

- Whether the LOP or TD lines need to be updated.

- How long the current stock will last for a given edition.

The NOS produces chart catalogues which list available charts in US Waters. These catalogues indicate those charts that have the Loran overlays, and are divided by regions. The catalogues are free of charge and may be obtained from:

Distribution Division (C-44)
National Ocean Survey
Riverdale, Maryland 20840

A final function of the NOS in the Loran charting program is to participate with the Coast Guard in verification surveys.

United States Coast Guard

From the very beginning, the Coast Guard has been an integral part in the development of Loran use in coastal waters. Not only has it been given the responsibility of establishing and maintaining the numerous Loran stations, but it has also been a key agency for supplying data essential for chart preparation and field testing the resulting chart grids.

Initial charts are tested in at-sea surveys to assure that the first editions meet the standards of accuracy within ¼ mile. In most cases this verification survey of grid predictions is necessary before the chart measures up to these standards. In addition to verification of first edition charts, the Coast Guard has been instrumental in updating charts to include corrections for additional secondary factors. Verification surveys were begun in 1977 and completed by mid-1982. They covered the entire CCZ and Great Lakes; not all other areas of the world have been so verified.

Steps in Loran Chart Construction

Sometimes it is easy to get the various agencies and their particular functions confused, so it may be beneficial at this point to have an overall look at the various steps used in constructing and printing Loran charts.

1. Computing LOPs or TD values on the basis of an all sea-water path.

2. Predicting ASF corrections mathematically and adjusting the original TDs.

3. Verification of above TDs by:

    a. measuring actual TDs in field surveys.

    b. modeling or determining ASF corrections for each location on basis of "a".

    c. adjusting the predicted LOPs to include the measured ASF correction in "b".

Fig. 4.2   Steps in Loran Chart Construction

1. Initially, the TD lines are computed as though the Loran signals travel only over sea-water. Many of the first edition Loran charts contained TD lines derived just from these calculations and did not reflect the errors which were due to the retardation of signals as they passed over land.

One of the problems with first edition charts is that, when they are first issued, the public begins to use them even though verification surveys may have not yet been completed. Although these charts are usually quite accurate, there have been cases in which the accuracy has been well outside of standard parameters. A good example of this was seen in the early days of Loran-C use on the West Coast. First edition charts, especially off the coast of California often had lines that were off by as much as one to two miles. Verification surveys of course take time, and the problem is further compounded in that the charts are published on a rotating schedule, so even after the survey has been conducted, it may be a few years before the corrections are reflected on the next edition.

2. The calculated or predicted TD lines are then adjusted for the delay of signal transmission caused by passing over land. The delay is called the Additional Secondary Phase Factor or ASF. At this point, this adjustment is done entirely by mathematical computations which predict what the amount of the delay should be. Unfortunately, it has been found that, in many areas, these predicted LOPs, which include the predicted ASF corrections, still yield position errors that exceed ¼ mile. Thus, there is a need to verify the predicted TDs along with their predicted ASF corrections by actual field testing.

3. To address the problem of position errors due to inaccurate ASF predictions, the Coast Guard has initiated a Chart Verification Program which consists of three basic phases.

A. Field testing or verification surveys are conducted on track lines which follow the U.S. coastline, usually about 10 - 20 miles offshore.

B. The next step is to model or develop the ASF corrections according to the TDs which were actually measured in A. In this phase, the ASF corrections made on the basis of observed data are compared with the predicted ASF corrections in step 2. The predicted ASF corrections are then adjusted to agree with the measured ASF corrections so that they result in position accuracy that is at least ¼ mile. (The Coast Guard collects the data, the Defense Mapping Agency (DMA) analyzes it and then sends recommended adjustments to NOS for printing on updated charts.)

C. The final step is to implement the corrected TD lines which are adjusted to the measured ASF corrections in B. The most common way to of doing this is to issue an updated edition of the chart. Another way to update the TD lines of original charts is to manually apply the corrections by using Correction Tables in which the ASF corrections are listed. However, this should only be done with original charts on which no corrections have been made. Since most charts now have at least predicted corrections, these tables have limited use in this respect. They are, however, useful for manually determining ASF corrections to Lat/Lon coordinates from receivers that do not automatically adjust for ASF. (See section on Correction Tables.)

In short there are two different ways in which Loran TD lines are adjusted for land path errors:

By predicted ASF, see step two.

By observed ASF, see step three.

These two ways of making corrections are indicated on those charts with corrected lattices by one of two notices:

> The Loran-C lines of position overprinted on this chart have been prepared for use with groundwave signals and are presently compensated only for **theoretical** propagation delays, which have not yet been verified by observed data. Mariners are cautioned not to rely entirely on the lattices in inshore waters. Skywave corrections are not provided.

> The Loran-C lines of position overprinted on this chart have been prepared for use with groundwave signals and are compensated with propagation delays computed from **observed** data. Mariners are cautioned not to rely entirely on the lattices in inshore waters. Skywave corrections are not provided.

The emphasized words in these notices are added here to point out the differences in the two and are not printed as such on the charts. At this book's publication only 3-5% of the charts printed with overlay lines have been verified by observed data. The notice printed on individual charts should be checked.

Other Agencies and Charts

The Defense Mapping Agency (DMA) produces and distributes navigational charts for those areas which are outside U.S. waters. It also publishes numerous specialty charts, sheets and tables, some of which have direct application for Loran use. The charts are organized according to specific regions. To order, it is necessary to have the region catalogue for a given area of cruising. A listing of these various catalogues is available from:

DMA Topographic Center (Attn:DDCP)
6500 Brooks Lane
Washington D.C. 20315

The Canadian Hydrographic Service issues charts for the Great Lakes and both coasts of Canada. Listings for these charts are in three different catalogues by region: Pacific Coast, Great Lakes, and Atlantic Coast. The catalogues are free of charge and can be obtained by sending to:

Hydrographic Chart Distribution Office
Department of Fisheries & Oceans
P.O. Box 8080
1875 Russel Road
Ottawa, Ontario
Canada, KLA 3H6

Private Chart Books

In the past few years there has been a flourish of activity in the area of privately published chart books. Various publishers have introduced books which feature charts reproduced from government originals. These are usually 12"x18" or larger and contain reproductions of general, coastal and harbor charts (depending on the publisher) for a specific cruising area. The inclusion of additional information and design reflect the priorities of the publishers.

Waterway Guide publishes a series of chart books in a form which use a system of accordion folds. When in use, each chart folds out of the book in a strip. While modestly priced, the Waterway Guide charts also contain the fewest detailed harbor charts. A companion book contains additional facility and other cruising information of interest to the skipper.

The Better Boating Association (a private business) publishes a series of large format chart books called Chart Kits. The charts are, depending on the government original, slightly reduced in size.

The Evergreen Cruising Atlas published by Straub Publishing, is available for the Pacific Northwest and the Canadian West Coast. It contains a complete series of charts plus cruising information.

Richardsons' CHARTBOOK & CRUISING Guides are available for each of the Great Lakes (except Superior). These are the most popular chartbooks in the Great Lakes Region. They feature a complete series of charts including all harbor charts and coast charts and in the same scale of the government originals. These books also feature facility listings for each harbor as well as aerial photos and ancillary information.

All of these publications represent good alternatives to the traditional government charts. All are much easier to use (than full size government charts) aboard small craft. All should be satisfactory for use with Lat/Lon Loran-C receivers. Whether or not these books contain TDs depends upon the government originals from which they were reproduced. All represent a substantial savings of dollars compared to the purchase of a similar set of government charts. These chart reproductions can be purchased from:

> **Better Boating Association**
> **Needham, MA**
> **02192**

> **Richardsons' Marine Publishing**
> **P.O. Box 23**
> **Streamwood, IL**
> **60103**

Straub Publishing
4535 union Bay Pl. NE
Seattle, WA

Waterway Guide
238 West St.
P.O. Box 1486
Annapolis, MD

Chart Characteristics

1. Scale. Charts with Loran-C overlays vary from small scale charts which cover a relatively large area to larger scale charts which cover smaller areas. The small scale charts are general charts which are used for coastal navigation outside of outlying reefs or shoals or for making open water passages. Scales for these charts with Loran overlays usually vary from 1:150,000 to 1:600,000. (The larger the number the smaller the scale.) However, there are a few Loran charts which represent very large areas such as those for the Gulf of Mexico (1:2,187,400), the Hawaiian Islands (1:3,121,170), and San Diego to the Aleutian and Hawaiian Islands (1:4,860,700). See Fig. 4.3.

Coast charts are those which are used for inshore navigation and entering large harbors and bays. These are larger scale charts which vary from 1:50,000 to 1:150,000. Most large scale Loran charts are from 1:80,000 to 1:120,000. TD fixes plotted on a large scale chart are more accurate than those on a small scale chart because the last few significant digits of the microsecond reading usually can be plotted on the large scale chart, whereas they just get lost on the small scale chart. This is because the actual line difference in microseconds is usually less on the large scale chart, i.e. 10 or 20 microsecond difference as opposed to 50 microseconds or greater. An example of this is seen in Figure 4.4 which shows two different Loran charts for the Western end of Lake Superior. In the first chart (A) which is small scale, the difference between the lines is 50 microseconds. In the large scale chart (B) the difference between the lines is 10 and 20 microseconds.

Harbor charts are those with very large scales, 1:50,000 and greater. These charts show fine detail of harbors, anchorages, and smaller waterways. At the time of this writing, none of these very large scale charts contain Loran overlay lines - and for very good reason. First of all, when Loran-C was adopted as the official National Radionavigational Aid in 1974, it was not intended for use in these areas. The Loran-C coverage begins at harbor entrances

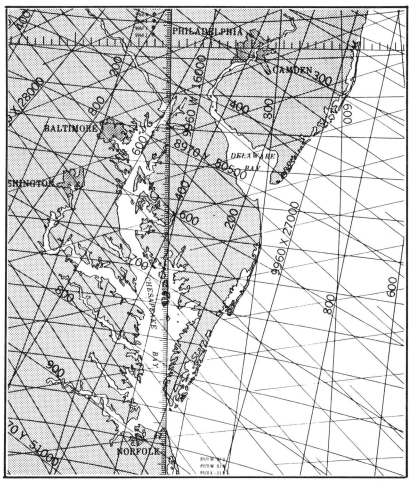

Fig. 4.3   A Small Scale Chart With Loran-C Overlay
(Northeastern United States) Scale 1:2,187,400   DMA STOCK NO. LORCX7822

and extends seaward. The second reason is that the goal for accuracy of the system is ¼ mile. A ¼ mile accuracy is not good enough to navigate in most of these inner harbor areas.

2. Line Characteristics. Although the overlay lines are in fact large hyperbolas, they appear as straight lines. This is because the hyperbolas stretch out over very large areas. Since most charts cover just a small area, this will cause the lines to appear almost straight. The overall distance between the TD lines does, however, vary (see Fig. 4.3) and even on large scale charts this can be quickly checked by using a pair of dividers and checking the distance between the two lines at one end of the chart as opposed to the other.

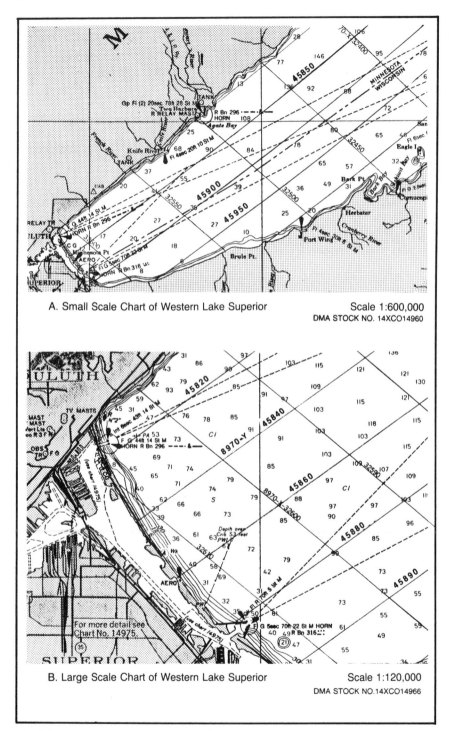

A. Small Scale Chart of Western Lake Superior   Scale 1:600,000
DMA STOCK NO. 14XCO14960

B. Large Scale Chart of Western Lake Superior   Scale 1:120,000
DMA STOCK NO.14XCO14966

Fig. 4.4

The number of microseconds between each line will also vary. Common intervals are 10, 20, and 25 microseconds between the lines on large scale charts. With smaller scale charts, the number of microseconds between the lines will usually get larger. In some of those very small scale charts, the difference between lines can be as much as 200 or 250 microseconds.

The number of microseconds between the lines of station pairs in the same chain may also be different. In Fig. 4.4 B the difference between the X lines is 10 microseconds and the difference between the Y lines is 20 microseconds. This difference in microsecond value between the lines in relation to the actual distance between the lines can affect the accuracy of plotted fixes and thus which station pairs to choose in a chain. (See Chapter Six on choosing station pairs.)

3. Secondary Identification. At first glance on reading some of the navigational charts containing Loran overlays, the initial effect may be somewhat overwhelming, particularly if the chart contains more than one GRI such as in Fig. 4.5 of the Cape Cod Area. This chart contains the X, Y, and Z secondaries for the Great

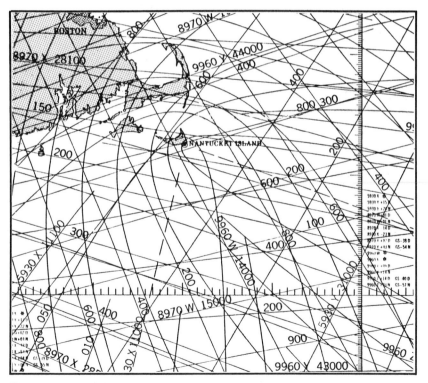

Fig. 4.5   A Loran Chart With LOPs From More Than One Chain

Lakes 8970 Chain; the W, X, Y, and Z secondaries for the Northeast US 9960 Chain, and the X and Y secondaries for the East Canadian Coast 5930 Chain, a total of nine lines which cross every which way.

As a result, it is helpful to note that these lines are color coded and that, regardless of the chain, the W lines are always turquoise, the X lines are purple, the Y lines are grey, and the Z lines are green. Although this is a great asset when it comes to plotting fixes, it is still easy to get the same color lines mixed up - for example, getting the Y lines from one chain confused with the Y lines of another chain. With poor lighting the colored lines will be difficult to read. Under red light conditions the lines will be difficult or impossible to read.

4. Loran Linear Interpolator. Charts which come with Loran overlay lines will also have printed off to one side a Loran Linear Interpolator. (See Fig. 6.5) This device is used along with a pair of dividers to break up the distance between the lines into even units so that the exact microsecond reading between the lines can be determined. Because it represents a sliding scale, it can be used for any given set of secondary lines, regardless of the number of micro-seconds between them. To find out how this technique and the interpolator work, see Chapter Six in sections on plotting fixes.

Section II: Other Resource Materials

Notices to Mariners

For updates on the Loran system and known discrepancies, there are some publications which can be helpful. One of these is the **Notices to Mariners**, a weekly publication produced by the DMAHTC in cooperation with the Coast Guard and NOS. It is geared primarily for mariners with extensive sea-going operations. Probably of more use to small craft operators, is the **Local Notice to Mariners** which is published by the U.S. Coast Guard in each Coast Guard District.

Radionavigation Bulletin

The Coast Guard publishes the **Radionavigation Bulletin** on a quarterly basis. This bulletin deals with all types of radionavigation (OMEGA, RACON, SAT NAV, GPS) in addition to Loran. It is quite useful in providing information on various aspects of radionavigation and system updates. The bulletin can be obtained free of charge by sending to:

COMMANDANT (G-NRN-3)
U.S. Coast Guard
Washington D.C. 20593

The Wild Goose Association

The Wild Goose Association, which was formed in 1972, takes its name from those "majestic birds that navigate thousands of miles with unerring accuracy." The membership includes hundreds of scientists, professional engineers, and interested personnel from all segments of government, industry, and the user community throughout the world. Membership is available to any individual or organization that has an interest in Loran. For additional information or to obtain a membership, write:

Wild Goose Association
P.O. Box 556
Bedford, MA 01730

One of the main activities of the WGA is its Annual Technical Symposium, which is held each fall, at which papers on various aspects of Loran are presented. These papers are recorded in the organizations's publication, "Proceedings of the Technical Symposium" and can be purchased.

Other publications of the WGA are a Radionavigation Journal and a Newsletter . The Journal is a yearly publication. It contains Loran related articles and system updates. The information provided in these publications is without doubt, some of the best that is available to the interested user who wants to keep abreast with current developments in the system. These Journals may also be purchased. Complementing the Journal is the WGA Newsletter which is published at least quarterly and sometimes monthly.

The Institute of Navigation

The Institute of Navigation is another organization which is dedicated to the advancement of navigation techniques. It deals with all aspects of navigation, not just radionavigation. It, too, publishes a journal, **Navigation: Journal of the Institute of Navigation**. One issue in particular is of interest to the Loran user, and that is the 1982 Spring issue, (Volume 29, #1) which is devoted entirely to Loran-C. Journals or membership can be obtained from:

The Institute of Navigation
Suite 832
815 15th Street, N.W.
Washington D.C. 20005

ASF Correction Tables

One of the functions of the DMAHTC is to prepare and publish correction tables for the ASF which produces an error in TD (and Lat/Lon) readings because radio waves travel travel at different speeds over varying terrains. These tables can be used to obtain more accurate fixes when using first edition charts which have not been corrected for the error. It is important to check the chart being used to see if it has already been corrected for ASF. If it has, it will contain one of the two notices printed earlier in this chapter. To use these tables with a chart that has already been corrected would literally be putting the ASF error back into a fix and give only the accuracy found with first edition uncorrected charts.

Since most charts are now corrected for ASF, a more common use for the Correction Tables is to correct TD readings before using them to convert to geographic (Lat/Lon) coordinates. This is especially useful for those receivers which display Lat/Lon but don't have the ASF corrections programmed in. The TDs which are received still contain the ASF error - TD fixes are only more accurate than uncorrected Lat/Lon fixes because they are plotted on corrected charts. The Lat/Lon coordinates are calculated from these erroneous TDs and the error is passed along. However, if the error is known in microseconds (which is what the tables give), the TD reading can be corrected and then the computer functions of the receiver can be used to give a more accurate Lat/Lon from the corrected TDs.

The ASF error is usually not greater than ±4 microseconds, so it may not be all that important to consider if small scale charts are being used - the error will be lost in the small scale and probably won't make much difference in plotted position. But, if large scale charts are being used, along with Lat/Lon coordinates, ASF correction will add another degree of precision for accurate navigation.

The Correction Tables can also be used to give an indication of a need to correct for ASF. A quick glance at the tables for the area of cruising will tell just how bad the error for that area is. If it is less

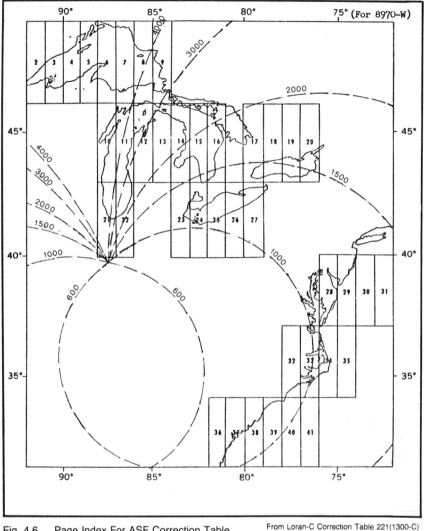

Fig. 4.6   Page Index For ASF Correction Table

From Loran-C Correction Table 221(1300-C)
Defense Mapping Agency
Hydrographic/ Topographic Center

than one microsecond, which it is in many areas, the error probably isn't even worth adjusting for. But if the tables show errors of 2 or 3 microseconds, then it may be wise to take them into consideration when using the Lat/Lon function of the receiver.

The tables are published in booklet form for each chain. For example, there is a different booklet for Great Lakes Chain #8970 and Northeast US Chain #9960. Each booklet is divided into separate tables for each station pair: one table for the master and the X secondary, another table for the master and the Y secondary, etc.

The areas of coverage are determined by the range of ground-wave transmissions for the individual chain. To find the table for a particular cruising area, there is a page index near the front of each booklet where the areas are divided according to sections which are assigned different page numbers. (See Fig. 4.6) If the area is in a given section, for example #15, there will be a separate page 15 for each secondary: i.e., 15W, 15X, 15Y, and 15Z. The tables run completely through all the sections for a given secondary before switching to another secondary.

9960-W   **17W**

LONGITUDE WEST

LATITUDE	68° 0'	55	50	45	40	35	30	25	20	15	10	5	67° 0'
45° 0'													
55													
50													
45													2.0
40												1.7	1.6
35									1.7	1.7	1.6	1.6	1.6
30							1.7	1.6	1.6	1.6	1.5	1.5	1.5
25					1.6	1.5	1.5	1.6	1.6	(1.6)	1.5	1.5	1.5
20	1.6	1.5	1.6	1.6	1.5	1.4	1.5	1.5	1.5	1.5	1.5	1.5	1.5
15	1.6	1.5	1.5	1.5	1.5	1.5	1.5	1.5	1.5	1.5	1.5	1.4	1.4
10	1.5	1.4	1.5	1.5	1.4	1.4	1.4	1.4	1.4	1.4	1.4	1.4	1.3
5	1.4	1.4	1.5	1.4	1.4	1.4	1.3	1.3	1.3	1.3	1.3	1.3	
44° 0'	1.3	1.3	1.3	1.3	1.3	1.3	1.3	1.3	1.2	1.3	1.3		
55	1.3	1.3	1.3	1.2	1.3	1.3	1.3	1.3	1.2				
50	1.3	1.3	1.3	1.3	1.3	1.3	1.3						
45	1.3	1.3	1.2	1.3	1.3	1.3							
40	1.2	1.2	1.3	1.3	1.3								
35	1.3	1.2	1.3										
30	1.3	1.3	1.3										
25	1.2	1.3	1.3										
20	1.2	1.3	1.3	1.3									
15	1.2	1.3	1.3	1.3	1.3								
10	1.2	1.2	1.3	1.3	1.3								
5	1.2	1.2	1.2	1.3	1.3	1.3							
43° 0'	1.2	1.2	1.2	1.2	1.3	1.3	1.3						
55	1.2	1.2	1.2	1.2	1.3	1.3	1.3						
50	1.2	1.2	1.2	1.2	1.2	1.3	1.3	1.3					
45	1.2	1.2	1.2	1.2	1.2	1.2	1.3	1.3	1.3				
40	1.2	1.2	1.2	1.2	1.2	1.2	1.3	1.3	1.3	1.3			
35	1.2	1.2	1.2	1.2	1.2	1.2	1.3	1.3	1.3	1.3			
30	1.3	1.2	1.2	1.2	1.2	1.2	1.2	1.2	1.3	1.3			
25	1.2	1.2	1.2	1.2	1.2	1.3	1.3	1.3	1.2	1.3	1.3	1.3	1.3
20	1.2	1.2	1.2	1.2	1.2	1.2	1.2	1.3	1.2	1.2	1.2	1.2	1.3
15	1.2	1.2	1.2	1.2	1.2	1.2	1.2	1.2	1.2	1.2	1.2	1.3	1.2
10	1.2	1.1	1.2	1.2	1.2	1.2	1.2	1.3	1.2	1.2	1.2	1.2	1.2
5	1.2	1.1	1.2	1.2	1.2	1.2	1.2	1.2	1.2	1.2	1.2	1.2	1.2
42° 0'	1.1	1.1	1.2	1.2	1.2	1.2	1.2	1.2	1.2	1.2	1.2	1.2	1.2

Fig. 4.7 A   Example Of ASF Correction Tables For GRI 9960: W Secondary

From Loran-C Correction Table 221(1300-C)   Defense Mapping Agency Hydrographic/Topographic Center

Each page covers 3 degrees latitude by one degree longitude. Areas which are only land are omitted. Those areas within the tables which are outside the CCZ, or represent land are left blank, i.e., the microsecond corrections represent only areas on the water. Latitude values are printed down the left side of each page; longitude values are printed across the top. Each is represented in increments of 5 minutes. The ASF errors for the Lat/Lon coordinates are given in a matrix form in ± microseconds. It is these values that are added algebraically to the TD readings.

9960-Y 17Y

LATITUDE NORTH	LONGITUDE WEST 68° 0'	55	50	45	40	35	30	25	20	15	10	5	67° 0'
45° 0'													
55													
50													
45			LAND										3.4
40												3.1	3.0
35									3.0	3.1	3.0	2.9	2.9
30							2.9	2.9	2.9	2.9	2.8	2.8	2.8
25					2.7	2.8	2.8	2.8	2.8	2.8	2.8	2.7	2.7
20	2.8	2.7	2.7	2.7	2.7	2.7	2.7	2.8	2.7	2.7	2.6	2.7	2.6
15	2.7	2.6	2.6	2.7	2.8	2.7	2.7	2.7	2.7	2.6	2.6	2.6	2.6
10	2.7	2.6	2.6	2.7	2.7	2.6	2.6	2.5	2.5	2.6	2.6	2.6	2.6
5	2.6	2.6	2.6	2.6	2.5	2.5	2.4	2.4	2.4	2.5	2.5	2.5	
44° 0'	2.5	2.5	2.5	2.5	2.4	2.4	2.4	2.3	2.4	2.4			
55	2.4	2.4	2.4	2.4	2.4	2.4	2.4	2.4	2.4				
50	2.4	2.4	2.4	2.4	2.4	2.4	2.4						
45	2.4	2.4	2.3	2.4	2.4	2.4							
40	2.3	2.3	2.3	2.4	2.4								
35	2.4	2.4	2.4										
30	2.4	2.4	2.4										
									OUTSIDE CCZ				
25	2.4	2.4	2.4										
20	2.4	2.4	2.4	2.4									
15	2.4	2.4	2.4	2.4	2.4								
10	2.4	2.4	2.4	2.4	2.4								
5	2.4	2.4	2.4	2.4	2.4	2.4							
43° 0'	2.4	2.4	2.4	2.4	2.4	2.4	2.4						
55	2.4	2.4	2.4	2.4	2.4	2.4	2.4						
50	2.4	2.4	2.4	2.4	2.4	2.4	2.4	2.4					
45	2.4	2.4	2.4	2.4	2.4	2.4	2.4	2.4	2.4				
40	2.4	2.4	2.4	2.4	2.4	2.4	2.4	2.4	2.4	2.4			
35	2.5	2.4	2.4	2.4	2.4	2.4	2.4	2.4	2.4	2.4			
30	2.5	2.5	2.4	2.4	2.4	2.4	2.4	2.4	2.4	2.4			
25	2.4	2.4	2.4	2.4	2.4	2.4	2.4	2.4	2.4	2.4	2.4	2.4	2.5
20	2.4	2.4	2.4	2.4	2.4	2.4	2.4	2.4	2.4	2.4	2.4	2.4	2.4
15	2.4	2.4	2.4	2.4	2.4	2.4	2.4	2.4	2.4	2.4	2.4	2.4	2.4
10	2.4	2.3	2.4	2.4	2.4	2.4	2.4	2.4	2.4	2.4	2.4	2.4	2.4
5	2.4	2.3	2.4	2.4	2.4	2.4	2.4	2.4	2.4	2.4	2.4	2.4	2.4
42° 0'	2.4	2.3	2.3	2.4	2.3	2.4	2.4	2.4	2.4	2.4	2.4	2.4	2.4

Fig. 4.7 B Example Of ASF Correction Tables For GRI 9960: Y Secondary

Taken from Loran-C Correction Table 221(1300-C) Defense Mapping Agency Hydrographic/Topographic Center

To enter a specific table, position must be known to the nearest 5 minutes in latitude and longitude. (Interpolation between these readings really isn't valid because the relationship of ASF error to position is not a linear one.) To see how the tables work an example of cruising off the coast of Maine can be used. The coordinates used might be the W and Y secondaries of the Northeast US Chain #9960. The Loran receiver displays Lat/Lon coordinates of 44°24.32'N and 67°16.21'W with the TDs of 12053.29 and 44471.68. Rounding the Lat/Lon reading off to the nearest 5 minutes will result in 44°25' and 67°15' which are the values which are used to enter the table for each secondary.

| | TDs | | Initial | Corrected |
	W	Y	Loran Lat/Lon	Lat/Lon
Initial TDs	12053.29	44471.68	44°24.32'N	44°24.66'N
ASF Correction	+ 1.6	+ 2.8	67°16.21'W	67°17.35'W
Corrected TDs	12054.89	44474.48		

Fig. 4.8   Using ASF Correction To Correct TDs And Lat/Lon Co-ordinates

For the W secondary the correction for these coordinates is: 1.6 microseconds; for the Y secondary the correction is 2.8 microseconds. (See again Fig. 4.7 A&B)

To make the correction, these values are added to the TD readings to get: 12054.89 and 44474.48. Using the computer functions of the receiver, the corrected TDs are converted to their Lat/Lon counterparts: 44°24.66'N and 67°17.35'W. (See Fig. 4.8) These Lat/Lon coordinates are now corrected for ASF and can be entered onto a chart for a position fix of greater accuracy than would result from the original Lat/Lon readings. In this particular example, the difference between the initial and corrected Lat/Lon coordinates is approximately one nautical mile.

Although the tables can be quite useful in precision navigation, as the above illustration indicates, they should be used with caution in areas that are within 10 miles of land. This is because these areas represent an unreliable zone where there are large variations that occur in the magnitude of correction.

Loran-C Tables For:
User Applied Overlay Lines/Plotting TDs
Without Chart Overlays.

The DMAHTC puts out another series of Loran tables that can be useful to the Loran user. These tables provide the Lat/Lon coordinates of TD overlay lines at given points. The tables can be used to either construct charts with overlay lines or to plot a TD fix on any chart - even those which do not have the Loran overlay. Lat/Lon coordinates can then be derived from the chart.

The tables are quite massive and come in different volumes for each secondary in a given chain. They are, however, conveniently punched with holes to fit a 3 ring binder. The tables for one secondary alone would easily fill a large 3 ring binder. Tables can be bought from any authorized sales agent of the Defense Mapping Agency Office of Distribution Services. There is a separate charge for each secondary table in the chain.

How to Apply Overlay Lines to a Chart.

There may be times when it may be advantageous to construct overlay lines on a given chart; for example, in an area where the overlay lines have not yet been added to large scale charts, but are available only on smaller scale charts. Another possibility is adding lines to a harbor chart or a home cruising area.

To some extent, plotting of TD lines may be assisted by intersection of the line with a known geographic position such as a specific land mass. But often there are areas miles off shore, where there are no identifying reference points. The tables provide lists of geographic coordinates of TD line positions at given points. When any two of these points for a specific TD line in an area of concern are known - the whole line can be drawn in. An example best illustrates these techniques and use of the tables.

If there are no Loran charts for a cruising area, and for some reason the Lat/Lon functions of the receiver have been lost, there would be only TD readouts to work with. Because continued navigation is desired in the area, the decision is made to add TD lines to the chart being used. The receiver is giving a TD reading of 31024.7 for one of the secondaries, so that gives a clue where to start, and it is known the chart must include those lines for TD 31020 and 31030. To construct a given TD line, it is necessary to have two sets of geographic coordinates to plot two different points on the line.

STEP ONE:
DETERMINING ONE POINT ON TD LINE 31020.

The easiest way to enter the table is to quickly flip through the pages for the X secondary table of the chain used and note the

TD microsecond values printed across the top of each page until finding those listing 31020 and 31030. (See Fig. 4.9) Actually, the same microsecond values will be seen on a number of pages, and to get the correct entry into the table the area of concern must be known to the nearest whole degree of latitude or longitude. These values will be printed either in the extreme left hand column (latitude) or the extreme right hand column (longitude). In this particular example, it is the latitude values which are printed, and a quick look at the chart being used (Fig. 4.10), shows that the position is somewhere in the area of 47°N latitude. From the table it can be determined that the TD line 31020 crosses latitude 47°00'N at a longitude of 84°41.9'W. These then are the first set of geographic coordinates, and from these it is now possible to plot a single point on that 31020 line. (See Fig. 4.10)

STEP TWO:
DETERMINING A SECOND POINT ON LINE 31020.

To determine the TD 31020 line itself, it is necessary to establish another geographic point on the line. To do this another set of coordinates is needed. Looking at the table again will show that the TD line 31020 crosses latitude 48°00'N at a longitude of 85°13.1'W. This, however, isn't going to do much good because the chart being used isn't big enough to include latitude 48°N. But, it can be seen that the next latitude line marked on the chart is 47°10'N. If it can be determined where TD 31020 crosses this second latitude line, that will give the needed second point to construct the TD line.

To find the longitude where TD 31020 crosses on latitude 47°10'N, it is necessary to interpolate between latitude 47°00' N and latitude 48°00'N. Since there are 60' (minutes) between each degree of latitude, and 10' is ⅙ of that, the difference between the two longitude readings at latitudes 47°N and 48°N should be divided by 6. This will give the change in longitude for each 10' change in latitude. In this case the value is 5.2, and this can be added to the longitude crossing point at 47°00'N to give the longitude crossing point at 47°10'. (For calculations see bottom section of Column A in Figure 4.9.) The second set of coordinates, to determine that second point, are thus Lat 47°10'N and Lon 84°47.1'W. With the second point plotted, the TD line of 31020 can be drawn. (See Fig. 4.10).

This procedure can be repeated with other TD lines in the area, such as 31030 and 31040. Of course to get plotted fixes, it will

	8970-X					DS 195
T	31000	31010	31020	31030	31040	**T**
Lat						**Long**
° ′	° ′ Δ	° ′ Δ	° ′ Δ	° ′ Δ	° ′ Δ	° ′
43 N	82 42.7W 12	82 44.0W 12	82 45.2W 12	82 46.4W 12	82 47.7W 12	
44 N	83 10.8W 13	83 12.1W 13	83 13.5W 13	83 14.9W 14	83 16.4W 14	
45 N	83 39.1W 15	83 40.7W 15	83 42.2W 16	83 43.9W 16	83 45.5W 16	
46 N	84 08.0W 18	84 09.9W 18	84 11.7W 18	84 13.5W 18	84 15.4W 18	
47 N	84 37.6W 21	84 39.7W 21	84 41.9W 21	84 44.0W 20	84 46.1W 21	
48 N	85 08.2W 23	85 10.6W 24	85 13.1W 24	85 15.5W 24	85 17.9W 23	
49 N	85 39.9W 27	85 42.6W 27	85 45.3W 27	85 48.2W 28	85 51.0W 27	
50 N	86 12.7W 31	86 15.9W 31	86 19.1W 31	86 22.1W 30	86 25.2W 31	
51 N	86 47.1W 35	86 50.6W 34	86 54.1W 34	86 57.5W 35	87 01.1W 35	
52 N	87 22.9W 38	87 26.8W 39	87 30.7W 39	87 34.7W 39	87 38.6W 38	

Taken from DMA. Stock No. LCPUB2211024 Pair 8970-X.

	(A) TD_x 31020	(B) TD_x 31030	(C) TD_x 31040
AT LAT 47°00'N	TABLE LON: 84°41.9'W	TABLE LON: 84°44.0'W	TABLE LON: 84°46.1'W
AT LAT 48°00'N	TABLE LON: 85°13.1'W	TABLE LON: 85°15.5'W	TABLE LON: 85°17.9'W
AT LAT 47°10'N	INTERPOLATED LON: 84°47.1'W	INTERPOLATED LON: 84°49.3'W	INTERPOLATED LON: 85°51.4'W

	(A)	(B)	(C)
Interpolation for longitude values at 47°10'N	85°13.1 (60) − 84°41.9 31.2 5.2 6)31.2 84°41.9 + 5.2 84°47.1	85°15.5 (60) − 84°44.0 31.5 5.25 or 5.3 6)31.5 84°44.0 + 5.3 84°49.3	85°17.9 (60) − 84°46.1 31.8 5.3 6)31.8 84°46.1 + 5.3 84°51.4

Fig. 4.9   Determining Co-ordinates For Plotting TD Lines

also be necessary to establish TD lines from another secondary, using another set of tables. With care, TD lines can thus be transferred to any chart. A word of caution, however, is necessary when using this technique. It will be up to the user to do his own field testing and to check the accuracy of plotted lines against known positions. Especially in those areas, such as harbors and areas close in to shore, lines may need to be corrected for variations from ASF, shore proximity errors, etc.

Using the Tables to Plot a TD Fix Without Overlay Lines.

The same conditions may exist as in the above example, (only TDs to work with and no Loran chart), but the intent may be to leave the area, making it not worthwhile to go to the bother of

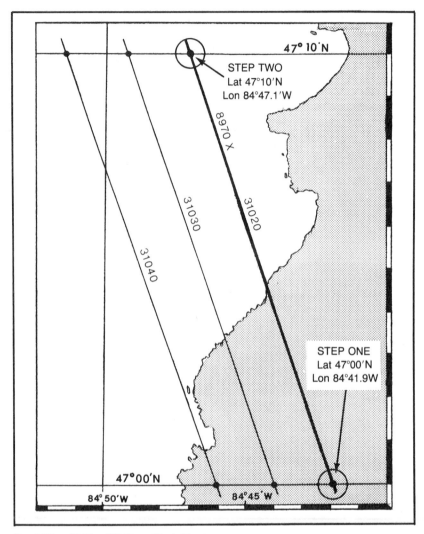

Fig. 4.10   Plotting TD Lines On A Chart

constructing all the TD lines on a chart. However, it is desirable to know the present position. The tables can then be used to determine position without using general TD lines at all. What is being done is essentially the same as the above procedure, but instead of constructing the general TD line 31020, the actual TD LOP 31024.7 is constructed. Again, it is necessary to have two sets of coordinates to determine the two points where the line 31024.7 would intersect two given latitudes OR longitudes in the area. To assist in determining these coordinates, it is required to use a Δ value which is also given in the tables.

The Δ listing is the rate of change in hundredths of degrees of latitude or longitude for each change of one microsecond. Again, an illustration will best explain the use of the tables to produce such a fix.

In this case, (cruising the same area) the TDs given are:

TD 31053.6 and TD 47462.8.

It is necessary to know the present position even though no Loran chart is available and it is not worthwhile to construct one. To

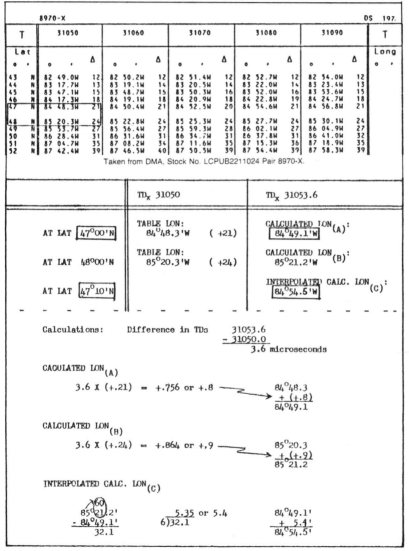

Fig. 4.11 Determining TDx LOP 31053.6

determine the fix, each TD LOP will have to be constructed. To construct one TD line, two geographic points will have to be determined. The difference from the method before is that an actual specific LOP is being constructed, not a general TD line.

STEP ONE:
DETERMINING ONE GEOGRAPHIC POINT ON TDx.

The procedure is to take the TDx LOP and enter the X secondary table by finding the TD line value that comes closest to that

8970-Y					DB 277
T	47450	47460	47470	47480	47490	T
Lat ° '	° ' Δ	° ' Δ	° ' Δ	° ' Δ	° ' Δ	Long ° '

	45 29.0N - 10	45 28.0N - 9	45 27.1N - 9	45 26.1N - 9	45 25.1N - 10	89 W
	45 53.3N - 10	45 52.3N - 10	45 51.3N - 10	45 50.3N - 10	45 49.2N - 10	88 W
	46 17.4N - 11	46 16.2N - 11	46 15.1N - 10	46 14.1N - 11	46 12.9N - 11	87 W
	46 40.9N - 12	46 39.7N - 11	46 38.5N - 11	46 37.4N - 11	46 36.1N - 12	86 W
	47 03.9N - 13	47 02.6N - 12	47 01.3N - 12	47 00.1N - 12	46 58.8N - 13	85 W
	47 26.3N - 13	47 24.9N - 14	47 23.5N - 13	47 22.2N - 13	47 20.9N - 13	84 W
	47 48.1N - 15	47 46.6N - 14	47 45.1N - 14	47 43.7N - 14	47 42.2N - 14	83 W
	48 09.2N - 15	48 07.6N - 15	48 06.1N - 15	48 04.5N - 16	48 02.9N - 15	82 W
	48 29.6N - 17	48 27.9N - 16	48 26.3N - 16	48 24.6N - 16	48 22.9N - 17	81 W
	48 49.3N - 17	48 47.6N - 17	48 45.8N - 17	48 44.0N - 18	48 42.2N - 17	80 W

Taken from DMA, Stock No, LCPUB2211024 Pair 8970-Y.

	TD$_y$ 47460	TD$_y$ 47462.8
AT LON 84°00'W	TABLE LAT: 47°24.9N (Δ -14)	CALCULATED LAT$_{(A)}$: 47°24.5'N (A)
AT LON 85°00'W	TABLE LAT: 47°02.6N (Δ -12)	CALCULATED LAT$_{(B)}$: 47°02.3'N (B)
AT LON 84°50'W		INTERPOLATED CALC. LAT$_{(C)}$: 47°06.0'N

Calculations:　Difference in TDs　47462.8
$$\begin{array}{r} 47462.8 \\ -\ 47460.0 \\ \hline +\ 2.8 \text{ microseconds} \end{array}$$

CALCULATED LAT$_{(A)}$

2.8 X (-.14) = -.392 or -.4 ⟶
$$\begin{array}{r} 47°24.9 \\ +\ (-.4) \\ \hline 47°24.5 \end{array}$$

CALCULATED LAT$_{(B)}$

2.8 X (-.12) = -.336 or -.3 ⟶
$$\begin{array}{r} 47°02.6N \\ +\ (-.3) \\ \hline 47°02.3N \end{array}$$

INTERPOLATED CALC. LAT$_{(C)}$

$$\begin{array}{r} 47°24.5 \\ -\ 47°02.3 \\ \hline 22.2 \end{array}$$　$6\overline{)22.2}$　$\dfrac{3.7}{}$　
$$\begin{array}{r} 47°02.3 \\ +\ 3.7 \\ \hline 47°06.0 \end{array}$$

Fig. 4.12　Determining TDy LOP 47462.8

reading. In this case it would be line 31050. Dead reckoning shows that the current position is somewhere north of latitude 47°00'N, but not as far north as latitude 48°00'N. From the table it can be seen that line 31050 crosses latitude 47°N at longitude 84°48.3'W. (See Fig. 4.11). But this isn't what is wanted. Instead, what is necessary to know is where the LOP 31053.6 crosses Lat 47°N. To find this out the Δ listed value is used to find out the change in longitude for each microsecond difference from 31050. In this case, the Δ value is +.21 which means that for each added microsecond there is an increase of +.21' longitude. The difference between the TD LOP 31503.6 and TD 31050 is 3.6 microseconds. The next step is to multiply 3.6 X +.21 to get a change of .756 or .8' longitude for the difference of 3.6 microseconds. (See calculation for calculated Lon (A) in Fig. 4.11) This longitude change is then added to the 31050 longitude value of 84°48.3' W and it is known

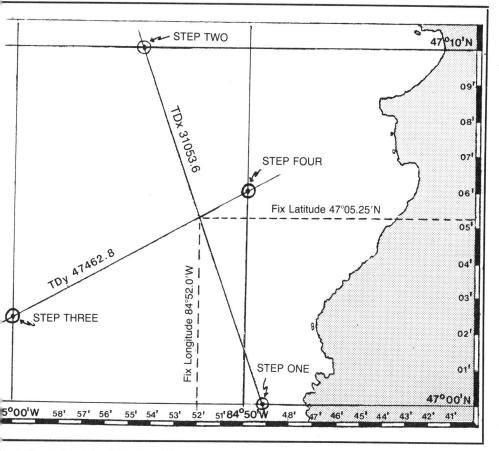

g. 4.13   Determining A Fix From TDs Without Chart Overlay Lines

113

that 31053.6 LOP crosses the 47°00'N latitude at a longitude of 84°49.1'W. With these two geographic coordinates it is now possible to plot the first point on the TD LOP. (See Fig. 4.13).

STEP TWO:
DETERMINING A SECOND GEOGRAPHIC POINT ON TDx.

It is again necessary to get a second set of coordinates to determine a second point on the TD LOP, so the line of position can be drawn. To do this, the table must be entered again, this time at the next latitude, which is 48°00'N. Using the same procedure, but a new Δ value (+ 24), the longitude is calculated where the TD line of 31053.6 crosses Lat 48°00'N. (See calculations for calculated LON (B) in Fig. 4.11). As before, Lat 48°00'N is too far away and off the chart, so interpolation is necessary to find where the TD LOP would cross on a closer latitude - again using 47°10'N. To interpolate, one must find the difference between the two calculated longitudes (that are at 47°N and 48°N) and divide by 6. This value is then added on to the longitude where the TD lop crosses at 47°00'N to give the longitude where the TD will cross at 47°10'N. This new longitude is 84°54.5'W and the other set of geographic points is available to plot a second point on the TD LOP: 47°10'N & 84°54.5'W. With the two points now established, the TDx LOP can be drawn and position is somewhere along that line. (See Fig. 4.13).

STEP THREE:
DETERMINING FIRST GEOGRAPHIC POINT ON TDy LOP.

To determine the fix, the whole procedure must be followed again with TDy 47462.8. Using the tables for the Y secondary, entry is made at the closest TD line value, which is 47460. (see Fig. 4.12) This time the initial reference points are given in longitude instead of latitude, which are found in the extreme right hand column of the table. Dead reckoning reveals that the ship's position is somewhere between 84° and 85°W, so this is where the values are taken. As before, the latitudes given are only where the general TD line 47460 crosses these longitudes. The information needed is where the TD LOP 47462.8 crosses these longitudes. To do this the Δ listing must be multiplied by the difference in microseconds between the actual TD LOP and line 47460. At longitude 85°W, this value is -.12. The difference between the TD LOP and the table TD is 2.8 microseconds. Multiplying 2.8 X -.12 gives a latitude change of -.336 or -.3 which is added algebraically to the latitude crossing at 85°W. (See calculations for calculated Lat (B) in Fig. 4.12.) This produces the first set of TD coordinates (85°00'W & 47°02.3'N.) which are plotted on the chart. (See Fig. 4.13.)

STEP FOUR:
DETERMINING A SECOND GEOGRAPHIC POINT ON TDy.

To get the second point on the LOP, the situation again exists that the chart isn't big enough to include the second set of coordinates at the next nearest longitude given on the table: 84°00'W. The position of the TD LOP is interpolated to a closer longitude, that of 84°50'W. The difference in the calculated latitude readings at the two given longitudes (84°N and 85°W) is found and divided by 6. Sometimes it is difficult to know whether to add or subtract the resulting value. A quick sketch of the relative positions of the initial coordinates will show that the interpolated position must be somewhere on a line between the two and, in this case, it is apparent that the change in latitude must be added to the latitude at 85° to give the latitude at 84°50'N where the TD LOP crosses (see Fig. 4.14). It is now possible to plot the second point on TDy with coordinates 84°50'W & 47°06.0'N. With the two points now established, TD LOP 47462.8 can be constructed.

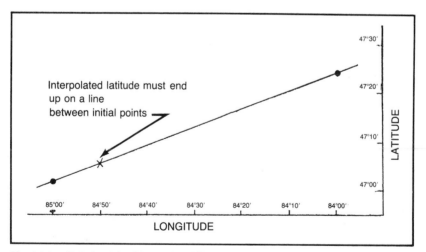

Fig. 4.14   Relationship of Interpolated Point To Initial Reference Points

The ship's position is where the two LOPs cross. Lat/Lon coordinates for the fix can be lifted directly off the chart.

If all this sounds like quite a bit of work to obtain a simple fix, it certainly has to be admitted that it is a lot more demanding than simply transferring TDs or Lat/Lon coordinates directly to a chart. The above procedure almost rivals taking a sight with a sextant and working through reduction tables and a maze of corrections to obtain a fix. Yet, it wasn't too many years back when a group of fellows were doing all their navigation in just this manner. They were forced to because they had a TD only receiver and they were cruising in an area where large scale Loran-C charts were yet to come. Now, with the abundance of Lat/Lon receivers, the technique is not as important as it used to be. However, it isn't a bad one to know, in case one is ever in a situation where this is the only way to obtain a fix. And, as with any other technique, the more it is used, the quicker running through a set of calculations to determine a fix can be done.

CHAPTER FIVE

Loran-C Chains

Loran-C chains are spread throughout the world, primarily in the Northern Hemisphere, where they provide coverage in most geographic areas. There are basically two types of chains: those which are established by governments, and those which are privately owned and operated. Some of the chains are in areas, such as in the USSR, where data is not yet complete or confirmed.

The United States Coast Guard has been the key agency for establishing US chains both in and outside the U.S. Privately owned chains are in operation in areas such as: Saudi Arabia, Gulf of Mexico, and the Java Sea. Along with future chains planned for Hudson Bay and the Celtic and North Seas, these chains usually operate with lower power than the main chains, resulting in smaller coverage areas. For an overall picture of world wide Loran-C coverage, see Fig. 1.3.

Section I: Station Characteristics

Within a given chain, stations can be classified according to their functions. There are two basic types: those which transmit signals, and those which do not. Transmitting stations may be further subdivided into two categories: the master station and its secondaries. In addition, there are two different non-transmitting functions: those which monitor other stations, and those which control other stations.

Transmitting	Non-Transmitting
Master	Monitor
Secondary	Control

Fig. 5.1   Types of Loran-C Stations

The stations may be assigned several functions. For example, the station at Seneca, NY, serves as the master for the

Northeast US 9960 Chain and as the X secondary for the Great Lakes 8970 Chain. A transmitting station may also be assigned non-transmitting functions and serve as a control station for other stations in the chain, or even stations in other chains. In the above example, this same station at Seneca, NY, is scheduled to become the remote operating control station for the stations at Dana, IN (Master 8970/Z secondary 9960), Baudette, MN (Y secondary 8970) Caribou, ME (W secondary 9960), and Nantuckett, MA (X secondary 8970/X secondary 5930). See Fig. 5.2

Master Stations

Master stations broadcast a series of 9 pulses that are coded in such a way that a Loran-C receiver can identify them as master stations. To accomplish this, the station has a number of different functions which include:

Transmitting signals of proper format within established tolerances.

Establishing the epoch time, repetition rate and carrier frequency for the chain.

Monitoring the signals of secondary stations.

Secondary Stations

Secondary stations also transmit pulse data. Through precision timing, they wait a specified time interval from the transmission of the master signal and then broadcast a series of 8 pulses. To accomplish this, the secondary has functions which are a little different from the master. They are:

Transmitting signals of the proper format within established tolerances.

Maintaining the proper emission delay.

Blinking signals for navigator warning when directed by a control station.

Monitoring the master-secondary time differences of stations.

Monitor Stations

Monitor stations do not transmit any signals to be picked up by a Loran-C receiver. Instead, these stations utilize specialized

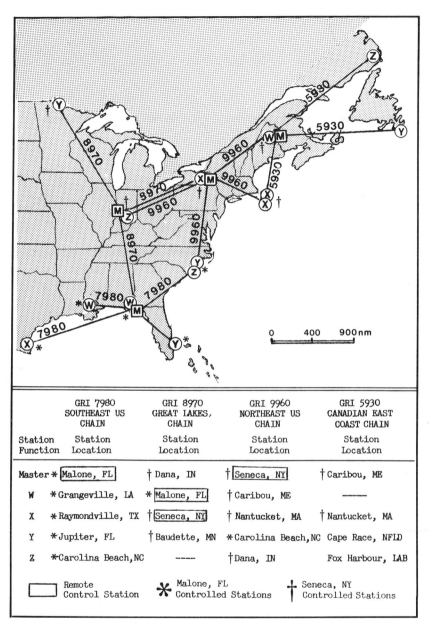

	GRI 7980 SOUTHEAST US CHAIN	GRI 8970 GREAT LAKES, CHAIN	GRI 9960 NORTHEAST US CHAIN	GRI 5930 CANADIAN EAST COAST CHAIN
Station Function	Station Location	Station Location	Station Location	Station Location
Master *	Malone, FL	† Dana, IN	† Seneca, NY	† Caribou, ME
W	* Grangeville, LA	* Malone, FL	† Caribou, ME	-----
X	* Raymondville, TX	† Seneca, NY	† Nantucket, MA	† Nantucket, MA
Y	* Jupiter, FL	† Baudette, MN	* Carolina Beach, NC	Cape Race, NFLD
Z	* Carolina Beach, NC	----	† Dana, IN	Fox Harbour, LAB

	Remote Control Station	✱ Malone, FL Controlled Stations	† Seneca, NY Controlled Stations

Fig. 5.2   Loran-C Coverage For The Eastern United States & Canada

receiving equipment to monitor signals from one or more master-secondary pairs. The monitor station's function is to insure that the transmitting stations are operating up to pre-determined standards within a prescribed tolerance. When adjustments are needed, this information is transferred to the specific station.

Control Stations

Control Stations, which are an integral part of the Remote Operating System (ROS), are a fairly new addition to the Loran system. The idea began in January of 1978 when, with the co-operation of the Canadian government, a new station was constructed on Vancouver Island. This station, which became the Z secondary for the Canadian West Coast 5990 Chain, obtained ROS status in November 1980 when all critical operational and control information was transferred to a remote monitor station at Alert Bay, British Columbia. These initial tests showed that a transmitting station could be operated with as few as 4 persons, as long as the station didn't have control responsibility for the whole chain. Through the use of remote control stations, the costly manpower within a given chain can be reduced.

A prime example of this concept in action is seen by looking at the 3 major US chains which cover an area from the Gulf of Mexico to the New England States. These 3 chains are made up of 3 master stations and 11 different secondaries. Yet, through overlap, or doubling of station functions - and the ROS, the whole Eastern half of the United States is scheduled to be controlled by two control stations: Seneca NY, and Malone, FL.(See Fig. 5.2)

Station Location

Primary requirements for station position are based on the desired geographic coverage and the ability to meet accuracy requirements.

Factors which affect a station's location are:

General noise in the area.

Availability of station sites and the possibility of sharing sites between adjacent sites.

Reliable over-water coverage for a given chain usually extends at least 600 nautical miles from the most distant transmitter. Usable coverage may extend to as much as 1000 miles, but in these fringe areas there is often the danger of cycle slip. When signals pass over rough terrain such as mountains, etc., reliable coverage may be reduced to only 400 miles.

Section II: Chains in the Atlantic and Adjacent Waters

The Loran-C chains and their coverage areas lie predominantly in the Northern Hemisphere. For convénience, they can be divided into two very large areas: those which provide coverage in the Atlantic Ocean and adjacent bodies of water, and those which provide coverage in the Central and Northern half of the Pacific Ocean. Beginning with the Atlantic Ocean, information on the chains will be provided in a geographically clockwise manner, beginning with coverage in the Gulf of Mexico.

Primary coverage in the Atlantic is from the Gulf of Mexico, up the Eastern United States and Canadian coasts to Greenland, Iceland, the Norwegian Coast and the British Isles. Three fourths of the Mediterranean also has primary coverage. By using skywaves, secondary coverage takes in most of the North Atlantic and those prime cruising areas in the Bahamas and even the Virgin Islands.

Southeast U.S. Chain: GRI 7980

The Eastern seaboard of the United States and Canada is one of the best areas for Loran-C coverage in the world. Three United States chains and one Canadian chain provide an overlapping network of station coverage for this area. (See Fig. 5.2.)

The southernmost of these chains is the Southeast US 7980 Chain. This chain became operational in December of 1979. It has its master at Malone, FL, and 4 secondaries: W at Grangeville, FL; X at Raymondville, TX; Y at Jupiter, FL; and Z at Carolina Beach, NC. In addition, the Malone site serves as the W secondary for the Great Lakes 8970 Chain and the Carolina Beach station doubles as the Y secondary for the Northeast US 9960 Chain. The station at Malone also controls the Y secondary for the 9960 chain and all of the stations in the 7980 chain. Monitors serving the chain are located at Mayport, FL, Destin, FL, and New Orleans, LA, with the last two also serving as monitors for the Great Lakes 8970 Chain. It is interesting to note that the site at Carolina Beach, which serves as the Z secondary in this chain and the Y secondary in the Northeast US 9960 Chain, was one of the original sites used when the Loran-C system was turned over to the Coast Guard in the mid-1950's, and first tested in 1957.

The primary coverage area of this chain is all of the Gulf of Mexico, except for the Southwest area, and in the Atlantic, offshore of Florida, Georga and South Carolina. A prime cruising area, of course, which falls close to this coverage area is the Bahamas and adjacent outlying island chains. While the primary coverage diagram for this chain includes only the Northern end of this area, it should be noted that secondary coverage is present for all of the Bahamas and beyond. With care, and using Loran-C skywaves, it is still possible to navigate with Loran-C well out into the far reaches of the islands. In fact, by adjusting for skywaves and cycle slip, there have been reports of those cruising with Loran-C using this chain as far away as the Virgin Islands. (See Fig. 5.3).

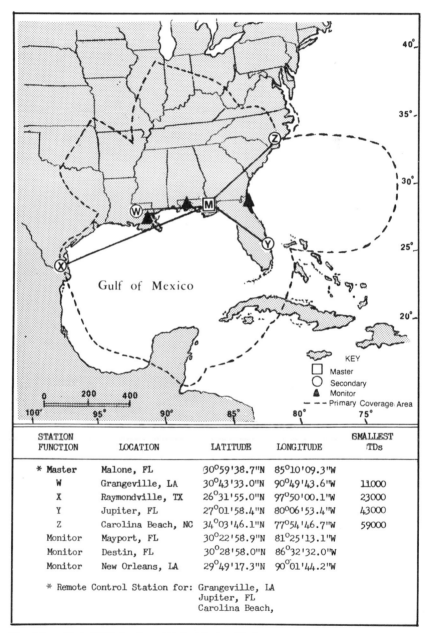

STATION FUNCTION	LOCATION	LATITUDE	LONGITUDE	SMALLEST TDs
* Master	Malone, FL	30°59'38.7"N	85°10'09.3"W	
W	Grangeville, LA	30°43'33.0"N	90°49'43.6"W	11000
X	Raymondville, TX	26°31'55.0"N	97°50'00.1"W	23000
Y	Jupiter, FL	27°01'58.4"N	80°06'53.4"W	43000
Z	Carolina Beach, NC	34°03'46.1"N	77°54'46.7"W	59000
Monitor	Mayport, FL	30°22'58.9"N	81°25'13.1"W	
Monitor	Destin, FL	30°28'58.0"N	86°32'32.0"W	
Monitor	New Orleans, LA	29°49'17.3"N	90°01'44.2"W	

* Remote Control Station for: Grangeville, LA
                              Jupiter, FL
                              Carolina Beach,

Fig. 5.3   Chain 7980 Southeast United States Chain

Northeast US Chain: GRI 9960

Other Eastern Seaboard coverage is provided by the Northeast US 9960 Chain. This chain essentially replaces the old 9930 chain which had served the US East Coast. The basic chain GRI 9960 became operational in 1977. The master station, which is located at Seneca, NY, also doubles as the X secondary for the Great Lakes 8970 Chain. There are 4 secondaries in the chain: W at Caribou, ME; X at Nantuckett, MA; Y at Carolina Beach, NC; and Z at Dana IN. In addition, the master station for this chain is one of the two control stations for the Eastern United States. Stations under its control are the station at Baudette, MN (GRI 8970) and all the stations in this chain (GRI 9960) except that at Carolina Beach. Monitors for the chain are located at Cape Elizabeth, ME; Sandy Hook, NJ; Plumbrook, OH; and Dunbar, MI. All of these except the station at Sandy Hook serve as monitors for other chains.

The primary coverage area for this chain is the entire Eastern United States from Georgia in the U.S. to Nova Scotia and Prince Edward Island in Canada. This coverage extends inland to Lakes Ontario, Erie, and the Eastern half of Lake Huron, including Georgian Bay. However, this chain is often picked up as far inland as the North Channel of Lake Huron and even Eastern Lake Superior. In fact, receivers which are set on automatic chain and secondary selection in these areas will often choose this 9960 chain over the Great Lakes 8970 Chain - even though the latter will give much more accurate results. In these areas it may become necessary for the operator to manually override the receiver's automatic chain selection. (See Fig. 5.4).

Great Lakes Chain: GRI 8970

This chain is one of the latest in the United States to become operational. This chain is also one which is spread over some of the largest geographic areas in the U.S. It has its master at Dana, IN; its W secondary at Malone, FL; and its X secondary at Seneca NY; the Y secondary is located at Baudette, MN. The station at Baudette, MN, is the only one in the chain which does not have a dual function. Monitor stations for the chain are at Dunbar Forest, MI; Plumbrook, OH; Destin, FL; and New Orleans, LA.

The primary area of this chain's coverage is, of course, The Great Lakes. It should be noted that the Eastern end of Lake Erie and Lake Ontario are not included in primary coverage for this chain. The Northeast US 9960 Chain will probably provide better coverage for these areas. It should also be noted that, while this chain is called The Great Lakes Chain, primary coverage does extend to include much of the Eastern seaboard from Georgia through New Jersey, and it offers another alternative to using chains 7980 and 9960. (See Fig. 5.5).

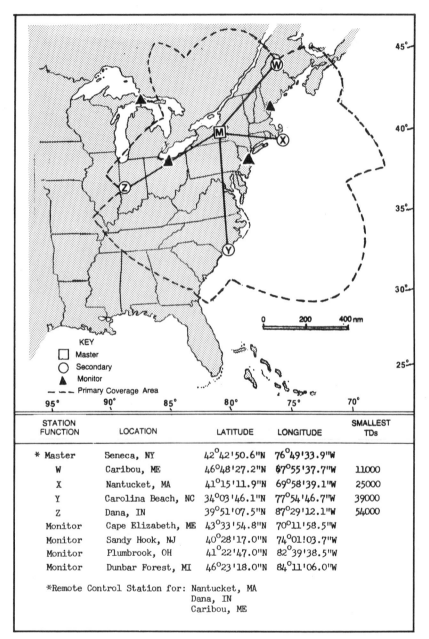

STATION FUNCTION	LOCATION	LATITUDE	LONGITUDE	SMALLEST TDs
* Master	Seneca, NY	42°42'50.6"N	76°49'33.9"W	
W	Caribou, ME	46°48'27.2"N	67°55'37.7"W	11000
X	Nantucket, MA	41°15'11.9"N	69°58'39.1"W	25000
Y	Carolina Beach, NC	34°03'46.1"N	77°54'46.7"W	39000
Z	Dana, IN	39°51'07.5"N	87°29'12.1"W	54000
Monitor	Cape Elizabeth, ME	43°33'54.8"N	70°11'58.5"W	
Monitor	Sandy Hook, NJ	40°28'17.0"N	74°01'03.7"W	
Monitor	Plumbrook, OH	41°22'47.0"N	82°39'38.5"W	
Monitor	Dunbar Forest, MI	46°23'18.0"N	84°11'06.0"W	

*Remote Control Station for: Nantucket, MA
Dana, IN
Caribou, ME

Fig. 5.4   GRI 9960 Northeast United States Chain

124

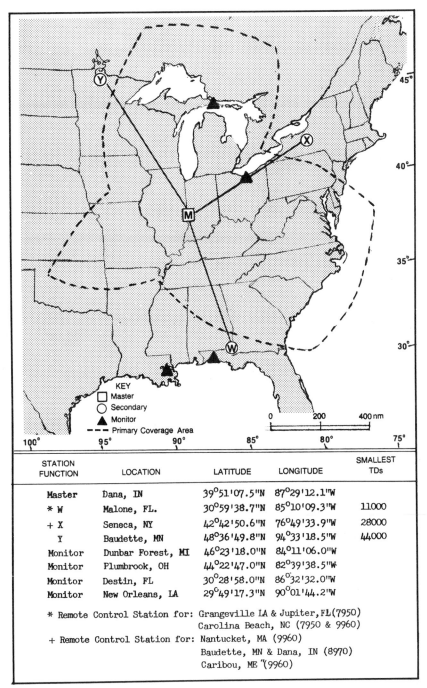

STATION FUNCTION	LOCATION	LATITUDE	LONGITUDE	SMALLEST TDs
Master	Dana, IN	39°51'07.5"N	87°29'12.1"W	
* W	Malone, FL.	30°59'38.7"N	85°10'09.3"W	11000
+ X	Seneca, NY	42°42'50.6"N	76°49'33.9"W	28000
Y	Baudette, MN	48°36'49.8"N	94°33'18.5"W	44000
Monitor	Dunbar Forest, MI	46°23'18.0"N	84°11'06.0"W	
Monitor	Plumbrook, OH	44°22'47.0"N	82°39'38.5"W	
Monitor	Destin, FL	30°28'58.0"N	86°32'32.0"W	
Monitor	New Orleans, LA	29°49'17.3"N	90°01'44.2"W	

* Remote Control Station for: Grangeville LA & Jupiter, FL (7950)
Carolina Beach, NC (7950 & 9960)
\+ Remote Control Station for: Nantucket, MA (9960)
Baudette, MN & Dana, IN (8970)
Caribou, ME "(9960)

Fig. 5.5   GRI 8970 Great Lakes Chain

Canadian East Coast Chain: GRI 5930

This chain was established in conjunction with the US government. It originally consisted of a master station, which was located at Caribou, ME, and two secondaries; X at Nantucket, MA, and Y at Cape Race Newfoundland, Canada. Then the chain underwent a reconfiguration when a new station, Z , was commissioned

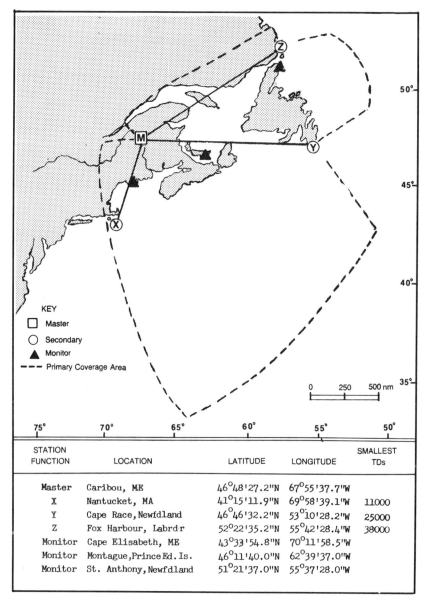

STATION FUNCTION	LOCATION	LATITUDE	LONGITUDE	SMALLEST TDs
Master	Caribou, ME	46°48'27.2"N	67°55'37.7"W	
X	Nantucket, MA	41°15'11.9"N	69°58'39.1"W	11000
Y	Cape Race, Newfdland	46°46'32.2"N	53°10'28.2"W	25000
Z	Fox Harbour, Labrdr	52°22'35.2"N	55°42'28.4"W	38000
Monitor	Cape Elisabeth, ME	43°33'54.8"N	70°11'58.5"W	
Monitor	Montague, Prince Ed. Is.	46°11'40.0"N	62°39'37.0"W	
Monitor	St. Anthony, Newfdland	51°21'37.0"N	55°37'28.0"W	

Fig. 5.6   GRI 5930 Canadian East Coast Chain

at Fox Harbour, Labrador, Canada. All four of the stations in the chain serve dual functions. Monitors for this chain are at Cape Elizabeth, ME; Montague, Prince Edward Island; and St. Anthony, Newfoundland, Canada.

The area of primary coverage used to include primarily the coastal waters off Maine in the U.S and Nova Scotia and Newfoundland Canada. With the addition of the station at Fox Harbour, this coverage has now been extended to include those waters northeast of Newfoundland where it overlaps and gives continuous coverage with the Labrador Sea Chain. (See Fig. 5.6).

NOTE: Because of the reconfiguration of this chain (along with the addition of the new Labrador Sea Chain and reconfiguration of station geometry in this North Atlantic area), those with receivers purchased prior to 1984 will be unable to use Loran in these areas unless they have their receivers reprogrammed by the manufacturer to accept the new data.

Labrador Sea Chain: GRI 7930

One of the newest chains to be added to the Loran system is the Labrador Sea Chain. It, along with the new configuration for the Icelandic 9980 chain, replaces the old North Atlantic (NOR-LANT) 7930 Chain. To get a better picture of what has been done it will help to see what prior North Atlantic coverage looked like.

The original 7930 North Atlantic Chain had its master at Angissoq, Greenland and 3 secondaries: W at Sandur, Iceland; X at the Faeroe Islands; and Z at Cape Race, Newfoundland. This configuration provided a very large coverage area - literally spanning the North Atlantic from Newfoundland to Ireland. Figure 5.7 shows this old configuration and those chains to each side of it: the Canadian East Coast Chain 5930 Chain on the west, and the Norwegian Sea 7970 Chain on the east. By adding the station at Fox Harbour, Labrador, coverage for the Canadian East Coast Chain was extended; a new chain (The Labrador Sea Chain - given the old GRI 7930) was created to give coverage to Greenland and beyond; and what was remaining of the old North Atlantic Chain became the Icelandic Chain with a new GRI 9980. Figure 5.8 shows this new configuration for the North Atlantic. The Norwegian Sea 7970 Chain remained unchanged, but is shown to illustrate the total coverage area.

Those cruising in this area, and owning receivers purchased before 1984, will most likely have to send those back to the manufacturer for reprogramming to accept the new station configuration.

The Labrador Sea Chain, which was assigned the old GRI 7930 from the North Atlantic Chain has a chain configuration with its master at Fox Harbour, Labrador and two secondaries. The W

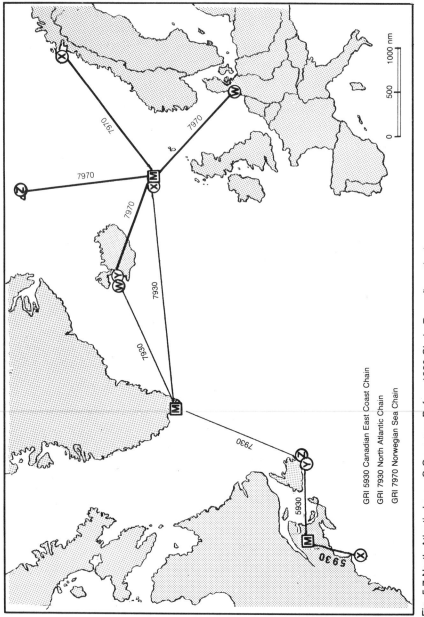

Fig. 5.7 North Atlantic Loran-C Coverage Before 1983 Chain Reconfiguration*
*See Fig. 5.8 for current chain configuration

GRI 5930 Canadian East Coast Chain
GRI 7930 North Atlantic Chain
GRI 7970 Norwegian Sea Chain

secondary is at Cape Race, Newfoundland, and the X secondary at Angissoq, Greenland. The Cape Race and Fox Harbour stations also double as secondaries for the Canadian East Coast Chain,

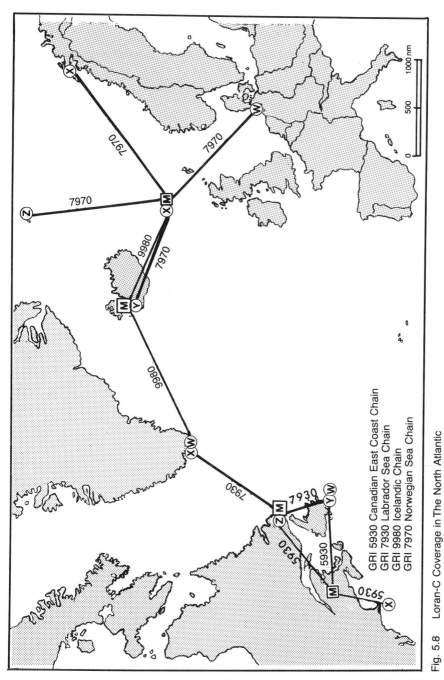

Fig. 5.8   Loran-C Coverage in The North Atlantic

GRI 5930 Canadian East Coast Chain
GRI 7930 Labrador Sea Chain
GRI 9980 Icelandic Chain
GRI 7970 Norwegian Sea Chain

while the Angissoq station, in addition serves as the W secondary for the Icelandic Chain. A monitor/control station is located at St. Anthony, Newfoundland, which also monitors the Canadian East Coast Chain.

Primary coverage for the Labrador Sea Chain includes most of the coastal waters of Newfoundland and a portion of Labrador. The sea coverage, however, extends to the Southern tip of Greenland and east of Newfoundland as far as longitude 25°W.

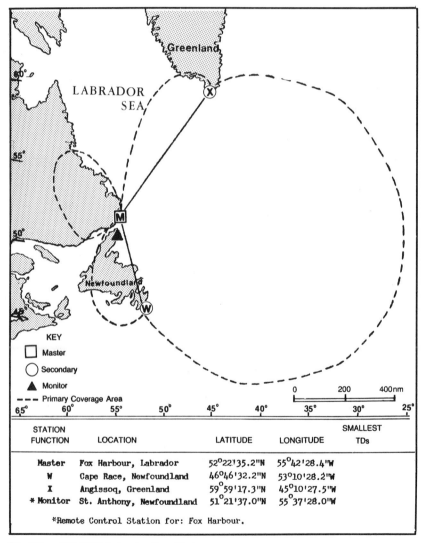

STATION FUNCTION	LOCATION	LATITUDE	LONGITUDE	SMALLEST TDs
Master	Fox Harbour, Labrador	52°22'35.2"N	55°42'28.4"W	
W	Cape Race, Newfoundland	46°46'32.2"N	53°10'28.2"W	
X	Angissoq, Greenland	59°59'17.3"N	45°10'27.5"W	
*Monitor	St. Anthony, Newfoundland	51°21'37.0"N	55°37'28.0"W	

*Remote Control Station for: Fox Harbour.

Fig. 5.9   GRI 7930 Labrador Sea Chain

Icelandic Chain: GRI 9980

The Icelandic Chain is also a result of the reconfiguration of the old North Atlantic Chain. Assigned a new GRI (9980), this chain essentially replaced the Eastern half of the old North Atlantic Chain. It has its master at Sandur, Iceland, and two secondaries: W at Angissoq, Greenland, and X at Ejde, in the Faeroe Islands. All stations in the chain serve dual functions. One monitor station is located at Keflavik, Iceland. This station also serves as a control station for the chain.

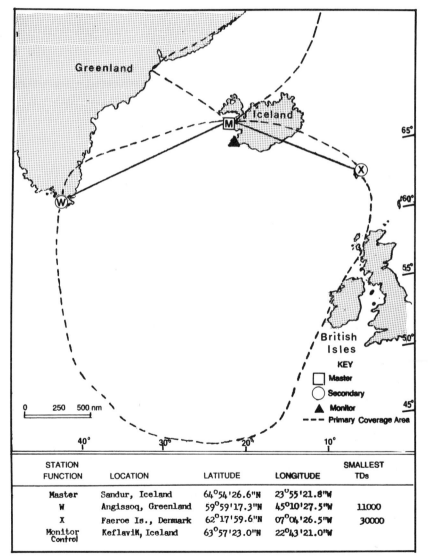

STATION FUNCTION	LOCATION	LATITUDE	LONGITUDE	SMALLEST TDs
Master	Sandur, Iceland	64°54'26.6"N	23°55'21.8"W	
W	Angissoq, Greenland	59°59'17.3"N	45°10'27.5"W	11000
X	Faeroe Is., Denmark	62°17'59.6"N	07°04'26.5"W	30000
Monitor Control	Keflavik, Iceland	63°57'23.0"N	22°43'21.0"W	

Fig. 5.10   GRI 9980 Icelandic Chain

The chain provides primary coverage from the Southern tip of Greenland to the Western shores of Ireland and Scotland, with considerable coverage extending south to approximately latitude 45°N. There is also a sector of coverage that extends up the Eastern coast of Greenland.

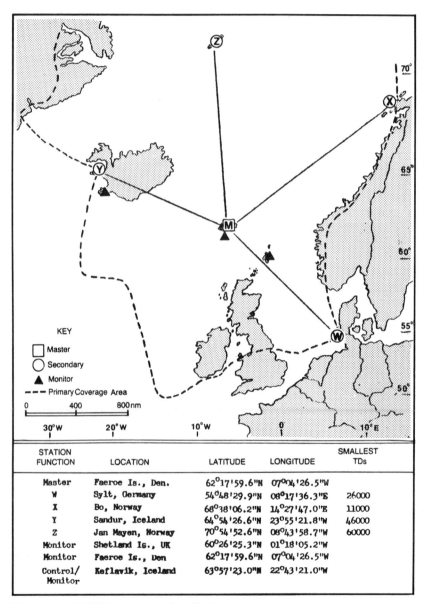

STATION FUNCTION	LOCATION	LATITUDE	LONGITUDE	SMALLEST TDs
Master	Faeroe Is., Den.	62°17'59.6"N	07°04'26.5"W	
W	Sylt, Germany	54°48'29.9"N	08°17'36.3"E	26000
X	Bo, Norway	68°38'06.2"N	14°27'47.0"E	11000
Y	Sandur, Iceland	64°54'26.6"N	23°55'21.8"W	46000
Z	Jan Mayen, Norway	70°54'52.6"N	08°43'58.7"W	60000
Monitor	Shetland Is., UK	60°26'25.3"N	01°18'05.2"W	
Monitor	Faeroe Is., Den	62°17'59.6"N	07°04'26.5"W	
Control/ Monitor	Keflavik, Iceland	63°57'23.0"N	22°43'21.0"W	

Fig. 5.11   GRI 7970 Norwegian Sea Chain

132

Norwegian Sea Chain: GRI 7980

The Norwegian Sea Chain is the only chain which has remained unchanged in the North Atlantic chain reconfiguration. It, along with other major European chains in current operation, is under the control of the US Coast Guard. From its office in London, the USCG exercises regional and chain manager functions. Although these chains were initiated to meet the precise navigation requirements of the Department of Defense, these chains are now receiving increased commercial and recreational use.

This chain is the result of the combined efforts of 6 different countries, with a master at Ejde in the Faeroe Islands (Denmark) and 4 secondaries: W at Sylt, Germany; X at Bo, Norway; Y at Sandur, Iceland; and Z at Jan Mayen, Norway. Two of these stations have dual functions with other chains. Monitors are located at the Shetland Islands (United Kingdom) and the Faeroe Islands. An additional monitor station is located at Keflavik, Iceland, which also serves as a control station for this chain and the Icelandic 9980 Chain.

The area of primary coverage includes part of the Eastern coast of Greenland along with most of the waters surrounding Iceland to the Atlantic coast of Norway. This coverage extends southward to include the Northern ⅔ of the British Isles and surrounding waters. (See Fig. 5.11)

Mediterranean Chain: GRI 7990

Coverage for the Mediterranean Sea is provided by the Mediterranean Chain with GRI 7990. Configuration for this chain consists of a master at Sellia Marina, Italy and 3 secondaries. The secondaries are located at: Lampedusea, Italy (X); Kargabarum, Turkey (Y); And Estartit, Spain (Z). Monitor stations are located in Italy at Sellia Marina and Crotone. Because there are no adjacent main Loran chains which are also under the control of the USCG, there is no overlap and all stations exhibit single functions.

As the name implies, primary coverage for this chain includes most of the Mediterranean Sea, with only the extreme Eastern and Western ends and a section off the African coast lying outside this area. Secondary coverage, which involves utilization of skywaves, provides coverage for all of the Mediterranean. (See Fig. 5.12)

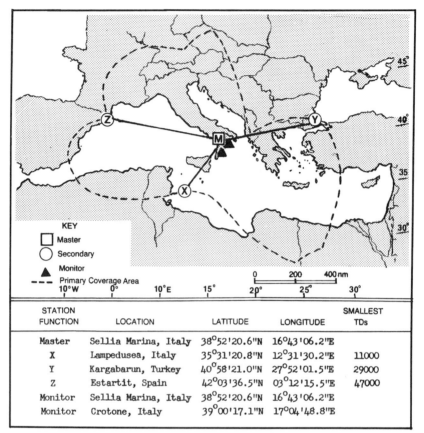

STATION FUNCTION	LOCATION	LATITUDE	LONGITUDE	SMALLEST TDs
Master	Sellia Marina, Italy	38°52'20.6"N	16°43'06.2"E	
X	Lampedusea, Italy	35°31'20.8"N	12°31'30.2"E	11000
Y	Kargabarun, Turkey	40°58'21.0"N	27°52'01.5"E	29000
Z	Estartit, Spain	42°03'36.5"N	03°12'15.5"E	47000
Monitor	Sellia Marina, Italy	38°52'20.6"N	16°43'06.2"E	
Monitor	Crotone, Italy	39°00'17.1"N	17°04'48.8"E	

Fig. 5.12   GRI 7990 Mediterranean Chain

Saudia Arabia Chains: GRI 8990: GRI 7170

The 1980's have seen the development of new chains in the Middle East. These chains differ from other major chains in that they are not controlled and operated by the United States Coast Guard. Instead, all the stations are located within and controlled by a single country, Saudi Arabia.

The North Chain, GRI 8990 was developed first, in the early 1980's. It consists of a master located in the central area of the country at Afif and a large number (5) of secondaries located at periphery points.

The South Chain, GRI 7170, was established by just adding one more station for the master at Al Khamasin and doubling up on station functions with some of those stations in the North Chain. The secondaries are shown in Fig. 5.13.

Between the two chains, the Saudi Arabia system provides primary coverage for all navigable waters surrounding Saudi Arabia and adjacent countries. These include the Red Sea, the Eastern end of the Mediterranean Sea, the Arabian Gulf, the Gulf of Aden and the Northern end of the Arabian Sea.

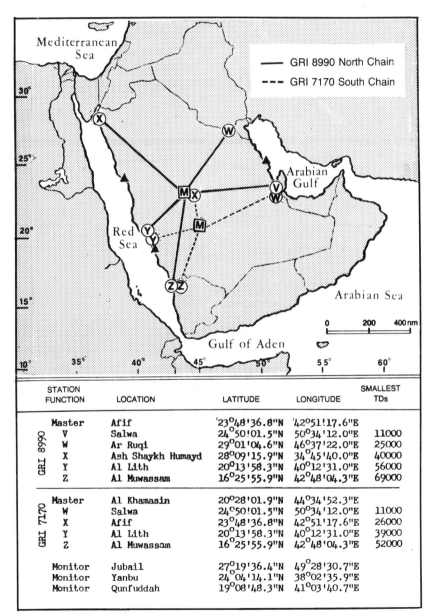

STATION FUNCTION	LOCATION	LATITUDE	LONGITUDE	SMALLEST TDs
Master	Afif	23°48'36.8"N	42°51'17.6"E	
V	Salwa	24°50'01.5"N	50°34'12.0"E	11000
W	Ar Ruqi	29°01'04.6"N	46°37'22.0"E	25000
X	Ash Shaykh Humayd	28°09'15.9"N	34°45'40.0"E	40000
Y	Al Lith	20°13'58.3"N	40°12'31.0"E	56000
Z	Al Muwassam	16°25'55.9"N	42°48'04.3"E	69000
Master	Al Khamasin	20°28'01.9"N	44°34'52.3"E	
W	Salwa	24°50'01.5"N	50°34'12.0"E	11000
X	Afif	23°48'36.8"N	42°51'17.6"E	26000
Y	Al Lith	20°13'58.3"N	40°12'31.0"E	39000
Z	Al Muwassam	16°25'55.9"N	42°48'04.3"E	52000
Monitor	Jubail	27°19'36.4"N	49°28'30.7"E	
Monitor	Yanbu	24°04'14.1"N	38°02'35.9"E	
Monitor	Qunfuddah	19°08'48.3"N	41°03'40.7"E	

(GRI 8990 labels the first group; GRI 7170 labels the second group)

Fig. 5.13   Saudi Arabian Chains

135

Section III: Main Chains in the Pacific

Loran coverage in the Pacific Ocean lies primarily in its Northern hemisphere. In only a few areas does coverage extend to the Southern latitudes below the equator. Primary coverage areas are in the central Pacific near the Hawaiian Islands, in the Western Pacific from the Philippines to Japan, and in the Northern latitudes from the Kamchatka Peninsula across to Alaska and down the West Coast of North America to the Baja Peninsula. Secondary coverage, which involves the utilization of skywaves, is even more extensive, providing coverage for 3/4 of the North Pacific Ocean. See Fig. 1.3.

Central Pacific Chain: GRI 4990

This chain, which is located in the Hawaiian Islands, consists of a master and two secondaries. The master station is located at Johnston Island; the X secondary is at Upolo Pt. on the island of Hawaii; and the Y secondary is on Kure Island. The Johnston Island site also serves as a monitor for the chain. (See Fig. 5.14)

The primary coverage area is for most of the Hawaiian Island chain and waters extending to the north and south. It extends roughly 800 to 1000 miles north of the islands and a little less than that to the south. The main islands in the group (Hawaii, Oahu, etc.) are outside the primary coverage area. Secondary coverage via skywaves takes in a much larger area; however, it should be noted that skywave coverage does not include those favorite cruising areas of the Marquesas, Tuamotus, and Society Islands.

Northwest Pacific Chain: GRI 9970

Moving westward, the next major Loran chain in the Pacific is the Northwest Pacific Chain. This chain consists of a master at Iwo Jima, Japan and four secondaries. The secondaries are located at Marcus Island, Japan (W); Hokkaido, Japan (X); Gesashi, Japan (Y); and Yap Island, a USA trust territory (Z). There are some station dual functions here as well. Monitors are located at Yakota, Japan, Chansan, Korea and Guam Island.

The primary coverage area for the chain extends from the Philippine Islands to the Northern islands of Japan. It also extends eastward in some areas by as much as 1500 - 2000 miles to include much of Micronesia. (See Fig. 5.15)

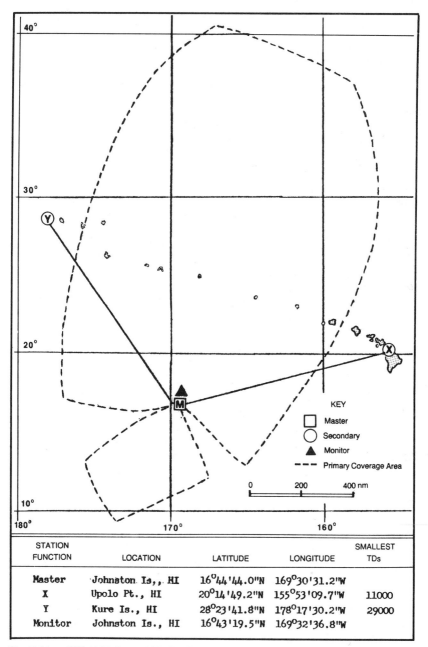

STATION FUNCTION	LOCATION	LATITUDE	LONGITUDE	SMALLEST TDs
Master	Johnston Is,, HI	16°44'44.0"N	169°30'31.2"W	
X	Upolo Pt., HI	20°14'49.2"N	155°53'09.7"W	11000
Y	Kure Is., HI	28°23'41.8"N	178°17'30.2"W	29000
Monitor	Johnston Is., HI	16°43'19.5"N	169°32'36.8"W	

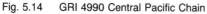

Fig. 5.14   GRI 4990 Central Pacific Chain

Commando Lion Chain: GRI 5970

Commando Lion Chain is a relatively new chain. It extends the coverage of the Northwest Pacific Chain by providing addition-

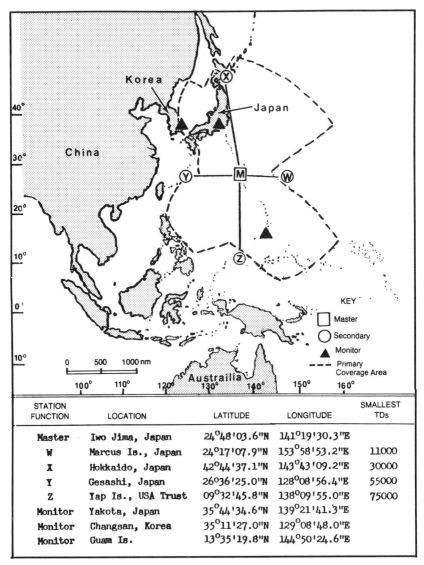

STATION FUNCTION	LOCATION	LATITUDE	LONGITUDE	SMALLEST TDs
Master	Iwo Jima, Japan	24°48'03.6"N	141°19'30.3"E	
W	Marcus Is., Japan	24°17'07.9"N	153°58'53.2"E	11000
X	Hokkaido, Japan	42°44'37.1"N	143°43'09.2"E	30000
Y	Gesashi, Japan	26°36'25.0"N	128°08'56.4"E	55000
Z	Yap Is., USA Trust	09°32'45.8"N	138°09'55.0"E	75000
Monitor	Yakota, Japan	35°44'34.6"N	139°21'41.3"E	
Monitor	Changsan, Korea	35°11'27.0"N	129°08'48.0"E	
Monitor	Guam Is.	13°35'19.8"N	144°50'24.6"E	

Fig. 5.15   GRI 9970 Northwest Pacific Chain

al coverage westward from that chain. The chain consists of a master, which is located at Pohong, Korea, and 3 secondaries. The secondaries are located at Hokkaido, Japan (W); Kwang Ju, Korea (X); and Gesashi, Japan (Y). Monitors are at Osan and Changsan, Korea, with the one at Changsan also doubling as a monitor for the Northwest Pacific Chain.

This chain has a much smaller coverage area than the Northwest Pacific Chain and concentrates mainly on the coastal

138

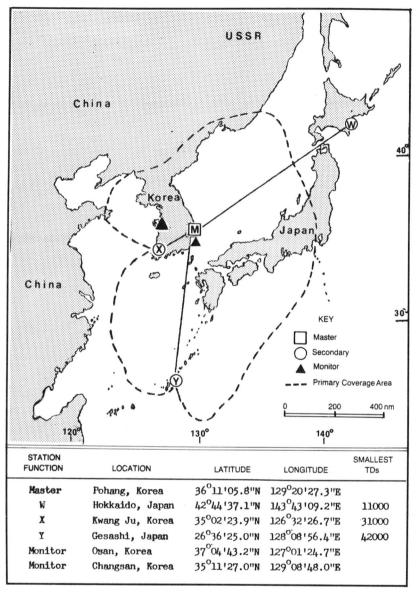

STATION FUNCTION	LOCATION	LATITUDE	LONGITUDE	SMALLEST TDs
Master	Pohang, Korea	36°11'05.8"N	129°20'27.3"E	
W	Hokkaido, Japan	42°44'37.1"N	143°43'09.2"E	11000
X	Kwang Ju, Korea	35°02'23.9"N	126°32'26.7"E	31000
Y	Gesashi, Japan	26°36'25.0"N	128°08'56.4"E	42000
Monitor	Osan, Korea	37°04'43.2"N	127°01'24.7"E	
Monitor	Changsan, Korea	35°11'27.0"N	129°08'48.0"E	

Fig. 5.16   GRI 5970 Commando Lion

waters off Korea and the main Islands of Japan. In the area between Japan and Korea, it provides another alternative to the Northwest Pacific Chain. (See Fig. 5.16)

North Pacific Chain: GRI 9990

The Northern part of the Pacific Ocean and the coastal waters of Western North America again present a vast network of

Loran chains which are interconnected to present continuous Loran coverage from the Aleutian Islands to the Baja Peninsula. The chains providing this coverage are four: the North Pacific Chain: GRI 9990; the Gulf of Alaska Chain: GRI 7960; the Canadian West Coast Chain: GRI 5990; and the US West Coast Chain: GRI 9940. Because the chains are inter-related with many stations again serving dual functions, it may be helpful to get an overall picture of this area and its chains. See Fig. 5.17

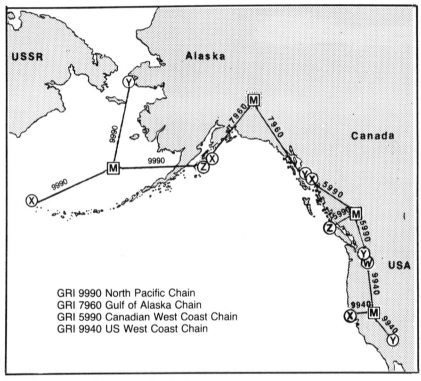

Fig. 5.17   Loran-C Chains in the Northeast Pacific

The first of these chains, the North Pacific Chain, consists of a master which is located on the island of St. Paul, Alaska, and 3 secondaries. The X secondary is located in the far reaches of the Aleutian Islands on the island of Attu. The Y secondary is located on the mainland at Port Clarence, Alaska, and the Z secondary is located at Narrow Cape, on Kodiak Island. Monitors are at Kodiak, Adak, and St. Paul, Alaska. The St. Paul site is also the master station for the chain. (See Fig. 5.18)

The primary coverage area for the chain is most of the area between Alaska and the USSR. It also extends well south, a thousand miles, of the Aleutian Islands. Secondary coverage extends much further, providing Loran use with skywaves for a great part of the North Pacific Ocean.

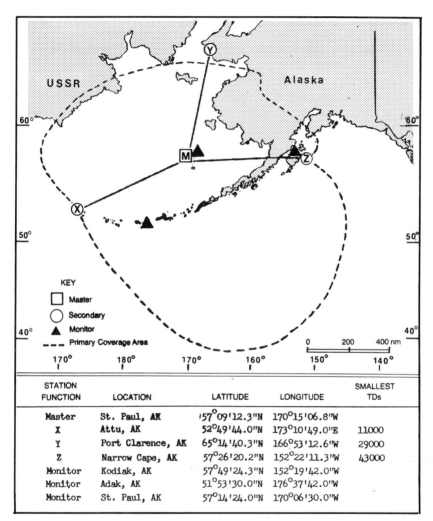

STATION FUNCTION	LOCATION	LATITUDE	LONGITUDE	SMALLEST TDs
Master	St. Paul, AK	57°09'12.3"N	170°15'06.8"W	
X	Attu, AK	52°49'44.0"N	173°10'49.0"E	11000
Y	Port Clarence, AK	65°14'40.3"N	166°53'12.6"W	29000
Z	Narrow Cape, AK	57°26'20.2"N	152°22'11.3"W	43000
Monitor	Kodiak, AK	57°49'24.3"N	152°19'42.0"W	
Monitor	Adak, AK	51°53'30.0"N	176°37'42.0"W	
Monitor	St. Paul, AK	57°14'24.0"N	170°06'30.0"W	

Fig. 5.18   GRI 9990 North Pacific Chain

Gulf of Alaska Chain: GRI 7960

This chain is smaller than the North Pacific Chain, but it provides important coverage for the gap between the North Pacific Chain and the Canadian West Coast Chain. Its master station is located at Tok, Alaska, with two secondaries: X at Narrow Cape, Alaska, and Y at Shoal Cove, Alaska. There are two monitors for the chain, one at Kodiak, Alaska, and one at Juneau, Alaska.

The primary coverage for this chain is the coastal waters of Alaska from Narrow Cape eastward to within 200 miles of the Southernmost tip of the state. Coverage extends offshore in this area, 300 to 400 miles. (See Fig. 5.19)

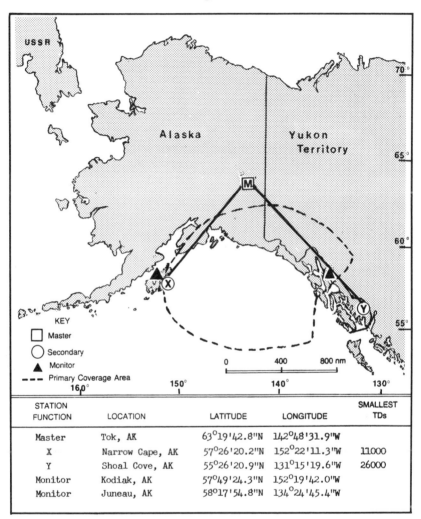

STATION FUNCTION	LOCATION	LATITUDE	LONGITUDE	SMALLEST TDs
Master	Tok, AK	63°19'42.8"N	142°48'31.9"W	
X	Narrow Cape, AK	57°26'20.2"N	152°22'11.3"W	11000
Y	Shoal Cove, AK	55°26'20.9"N	131°15'19.6"W	26000
Monitor	Kodiak, AK	57°49'24.3"N	152°19'42.0"W	
Monitor	Juneau, AK	58°17'54.8"N	134°24'45.4"W	

Fig. 5.19   GRI 7960 Gulf of Alaska Chain

Canadian West Coast Chain: GRI 5990

The Canadian West Coast Chain consists of a master and 3 secondaries. The master is located inland at Williams Lake, British Columbia, and the secondaries are located at: Shoal Cove, AK (X); George, WA (Y); and Port Hardy, British Columbia (Z). Monitor stations are located at Alert Bay, Whidbey Island, and Sand Spit, British Columbia.

The primary coverage area is for the coastal waters of the state of Washington and British Columbia, north to the Southern tip of Alaska. This coverage extends approximately 300 miles offshore. (See Fig. 5.20)

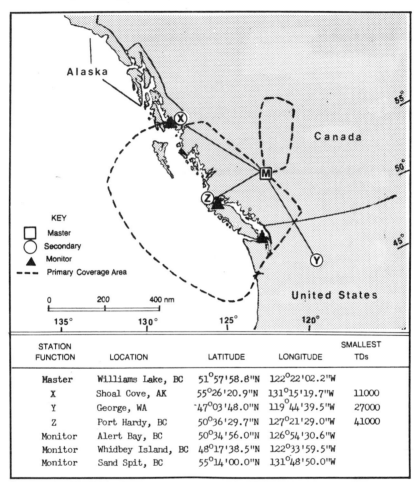

STATION FUNCTION	LOCATION	LATITUDE	LONGITUDE	SMALLEST TDs
Master	Williams Lake, BC	51°57'58.8"N	122°22'02.2"W	
X	Shoal Cove, AK	55°26'20.9"N	131°15'19.7"W	11000
Y	George, WA	⁻47°03'48.0"N	119°44'39.5"W	27000
Z	Port Hardy, BC	50°36'29.7"N	127°21'29.0"W	41000
Monitor	Alert Bay, BC	50°34'56.0"N	126°54'30.6"W	
Monitor	Whidbey Island, BC	48°17'38.5"N	122°33'59.5"W	
Monitor	Sand Spit, BC	55°14'00.0"N	131°48'50.0"W	

Fig. 5.20   GRI 5990 Canadian West Coast Chain

US West Coast Chain: GRI 9940

This was the first Loran-C chain to be developed in the U.S. waters because the West Coast, unlike the East Coast, did not have the extensive Loran-A coverage. It also was an area that was experiencing increased shipping. The chain consists of a master which is located at Fallon, NV, and 3 secondaries. The secondaries are located at: George, WA (W); Middletown, CA (X); and Searchlight, NV (Y). Monitors are located at North Bend, OR and Pt. Pinos, CA.

The area of primary coverage is the coastal waters off the Western United States, extending seaward 200 - 400 miles. Much of the coverage for this chain extends inland, which has lead many to believe that this chain could also be used for land use: air traffic, monitoring vehicles in congested areas, emergency vehicle dispatching, etc. (See Fig. 5.21)

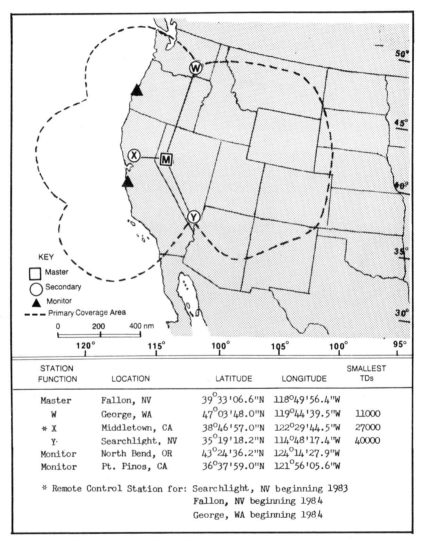

STATION FUNCTION	LOCATION	LATITUDE	LONGITUDE	SMALLEST TDs
Master	Fallon, NV	39°33'06.6"N	118°49'56.4"W	
W	George, WA	47°03'48.0"N	119°44'39.5"W	11000
* X	Middletown, CA	38°46'57.0"N	122°29'44.5"W	27000
Y·	Searchlight, NV	35°19'18.2"N	114°48'17.4"W	40000
Monitor	North Bend, OR	43°24'36.2"N	124°14'27.9"W	
Monitor	Pt. Pinos, CA	36°37'59.0"N	121°56'05.6"W	

* Remote Control Station for: Searchlight, NV beginning 1983
Fallon, NV beginning 1984
George, WA beginning 1984

Fig. 5.21   GRI 9940 United States West Coast Chain

Section IV: Other Loran Chains

In various areas of the world there are other Loran chains. Many of these are of the mini chain variety, such as those established in European waters. These are commercial systems which have been established primarily to provide accurate position fixing for the oil exploration industry. The future for mini chains looks bright because they can be established for just those areas where coverage is needed and with much less expense than that which is required to establish and maintain major chains.

There has been increasing pressure among those in the commercial fishing and oil industries to expand the present European main chain coverage. Countries such as France have begun building new stations and indicated their willingness to tie in with already existing chains to give more complete coverage in European waters.

Two of these stations, at Soustons (43°44′ 23″N; 01°22′ 37″W) and Lessay (49°08′52″N; 01°30′14″W), began transmitting on an intermittent schedule for testing purposes in 1984. Using GRI 8940, when the stations become operational for navigation, the chain will provide hyperbolic users with only one line of position (because there are only two stations). To get a fix, another LOP from some other source will be needed until more stations are established.

Other countries have also expressed an interest in adding stations and possibly reconfiguring present chains to improve coverage. At the time of this writing, a number of different possibilities exist, such as adding stations in Southern Ireland, Belgium, Bergen, Norway, or some of the islands off Norway's Northern coast. Thus, the remainder of the 80's may see some chain reconfiguration in European waters such as that which occurred in the North Atlantic in 1983-84.

The Soviet Union also has two chains, both in the Western and Eastern sections of their country. The USSR has also indicated an interest in joint chain operation and has proposed dual rate operations, particularly in the Northwest Pacific.

CHAPTER SIX

Mechanics

Getting Started

Once a Loran receiver has been properly installed and checked for interference (signal to noise ratio etc.), the next step is to acquire Loran signals in a given chain so that position can be established. There are two basic ways this is done: automatically by the receiver or manually by the operator.

Many receivers have automatic chain and station selection. With this function, the receiver will automatically select the chain and station pairs which will usually provide the best fix for a given area. However, to utilize this function, the receiver must have some idea of the present location so that it can make this selection. It may be necessary for the operator to initially program in a rough idea of position. This may be done by entering in the latitude and longitude from a chart to the nearest degree or within 200 - 300 miles of position.

Sometimes a receiver will not choose the best station pairs making it necessary to override the automatic function of chain and station selection with manual input. Other receivers that do not have automatic selection need to have the Group Repetition Interval (GRI), and sometimes even the secondaries to be tracked, entered manually. Some receivers require that the operator manually input only the GRI for the current cruising area. The available secondaries for the chain will then be displayed and the option of choosing secondaries is available. On other receivers, even the secondaries may need to be entered. This is done by using secondary identification which may be specific to each individual receiver, so the owner's manual must be consulted for the proper procedure for entering which secondaries are to be used. Regardless of the mode of manual selection, an important factor is to decide on which chain to use and those secondaries which will provide the most accurate fixes.

Choosing the Best Station Pairs

In choosing which GRI chain and station pairs to use, there are several considerations to be made. Certainly the main determinant will be location relative to available stations. Sometimes there will be only one chain serving a given area, but often there may be more than one.

One of the first considerations is to pick a chain and stations which can be used for the duration of the voyage so that there doesn't have to be a change midway in a day's run. Common sense dictates that, if all other factors are equal, a nearby transmitter should be used in order to have stronger signal reception. However, there are often other factors which affect station selection and the expected accuracy from a station pair. These factors are: the relationship of ship's position to the transmitting stations (station geometry); the size of the crossing angles between the hyperbolic lines; and the gradient, or distance between the lines.

Station Geometry

Ideally, the ship's position should be somewhere within an arc between the two stations of a given master - secondary pair. One area in which signals should not be used is in the extension of the baseline beyond a given station. There are two reasons why this is important and why signals in these areas produce inaccurate fixes. One is that, in the general vicinity of a baseline extension, a

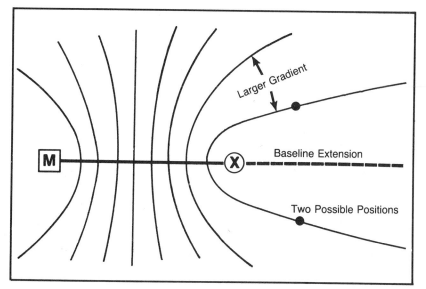

Fig. 6.1   Baseline Extensions

given TD (Time Delay) reading can actually represent two different positions - one on each side of the baseline. Another reason is that, in these areas the distance between adjacent hyperbolic lines spreads out and the gradient here becomes much larger then is desirable, so fixes will be less accurate. (See page 149, Gradients.)

The reliability of readings deteriorates the closer one comes to a baseline extension and the Loran receiver will respond sluggishly to large changes in position. The resulting fixes will be many miles off actual position. A general rule is that the ship's position should be at least 20 microseconds to either side of a baseline extension. The further away it is the more accurate the fixes will be from receiver readings. (See Fig. 6.1)

Crossing Angles.

Another factor to consider in choosing a set of secondaries is that the hyperbolic lines of different secondaries should cross each other as close to a 90 degree angle (right angles) as possible. Lines which cross at less that 30 degrees should not be used. (See explanation in Chapter Two). In other words, the greater the crossing angles between secondary lines, the better the position fix; accuracy is reduced with smaller crossing angles between the lines. In the

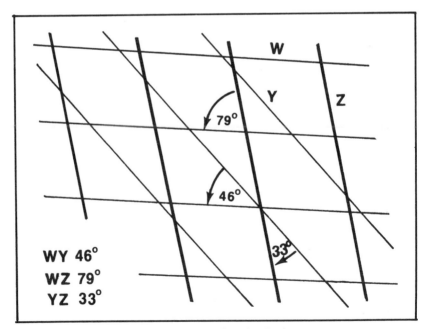

Fig. 6.2   Choosing Secondaries By Using Crossing Angles

example shown, Fig. 6.2, the WZ secondaries would be the best choice since they display the largest crossing angle. This, however, assumes that the gradients between each set of lines are equal.

Gradient

The gradient is a measure of the distance between the overlay lines in proportion to the number of microseconds represented between the lines, i.e., the distance each microsecond is worth. Checking with Fig. 2.3 (Chap. 2) shows that the distance between hyperbolic lines does vary.The separation is least along the baseline between the master and a given secondary, and becomes greater as the hyperbolic lines spread out.

Another factor which affects the gradient is that the microsecond value between the lines also varies. For example, for one secondary there may be 10 microseconds between the TD lines, while for another there may be 20 microseconds between them. Basically, the smaller the distance per microsecond, the more accurate the Loran readings will be.

Generally speaking it is best not to use secondaries in which the distance between the TD lines exceeds 6 miles/10 microsecond change in readings. For example, if the lines being used are in increments of 20 microseconds (i.e., 32520, 32540) the actual distance between the lines should not exceed 12 miles. Sometimes, however, this may not be possible because some small scale charts will exceed 6 miles/10 microseconds, and they may be the only charts available.

To get a rough idea of the gradient for a particular set of TD lines, one merely measures the distance between the lines with a divider (in the area of current position, as this distance does vary) and transfers it to the scale in feet or yards printed on the chart. (See Fig. 6.3) Since a rough working error of $\pm$ 0.1 microseconds can be assumed, the operator can get an idea of the degree of accuracy which is available with a given station pair. In this particular example, LOP would have the capability of being accurate to within 65 feet.

Note: In this example this degree of accuracy does not take into account distortion from secondary land factors (ASF), but just provides an idea of the potential accuracy of a fix from the simple factor of gradient alone.

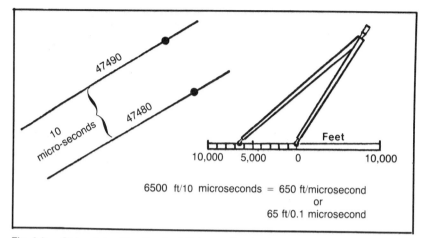

Fig. 6.3   Determining The Gradient Between Overlay Lines

Since all of these factors work together to determine the choice of station pairs, an example will best illustrate these concepts. If the cruising area is the Eastern end of the North Channel, on the Northern end of Lake Huron, there is the possibility of using X,Y,Z secondaries from the Northeast US Chain 9960 and the X,Y, secondaries from the Great Lakes Chain 8970. (See Fig. 6.4) In using the small scale chart for this area NOS CHART 14860, on the single criteria of crossing angles alone, the YZ combination in the 9960 chain is ruled out because the angle is too small (25 degrees). In this case the WZ secondaries would be the better choice over the remaining WY combination because the angles between the WZ secondaries are much larger (67 degrees versus 41 degrees). However, a look at the XY secondaries for the 8970 chain will show that, in this area, their crossing angles is 83 degrees, making this set by far the best choice.

A check of the gradients in this same example will show that the different sets of lines represent different time differences. The actual distance between the lines also varies, so that when these are divided out, the distance each microsecond is worth varies considerably. (Because of the small scale in this particular example, the distance between the lines is quite large. It is more convenient in this case to measure this distance in nautical miles or yards.) A gradient of so many yards/microsecond, and thus feet/0.1 microseconds can then be calculated. Again, with a working error or ± 0.1 microseconds, an idea of the potential accuracy of the different secondaries can be obtained. In the 9960 example

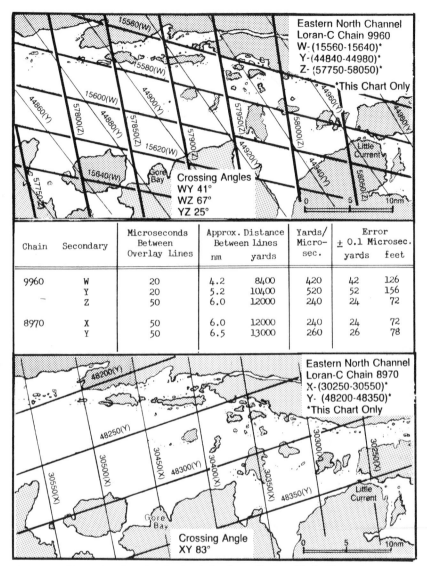

Chain	Secondary	Microseconds Between Overlay Lines	Approx. Distance Between Lines		Yards/ Micro- sec.	Error ± 0.1 Microsec.	
			nm	yards		yards	feet
9960	W	20	4.2	8400	420	42	126
	Y	20	5.2	10400	520	52	156
—	Z	50	6.0	12000	240	24	72
8970	X	50	6.0	12000	240	24	72
	Y	50	6.5	13000	260	26	78

Fig. 6.4   Comparing Crossing Angles & Gradients, Eastern North Channel

the Z secondary has the smallest gradient (72 feet/0.1 micro-second) and it would appear to have the greater accuracy. However, if the Z secondary is chosen, then because of the crossing angles as indicated above, the other secondary should be the W, which yields a crossing angle of 67 degrees as opposed to 25 degrees with the YZ combination. The gradients in the 8970 chain are quite a bit smaller than the W and Y gradients of the 9960 chain. The 8970 chain, with its two X and Y secondaries would be the better choice.

151

One of the nice things about having an overlap of the two chains or the possibility of using other station pairs is that, occasionally a station from a given pair may not be received and it is advantageous to use another pair as a backup. However, if this change is made, it is important to note that, because of the above factors, (gradient, crossing angles), the inherent accuracy of readouts may be different.

Plotting a Fix With TDs

There are two different ways to plot a fix; with TDs (time difference readings) or with geographic (latitude/longitude) coordinates. TD readings are in microseconds and require the use of special Loran charts printed with the hyperbolic overlay lines; geographic coordinates (readouts expressed in latitude/longitude, Lat/Lon) can be plotted on any chart.

The trend towards using receivers with Lat/Lon capabilities is increasing, so this method of plotting fixes as geographic coordinates is becoming the most popular method. Some skippers even boast of not owning a single Loran chart! They do all of their Loran work with only geographic coordinates. It is generally easier to visualize geographic coordinates, and they do have distinct advantages. But, it should be noted that it may be an undesirable practice to become too dependent on using only Lat/Lon readings. For example, there are areas which are known for large ASF (Additional Secondary Factors) errors. Unless the receiver automatically compensates for ASF, the fixes will be more accurate if they are plotted with TDs as opposed to Lat/Lon - providing the Loran charts are corrected. A skipper might also find himself in the position in which, through receiver malfunction, only TDs are displayed. The prudent navigator ought to learn how to plot fixes in TDs and gain confidence in the technique, so that, if the need should arise, the ship may be successfully navigated with just TDs.

A typical TD reading will be expressed as a 6 digit number to the nearest $\frac{1}{10}$ of a microsecond. Some sets will express these readings as 7 digits to the nearest $\frac{1}{100}$ microsecond, but the addition of this last digit does not make the reading much more accurate, for it usually isn't consistent, but will blink or jump around. Also, because of the scale used on the navigational charts with overlays, these fractions of microseconds usually get lost in the plotting and are not necessary in establishing position. The extra digit is only useful when using TD readings to return to a previous position. An example of a TD reading is 47627.3 microseconds.

Interpolation of TD Lines

   Rarely will the microsecond reading fall exactly on a printed overlay line, so to plot a reading, it is necessary to determine how many microseconds there are between the overlay lines for a particular secondary and then interpolate the position of the reading between those lines. Interpolating is giving an intermediate value to something between known or given values. In this example the chart used has 10 microseconds between each set of adjacent TD lines. To establish the LOP (line of position) from the above reading the navigator must interpolate the equivalent of 7.3 microseconds between lines 47620 and 47630. To do this there are two options; to use the Loran Linear Interpolator which is printed on the chart or a homemade or plastic plotting device which may be obtained from various Loran dealers.

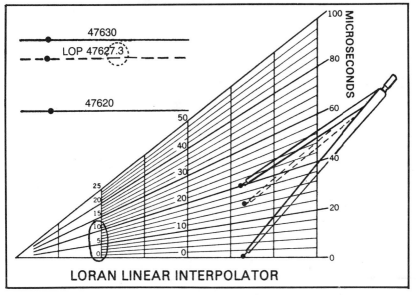

Fig. 6.5   Plotting a TD LOP Using a Linear Interopolator

   To use the Loran Linear Interpolator a pair of dividers is necessary. The first step is to measure off the distance between the lines which come closest to the reading in the area of approximated position. This distance is then transposed with dividers to that position on the interpolator where the dividers match up with the same number of microseconds for the distance being measured. By doing this the part of the interpolator to be used will be established. Then it must be determined which of the 3 interpolator scales matches with the number of microseconds between the chart overlay lines. In this case the smallest scale will be used where the distance measured by the dividers equals 10 microseconds, and each unit of measurement represents 1 microsecond. The next step is to bring the pointer down so the 7.3 microseconds are being measured and that distance is transferred back to the chart. A line is then drawn parallel to the printed overlay lines and position is somewhere along this line. The process is repeated with the second TD reading to determine a second LOP resulting in the fix, where the two LOPs cross.

Another method used to plot TDs is to use a card with different sets of divisions which will conveniently fit with the overlay lines being used. Cards with varying scales can often be obtained from Loran dealers or may be home made.

Plastic plotters such as this one by Si-Tex® are often used as promotional items by dealers.　With permssion by SI-Tex ®

The various scales should differ in size and be divided so that the resulting divisions are easy to count. A common way of dividing is by tens; this type scale is especially useful for charts with lines which are printed every 10 or 20 microseconds. For those charts on which there are 50 microseconds between each line, it may be easier to use a scale with only 5 divisions, with each division representing 10 microseconds. To use this method the scale is placed directly on the overlay lines an the approximate area of position, with the outer ends of the scale lined up on the two adjacent TD overlay lines closest to the Loran readout. The scale usually has to be tilted at an angle to achieve this.

An illustration of this technique can be shown with a reading of 31435.5 microseconds and a chart with a distance of 50 microseconds between each set of lines. To establish the LOP, 35.5 microseconds must be interpolated between lines 31400 and 31450. In this case it may be easiest to use a scale with 5 equal parts where each division represents 10 microseconds, and count up to halfway between the 3rd and 4th mark for 35 microseconds. (Because of the chart scale, the fraction of a microsecond usually does not register). See Fig. 6.6A

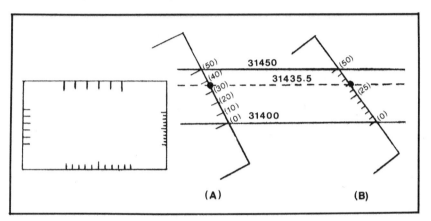

Fig. 6.6   Plotting A TD LOP Using A Homemade Plotter

It is also possible to use a scale divided into 10 equal parts such as in Fig. 6.6B, in which each division equals 5 microseconds. But here the counting may be a little confusing and prone to produce errors because most people are used to thinking in base 10 with a scale where each division would equal 1 or 10 microseconds. Whichever scale is used, once the interpolation is made on the chart, the card is turned so that its edge lies parallel to the overlay line and a line is drawn at that point parallel to the chart overlay lines. Position is somewhere along that line. To get a fix, the procedure is repeated with the second TD reading.

Plotting a Fix With Lat/Lon Coordinates

Many of the receivers on the market today will give position fixing information in the form of geographic coordinates (Lat/Lon) in addition to TDs. With its computer functions, the Loran receiver translates the TDs for a given position to the corresponding Lat/Lon coordinates. The operator then has the option of plotting a fix with either TDs or the Lat/Lon coordinates on any chart. To use Lat/Lon readouts in plotting fixes, there are several factors and techniques to consider.

Some receivers offer the option of having the Lat/Lon readings expressed in two different ways. These deal with how the fractions of a minute are represented: as hundredths of minutes or divided into seconds. If hundredths of minutes are used, the fractions of a minute are represented as a decimal to the nearest $1/100$ (.01) minutes. If seconds are used the fractions of a minute are expressed as seconds - there being 60″ to one minute or 30″ in a half minute, etc.

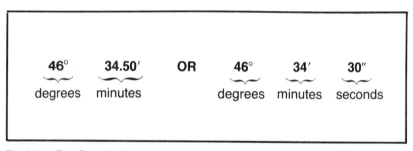

Fig. 6.7   Two Possible Ways of Expressing Latitude/Longitude Readings

If the receiver offers both ways of expressing Lat/Lon, which is chosen depends largely on how these units are represented on the charts. On some charts, the minutes are expressed as a derivative of base 10, so then it would be more convenient to work with Loran readings that are expressed to the nearest 0.01 minute. On other charts, the minutes are divided into 6 equal parts and these lend themselves to expressing the fractions of a minute as seconds: i.e., 10,20,30, etc. (See Fig. 6.8). If the receiver offers both these options, it will have to programmed in the way the Lat/Lon readings are expressed.

There are some receivers which give Lat/Lon readouts, but only in one or the other of the two forms. Then, of course, there is no choice. The chart will have to be carefully checked to see which method is used to insure that position will be accurately plotted. For example, the receiver displays the above latitude reading of 46°34.50′N and on the chart in use the minutes are divided into 6 equal parts as in Fig. 6.8B. The .50′ readout on the receiver equals ½ minute or 30″ (seconds) and would have to be plotted at the 3rd mark on the minute subdivision on the chart, not the 5th mark as

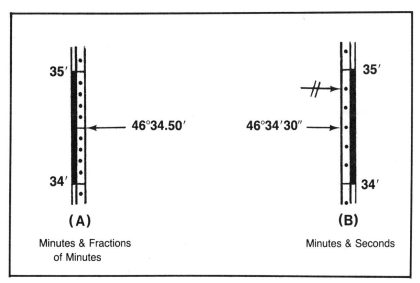

Fig. 6.8   Two Different Ways of Plotting Latitude/Longtitude Readings

it would be if the scale used were divided into 10 equal parts. If this error were made and plotted on the chart, the fix would be a approximately ⅓ mile too far north.

If the Lat/Lon chart scale is different from that of the Loran readout, the Loran readout will have to be converted to its chart equivalent before the fix is plotted. To change from hundredths of minutes to seconds, the minute fraction is multiplied by 60; to change from seconds to hundredths of minutes, the second value is divided by 60. See Fig. 6.9

A. To change from hundredths of minutes to seconds:

Seconds = minutes hundredths X 60

Example: .75 minutes = ? seconds
seconds = .75 min X 60 seconds = 45
OR .75 min = 45 seconds

B. To change from seconds to hundredths of minutes :

Minute hundredths = seconds/60

Example: 15 seconds = ? hundredths of minutes
minute fraction = ¹⁵/₆₀ = .25
OR 15 sec = .25 min

Fig. 6.9   Conversions For Minute Fractions

The relationship between hundredths of minutes and seconds is also shown on the following table.

CONVERSION TABLE

Hundredths of Minutes To Seconds

Minute (Hundredths) = Seconds

.05	3	.55	33
.10	6	.60	36
.15	9	.65	39
.20	12	.70	42
.25	15	.75	45
.30	18	.80	48
.35	21	.85	51
.40	24	.90	54
.45	27	.95	57
.50	30	1.00 minute	60 seconds

Fig. 6.9B   Quick Conversion Table

There are two different methods to plot a Lat/Lon fix. One uses a parallel rules; the other uses a pair of dividers and a linear interpolator similar to that used in plotting TDs. With the parallel rules all that is needed is to find the value at the side of the chart (if it is latitude) or on the top or bottom scale (if it is longitude) and "walk" that reading across the chart to the area of approximate position. This will give an LOP which is similar to that determined from a TD reading i.e, position is somewhere along that line of latitude or longitude. To establish position a second LOP must be determined from the remaining latitude or longitude. See Fig. 6.10

On some charts there is a Lat/Lon Interpolator which is similar to the Loran Linear Interpolator. This device can be used to determine the minutes and fractions of minutes between those latitude and longitude lines which are printed on the chart. Depending on the scale of the chart, the number of minutes between these lines will vary: i.e. 5, 10, 30 etc. minutes apart. The distance between latitude and longitude lines will also vary, so the interpolator is also an expanding scale that can be used to measure the different distances between the lines.

To use the interpolator, the first step is to measure the distance on the chart with a pair of dividers between two adjacent latitude or longitude lines. This distance is then transferred to the corresponding distance on a section of the interpolator. This step

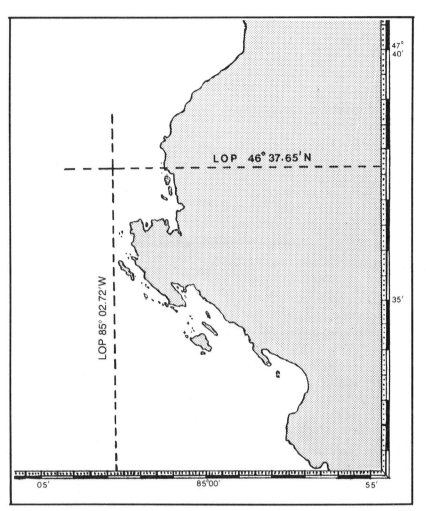

LOP 46° 37.65' N

LOP 85° 02.72' W

47°
40'

35'

05'   85°00'   55'

Fig. 6.10   Plotting A Fix With Latitude/Longitude Co-ordinates

determines which part of the interpolator matches up with the distance between the printed lines. One end of the dividers is then moved, in this same section of the interpolator, to measure off the minutes and fractions of the reading. This new distance representing individual minutes and fractions of minutes is then transferred back to the chart and added to the line with the lowest reading.

To illustrate this technique, suppose there is a need to plot a longitude reading of 87°53.40′W as in Fig. 6.11. The two longitude lines which are printed on the chart that come closest to this reading are 87°50′ and 88°00′. To chart longitude 87°53.4′W, it is necessary to know the distance represented by 3.4′ so that it can be added to the 87°50′ longitude value.

With dividers, the distance between longitude 87°50′ and 88°00′ at points A and B is measured. This distance is then transferred to the interpolator. The dividers are next moved to measure 3.40′ and this new distance is transferred back to the chart and added to the 87°50′ line to give an LOP of 87°53.40′. (Note, in this case, the minutes are divided into 5 parts so that each division represents 0.2 minute). To determine the fix, the same technique is used to determine the latitude LOP.

Keeping Records

One thing will become quickly apparent when one is working with Loran, and that is the need to develop some method for recording accumulated data. This is because one of the greatest assets in Loran navigation is its repeatable accuracy - the ability to go back to a previous position. Time difference readings at strategic points such as harbor entrances, channel openings, buoys etc. become important numbers to home-in on at a future date. Lat/Lon offsets which update and correct Lat/Lon readings for the difference in propagation errors (ASF) are also important for accurate Lat/Lon navigation in a given area. If the error is recorded the first time through, then it can be used when a return trip is made to the same general location. The information should be tabulated in a quickly retrievable form, and there are a number of ways in which this can be done.

The easiest method of recording some of the data is to enter it directly on the navigational chart. This is especially useful in identifying specific spots such as entrances to anchorages or channels. It is then there for ready reference and future use. An "X" is usually all that is needed to mark the position and then the TD numbers can be written in a blank spot off to the side. See Fig. 6.12.

Another way of recording the information is to keep a running log in which all information such as time, distance made good, course, cross track etc., are kept along with TDs and Lat/Lon readings. This is particularly helpful in identifying errors in plotting fixes or programming in waypoints. Since operator error is a common source of discrepancies, the value of keeping a running log is that it gives something concrete to go back to and retrace steps.

In addition to keeping a running log, it is often prudent to do the necessary homework before the day's run begins. If it is known

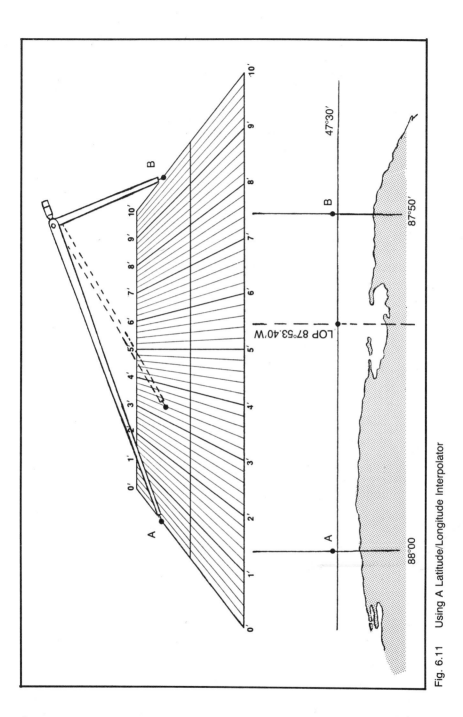

Fig. 6.11 Using A Latitude/Longitude Interpolator

that the destination will require a number of course changes, these can be programmed into the receiver ahead of time. Alternative courses can be anticipated in case weather conditions call for a

161

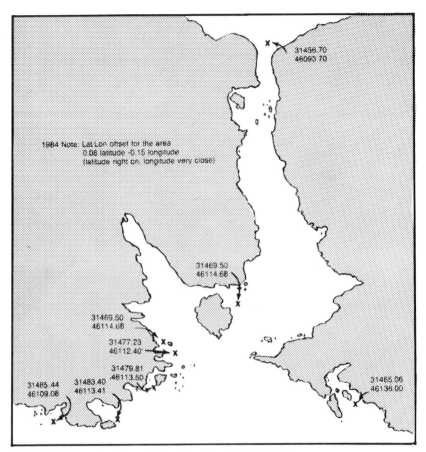

Fig. 6.12   Recording Loran Information Directly On A Chart

different course or anchorage. It certainly is a lot easier to look up coordinates and do chart work when at rest at anchor as opposed to while bouncing around in a chop. It is important to have some method of recording this information, particularly with waypoints as they may not be geographically marked, but just a set of coordinates out in an open stretch of water. One method which works well is to mark the waypoints ahead of time, both on the chart and a special waypoint notepad or in the running log. This way there is both a visual check and a record, so waypoints can be confirmed and/or chartwork retraced. (See Fig. 6.13)

Because the running log keeps a large amount of information, most of which is pertinent only to a particular day's run, it becomes advantageous to sift out just that data which is important for future reference, i.e., numbers for harbor entrances, Lat/Lon off-sets etc. One way to tabulate this data is to have a separate small book in which harbors and anchorages are entered alphabetically

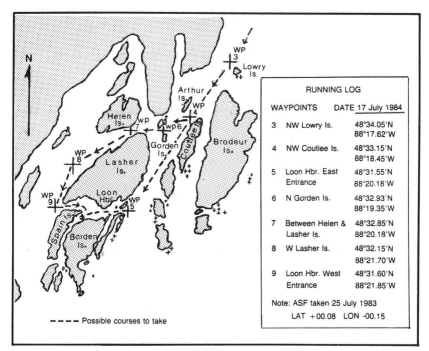

RUNNING LOG

WAYPOINTS   DATE 17 July 1984

3	NW Lowry Is.	48°34.05'N
		88°17.62'W
4	NW Coutlee Is.	48°33.15'N
		88°18.45'W
5	Loon Hbr. East	48°31.55'N
	Entrance	88°20.18'W
6	N Gorden Is.	48°32.93'N
		88°19.35'W
7	Between Helen &	48°32.85'N
	Lasher Is.	88°20.18'W
8	W Lasher Is.	48°32.15'N
		88°21.70'W
9	Loon Hbr. West	48°31.60'N
	Entrance	88°21.85'W

Note: ASF taken 25 July 1983

LAT +00.08   LON -00.15

– – – – Possible courses to take

Fig. 6.13   Charting & Recording Waypoint Navigation Using Alternative Routes

along with their entrance TDs, Lat/Lon coordinates and offset if there is one. Alphabetical dividers make this information available for quick reference.

Another method uses a small card file, again with alphabetical dividers and blank index cards. Each time a new anchorage is visited or channel navigated, a new card is made out. Specific anchorages can be distinguished from an area navigation by a special symbol such as an asterisk. The card can then be identified with the name of the anchorage at the top followed by a listing of specific data such as TDs, Lat/Lon coordinates, area offsets etc. In particular, those coordinates which are important as key points in approaches and entrances to the anchorage should be recorded. If a coordinate is left permanently in the receiver's memory as a waypoint, its identifying number should likewise be recorded for quick retrieval. With wilderness anchorages, a rough sketch may be drawn, along with other pertinent information given, such as uncharted rocks, outlying shoals, etc. Using the computer functions of the Loran will make it possible to calculate and include range and bearings to nearby or key anchorages. (See Fig. 6.14).

Cards can also be made for important cruising areas such as channels, through island chains where bouys and positions for

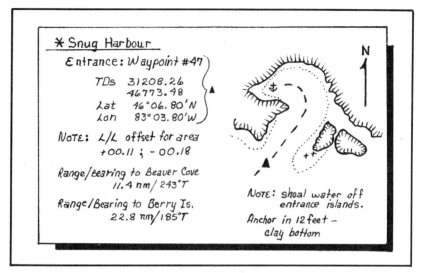

Fig. 6.14   Using A Card File For Storing Data

changing course etc. are marked with TDs or Lat/Lon coordinates. If the latter are used, it is important to note the ASF or Lat/Lon offset for the area. For, if the coordinates are recorded at a particular bouy, with a given offset in the receiver, and then an attempt is made to go back to that bouy forgetting to put in that offset, the attempt will fail.

With a Loran receiver which has 30 or more waypoints, there should be a way of cataloging those waypoints which are used often and kept in the receiver memory for future use. Waypoints 1-10 or 1-20 may be set aside as working waypoints which are changed for daily navigation. The remaining waypoints may be utilized as permanent waypoints for future use. In any event, these too need to be recorded. One possibility is to have a separate section at the back of the book or card file which keeps track of the permanently programmed waypoints.

CHAPTER SEVEN

How Exact is Exact? Accuracy

Section 1: General Concepts

Somewhere in the annals of navigation, there is a story which depicts nicely the concept of the reliability, or accuracy, of fixes. It concerns first a young lieutenant in the midst of his training who, in the course of his duties, must determine ship's position. Following all the rules of carefully learned lessons, he carefully runs through the calculations, adding for this, subtracting for that. Finally, with a well-sharpened pencil, he makes a fine mark on the chart and proudly claims that ship's position is at that point. The first mate, under whom the younger officer is taking his instruction, then comes to check through his calculations and draws a large circle around the pinpoint fix, declaring that ship's position is somewhere within a five mile circle of the point. Now a third person enters the scene. He is ship's captain, a salty old codger with a deeply lined face, weathered from years on the open sea. With a gruff mumble he moves a well worn pipe from his mouth, reaches across the chart and roughly twists his thumb on the fix, first in this direction and then that, leaving a large irregular smudge extending beyond the mate's circle: ship's position could be somewhere in the smudge area.

Supposedly, the moral of the story is that navigation is often more an art than a science and, even with solicitous attention to every detail, experience often proves that the accuracy of one's fix may not be as exact as one would like to believe. As in the story, the word "exact" may have different meanings for different people. Accuracy is often a relative thing and is affected as much by location and individual requirements as anything else. For example, for those who are navigating in the vast expanses of the open ocean, to come within a few miles of actual position in plotting a fix would be considered highly accurate. Yet, for the coastal sailor such accuracy is not good enough.

Before the days of Loran, for many, navigation was done primarily with dead reckoning. In those days to have a ¼ mile accuracy was considered "right on." Now, with Loran, ¼ mile accuracy often is not good enough - such as when approaching a tight entrance in the fog or skirting between two close underwater shoals. Of course, things are being done now which weren't done before the Loran system was available. That brings up another point; because of the inherent capabilities of the system, use of Loran may foster a false sense of security.

A case in point happened a few years ago when an approach was being made to the shoal strewn waters off the Southern end of Isle Royale in Lake Superior. Because of hidden rocks (a four foot shoal in particular) and poor visual points of reference, the safer approach had always been chosen previously. But this time it was on a close reach and there was a desire to avoid tacking out - besides Loran was available. Many months of constant Loran use had led to a confidence in the system.

As the area in question was approached, a captain on a passing excursion boat made radio contact to warn of a dangerously close shoaling area. A quick Loran fix showed the shoal area to be ½ mile off which was reported back to the excursion boat. The captain was not convinced, however, as his years of experience had led him to be more cautious. His last words on the radio were, "You are awfully close - awfully close." Luckily, the shoal was never seen, but there is no doubt the captain was probably right, and in this case the over reliance on the Loran was wrong - and not too smart. In retrospect, there is a realization of all the things that could have been wrong with that fix. The Loran signal may not have been tracked properly; the receiver could have been experiencing cycle slip and been off 10 or 20 microseconds; perhaps the right ASF correction for that area hadn't been made; or maybe there had been a mistake in transferring coordinates to the chart.

The lesson to be learned, of course, is that no system of navigation, no matter how accurate, should be so trusted or used exclusively of others. Loran-C is good, and usually it is incredibly accurate. Yet, there are factors which do affect its accuracy, and to use the system without the checks and balances of other navigational aids, is an invitation to danger, if not pure folly.

Accuracy Parameters

Before looking much further at the concept of accuracy and those factors which affect it, it will be beneficial to review the original guidelines under which the Loran system was established.

According to the National Plan for Navigation in 1972, the accuracy requirements determined for the newly proposed Loran-

C system were that a vessel would be able to fix its position with an accuracy of ¼ mile, 95% of the time, in the Coastal Confluent Zone. The CCZ is that area extending seaward from a harbor entrance to 50 nm offshore, or the outer edge of the continental shelf, or the 100 fathom curve, whichever is greater. When figured out on the basis of a nautical mile, this means that 1,518 feet or 467 meters equal ¼ mile. A fix accurate to 1500 feet certainly is a lot different from the 200 - 500 foot accuracy so often seen in the Loran literature.

Yet, as many are finding out - it is possible to obtain Loran fixes that are much more accurate than within ¼ mile. Even without ASF corrections, in many areas, more accurate fixes are often possible. As more receivers now have the automatic correction for the ASF built in, fix accuracy, even in areas with high propagation distortion, is being constantly improved. This has lead the user community to become accustomed to, and sometimes demanding of, accuracy parameters which are well beyond the original designs of the system. For those who are disappointed that they can't get 200 foot accuracy consistently, it is important to note that the system was never intended to deliver that degree of accuracy. While it often is possible to attain such fixes, the original intent of the system was to attain at least ¼ mile accuracy.

Some of the confusion in talking about Loran accuracy may stem from the fact that there are actually two different types of accuracy: absolute and relative. Which is being referred to makes a big difference in the degree of accuracy and the factors which affect it.

Absolute Accuracy

Absolute accuracy (which may also be called predictable or geodetic accuracy) is a measurement of the ability to determine actual or true geographic position. In other words, is the position exactly where the calculations say it is? If the boat is tucked into a little cove in a remote anchorage, does the Loran readout position it on the chart in this little cove or does it put it ½ mile inland? In navigating, absolute accuracy is what is being used when making a first time trip to a new location.

With Loran-C absolute accuracy usually varies between 0.1 to 0.25 nautical miles of actual position. It is absolute accuracy which is meant in the National Plan for Navigation goal within the Coastal Confluence Zone of ¼ (or 0.25) nm, 95% of the time. In many areas, an absolute accuracy of 0.1 nm (600 feet) is quite common. It is even possible to get absolute accuracies of 200 feet, if corrections are known and made for signal propagation distortion (ASF) over land.

There are a number of factors which can affect absolute accuracy such as: receiver installation, signal stability, geometric location in relation to transmitting stations, signal interference, cycle slip, land propagation errors, operator error, and sometimes weather. Land propagation error, in particular, is one of the greatest variance factors and, because of it, absolute accuracy may differ considerably from one area to another. It is because of this that in certain trouble areas (one example are some areas off the coast of California and Texas) fixes which have not been corrected for ASF will give an absolute accuracy that is one, and maybe even two, miles off.

Repeatable Accuracy

Repeatable accuracy is a measurement of the ability to go back to a given location on the basis of previous readings. It is repeatable accuracy that the lobster fisherman uses to return to his traps. It is repeatable accuracy that allows a return to the entrance of a hidden anchorage time after time, regardless of visibility or inadequate visual bearings. This type of accuracy is important to the Loran user because it is here that the Loran system really excels - for repeatable accuracy is much better than ¼ mile. In fact, when returning to a previous position, accuracy may range anywhere from ± 25 meters (75 feet) to ± 200 meters (600 feet).

To use repeatable accuracy one must have been to the location before and recorded the particular coordinates, whether they are in Lat/Lon or TDs, so they can be "homed in on." This then is another good reason for developing some method (log book/card file) for tabulating collected data. With repeatable accuracy, no special charts are needed. Repeatable accuracy can be obtained with no charts at all - simply by homing in on previous coordinates. Because of this it is becoming common practice for sailors to exchange coordinates at various strategic points, harbor entrances etc. In some areas, the Coast Guard and various organizations (yacht clubs etc.) will even produce lists of the coordinates at various channel markers and points of reference. For example, the Coast Guard has conducted a number of Loran-C waypoint surveys called Harbor and Harbor Entrance Surveys or HHE Surveys in which listings for various waypoints are included. These have been published in various issues of the *Radionavigation Bulletin.*

Although repeatable accuracy can vary depending on position within Loran coverage, it usually isn't subject to the large errors from ASF as absolute accuracy is. This is because the ASF error is fairly constant for a given locality: repeated readings for a specific point will contain the same error as the first time around, i.e., the errors will cancel each other out. However, if a manual ASF correction for the area has been programmed in, it is important that the correction be noted and made for subsequent readings or the error difference will be introduced in the readouts.

Other factors which can affect repeatable accuracy are those which affect signal transmission and reception, position in relation to transmitting stations, and those uncontrollable factors, such as weather, which can cause minute changes from one moment to another in signal propagation speed.

To determine precisely the repeatable accuracy for a given location it is necessary to set up a receiver at an established site and monitor signal transmissions over a given period of time. This, in fact, is what the Coast Guard does with its Harbor Monitor Program. Approximately 35 monitor stations have been established in the various chains.

Section II: Factors Which Affect Accuracy

Operator

One of the most important contributing factors in determining the accuracy of a plotted fix lies within the operator himself. All have experienced mistakes when updating a running fix or walking a course off a compass rose. Whereas, a certain degree of operator error may be acceptable in using some navigation techniques, because of the accuracy possibilities of Loran, it doesn't take much of a plotting error to defeat the inherent capabilities of the system.

Common sources of error are often found in simply misreading TD lines or the scales for latitude and longitude. With TDs, working on one side of the chart while the TD labels are on the other makes it easy to get one line mixed up with another. A simple way to solve this problem is to rewrite the line numbers closer to those areas being worked. Sometimes interpolation between the lines can also be another problem as it is possible to use the wrong scale, or count the wrong number of microseconds. Particularly if the number of microseconds between the lines of different secondaries are not the same, it is easy to get confused when interpolating TD readings. For example, see Fig. 4.3B which depicts the X and Y secondaries for the 8970 Great Lakes Chain. Note that the microsecond increments are different for each secondary: for the X secondary there are 10 microseconds between the lines, for the Y secondary there are 20 microseconds between the lines. In plotting lines of position (LOPs), first with one secondary and then with the other, the interpolation with the two different increments will be different - which lends itself to the good possibility of making interpolation errors.

In using Lat/Lon coordinates it is also possible to get mixed up as the scales may change from one chart to another. On small scale charts, charts which cover a large geographic area, the divisions will represent whole degrees or even groups of degrees. On large scale charts, those covering a small area in great depth, the divisions may represent minutes or half minutes. Simply adding in numbers will make the scale easier to read and reduce the chance of making errors. (See Fig. 7.1)

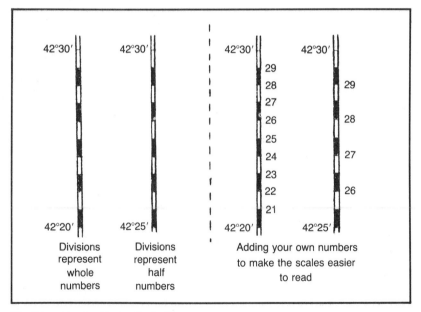

Fig. 7.1   Varying Scales For Lat/Lon

It goes without saying that, especially when working with Loran it is important to strive for accurate measuring techniques when using position fixing tools such as the dividers and parallel rules. It doesn't take much of a slip of either to throw plotted position off and introduce error in fixes and further navigation.

One of the best ways in dealing with all of these problems is to write all the coordinates down in a running log instead of plotting them directly from the receiver. Then there is something to fall back on to check chart work. Another excellent way of spotting errors is to use other navigational aids and techniques independently, but simultaneously with Loran. Loran position can then be checked against an advanced running fix kept by dead reckoning. Receiver data such as range and bearing can be checked by taking bearings with an RDF or hand bearing compass from known points of reference. When things don't match up, it is a signal that an error has been made somewhere and it is time to start rechecking.

Charts

The kind of chart upon which a fix is plotted will also affect the accuracy of that fix. Larger scale charts will yield more accurate fixes. This is because large scale charts have smaller gradients - the distance a given segment of that chart is worth. Whether that segment is measured in a specified number of microseconds or inches, if the segment represents a smaller distance, LOPs and their resulting fixes will be more accurate. For example, on a small scale chart such as 1:500,000 or 1:600,000, a small segment of the chart represents a very sizeable area so that an error of even the width of a pencil line could place position off by as much as ¼ mile. Another advantage, of course, in using large scale charts is that, because a given area is expanded, the chart provides greater detail, such as harbor entrances, shoal areas etc.

If TDs are being used to plot fixes, those charts with corrected lattices for ASF will produce more accurate fixes than uncorrected charts. There are two ways in which these corrections are made: by theoretical corrections and by observed data. If the chart is corrected by one of these ways, it will contain one of the verification notes. Examples of these notes are shown in Chapter 4. Charts with Loran lines that have ASF corrections made from observed data are more accurate than those which contain corrected lattices derived from theoretical predictions. According to the Coast Guard in the *Radionavigation Bulletin No. 15*, all charts corrected by observed propagation delays have at least ¼ mile accuracy or better. Those Loran-C charts with corrected lattices derived from theoretical calculations for the most part, yield ¼ mile accuracy. There are, however, some trouble spots where chart accuracy, even with predicted ASF corrections, is much worse than ¼ mile. These are often in fringe areas which are at the extremities of primary coverage. Examples of those areas where chart accuracy at this time exceeds standard parameters are the coastal waters off parts of Texas and the US/Mexican border on the Pacific Coast.

Using an early edition of a chart which is not corrected for ASF, either by predicted or observed data, will cause the accuracy of plotted fixes to suffer considerably. It may be necessary to correct TD readings before plotting them by using Correction Tables published by the DMAHTC.

In plotting Lat/Lon coordinates it doesn't matter what kind of charts are used as the latitude and longitude scales printed on the charts are actual geographic coordinates, and they have not been changed to adjust for an ASF error. Note that, even though plotting with geographic coordinates, fixes will not be corrected for ASF unless the receiver has the automatic correction feature, or they have been manually corrected by using the Correction Tables as illustrated in Chapter Four.

Ship's Location/Receiver Position

The position of the receiver in relation to those stations that are transmitting the Loran signals (station geometry), the distance from the transmitter, and even position in relation to certain land masses all have a bearing on the accuracy of fixes.

1. **Station Geometry.** Ship's position in relation to the transmitting stations can affect accuracy in a number of ways. One of these relates to the size of the crossing angles of the printed hyperbolic TD lines on the chart. Basically, position should be such that these lines from the transmitting secondaries have crossing angles which are greater than 30° and are as close to crossing at right angles, or 90° as possible. Especially in moving from one area to another, the relationship to the transmitting stations will change and so will the crossing angles. Even if TD readings are not being used, and all chart work is done with Lat/Lon coordinates, these values are derived from TDs and any degree of error in the TDs will be reflected in the computed geographical coordinates. A Loran overlay chart is helpful, if for nothing more than assisting in a decision based on station geometry on which are the preferred secondaries to use. As the crossing angles decrease, fix accuracy will likewise deteriorate.

A good example of the effect of crossing angle size is seen when cruising on Lake Ontario, an area where it is sometimes difficult to obtain good accuracy. This is outside the primary coverage area for the 8970 Great Lakes Chain so the 9960 Northeast US Chain must be relied upon. In this chain, there are four stations to choose from, but the two which exhibit the best crossing angles throughout the lake are the W and Z secondaries. The X secondary gives reliable LOPs only in the Eastern end of the lake and the Y secondary in the Western end.

Another way in which receiver position can affect the accuracy of plotted fixes is by ship's location within the actual grid of hyperbolic lines. The distance between the lines does vary with location. As the gradient (a measure of how much actual distance is represented by a given number of microseconds) gets larger, accuracy will decline. A general rule to remember is that the distance between the hyperbolic lines should not be more than six miles for a change of 10 microseconds.

An example of this type of accuracy deterioration is seen in those areas which are known as baseline extensions. Here, because the gradients become very large, readings will often be sluggish and a fix may be miles off from actual position: a deviation of just one microsecond can produce a position error of tens of miles. Another disadvantage in using readings within an area of a baseline extension is that it is actually possible to plot a reciprocal position on the other side of the baseline (See Fig. 6.1) so that the fix may be off by as much as 100 miles or more.

An illustration of this phenomenon is seen in the area of Nantucket Shoals and Georges Bank off the coast of Massachusetts. Although the area is well covered by the 9960 Northeast US Chain (See Fig. 5.4), use of the 9960 X secondary should be avoided in these areas because of close proximity to the X baseline extension. A similar situation occurs on the North end of Vancouver Island in British Columbia. Here the chain which gives the best signal strength is the 5990 Canadian West Coast Chain (See Fig. 5.20). It has three secondaries, but the Z secondary should not be used in those waters which lie to the West and Southwest of the North end of Vancouver Island because they are in the baseline extension zone for that secondary.

In summary, three of the factors which contribute to the effect that ship's location has on the degree of accuracy of a Loran reading are: A. the size of the crossing angles between the hyperbolic lines from two different secondaries. B. the size of the gradient between the lines of a single secondary. C. the proximity of ship's position to a baseline extension from a transmitting station. Fig. 7.2 lists the general rules for station selection which reflect these factors.

1. The angle between hyperbolic lines from different secondaries should be greater than 30°.

2. The distance between adjacent hyperbolic lines should not exceed 6 miles or 9.6 km for each 10 microseconds.

3. Readings within 20 microseconds of a baseline extension from a transmitting station should be avoided.

Fig. 7.2   General Rules For Obtaining Greater Accuracy By Station Selection.

When the above criteria are all satisfied, then the next factor which should be considered in reference to fix accuracy is the distance from the transmitter.

2. Distance from transmitter and signal strength. It stands to reason that the closer one is to a transmitter, the stronger the signal will be for the receiver to track. Reliable coverage usually will extend at least 600 miles over an all sea-water path and 400 miles over land. Signals that travel over land are further affected by the type of terrain, with rugged mountainous areas providing the greatest reduction in signal reliability.

Signal strength is also dependent on transmitted power which varies from station to station - anywhere from 165 to 1800 kW. Naturally, those stations with greater power output will provide greater range.

In remote or fringe areas the signal may become so weak that the signal to noise ratio (SNR) drops below 1:3. When this happens many receivers which are in an automatic cycle tracking mode are not able to track the correct cycle and will move further into the transmitted pulse where there is increased power to compensate for the lower power it is receiving from the incoming signal. This results in the phenomenon known as cycle slip in which the subsequent readouts are off by increments of 10 microseconds. If the weak pulse comes from a master station, accuracy will be affected by being 10 or 20 microseconds too low. If the pulse in question is from a secondary station, readouts will be 10 or 20 microseconds too high. If both master and secondary signals are weak and are tracked at the same cycle in the pulse - even though it is the wrong one, the errors will cancel each other out and the reading will be just as accurate as though there were no cycle slip. (See Chap. Two).

Once it is known that the receiver is experiencing cycle slip and by how much, this amount can then be mathematically added or subtracted to correct subsequent readings. With some receivers, it is possible to put the set in a "lock" or "track" mode to prevent cycle slip from occurring. Another trick with some receivers is to use a cycle stepping feature which allows manual input to improve receiver reception and, as a result, accuracy of readings from distant transmitters. For further discussion on using these techniques and improving accuracy in remote areas, see chapter eight.

Another effect of receiver distance from a transmitter on accuracy is that of skywave interference. Fig. 2.7 shows how skywaves are transmitted simultaneously with groundwaves. Because they travel a longer distance (to the ionosphere and back), the time it takes them to reach a given location will be greater than groundwaves transmitted at the same time. Since these waves are of the same signal frequency as their groundwave counterparts, they too can be received by a Loran set. If the skywaves are unknowingly read instead of groundwaves, position fixes may be off by many miles.

In normal propagation areas (primary coverage areas), skywaves are prevented from being read by the receiver in two ways: by tracking at a specific cycle in the pulse that reaches the receiver before the incoming skywaves and phase coding. (See Chap. Two). However, as the dstance from the receiver to the transmitter increases, sometimes these precautions are not enough and the receiver may begin tracking skywaves instead of groundwaves. This is particularly true in those fringe areas where the groundwave signal is weak and unable to compete with the stronger incoming skywave signal. Skywave interference is also stronger at night (See Fig. 2.9) and can be particularly troublesome a half hour before and after sunrise and sunset, so that readouts taken during these times may not be as accurate as those taken during other times of the day.

Because the skywave has traveled a longer distance, its travel time will be proportionately greater and the resulting TDs will reflect this error. Fortunately, many receivers have special warning indicators that tell if a skywave signal is being used instead of a groundwave signal to produce readouts. While coordinates which are derived from skywaves may reflect large position errors, there is nothing wrong with using skywaves for navigation. In fact, because these signals are often received in areas which are well beyond groundwave coverage (See Fig. 2.7), they are used to extend Loran coverage in remote areas. The trick is that, as with other position errors (cycle slip, ASF), the operator must be able to compare the readout which contains the error with known coordinates, a landmark, island, etc., for the position. Once the error is determined, the correction can be computed and programmed into the receiver to be used for subsequent readings.

3. Shore proximity errors. Another contributing factor of receiver location to the accuracy of Loran readouts is seen in the relationship of ship's position to some coastlines. Often the accuracy of a reading will be seen to change rapidly close in to shore in some coastal areas. This is especially true near large cliffs or headlands. (There are even some places, such as close in beneath cliffs or large buildings where a Loran signal cannot be received.) Unfortunately, this error usually has the distressing effect of making the position of the boat seem farther to seaward than it actually is, which can be dangerous.

An example of this phenomenon happened one summer on a cruise in the area of Lake Superior's Eastern shore with the crews on two other boats. Fog set in at the time of closing in on the next anchorage, but it was an easy approach - and all three boats had Loran. All were on a close reach and the attempt was made to make the anchorage without having to tack out, even though it was known that the boats were closing in to shore. But in this section of the lake it was very deep, right up to shore - which also made it difficult to follow contour lines with the depth sounder. About a mile from the destination the depthsounder on the first boat suddenly read only 15 feet and a rock cliff loomed overhead - while the Loran showed position to be a good half mile off shore. This was reported to the other boats and use of the log led to a safer distance off shore. At first it was assumed there was a malfunction with the receiver, as is so often the first thought when something goes wrong. But then, 10 minutes later, the same thing happened to the 2nd boat, while their receiver, which was a different make, showed them again to be a half mile off shore. The skipper in the 3rd boat wisely took heed of the situation, came about and headed offshore.

On many Loran charts, the possibility of shore proximity errors is suggested in that the lines are not extended or printed to include the coastline - an indication that use of Loran in these areas should be with caution. In fact, printed on most charts in the notice on lattice verification is the statement, "Mariners are cautioned not to rely entirely on the lattices on inshore waters." On the plus side however, it should be noted that these errors for a given area are consistent, so that once they are known they can be used to correct future readings - another illustration that it is with repeatable accuracy that the Loran system really excels.

176

Interference

As with any form of radio signal propagation, there are different kinds of interference which will affect reception of that signal. In the case of Loran-C, this interference can effect the accuracy of readouts and plotted position. This interference is in the form of electrical noise.

1. Atmospheric interference - weather. One of the selling points of Loran-C is its accurate position fixing capabilities regardless of weather. While this is true most of the time, it should be noted that there are some situations in which atmospheric conditions may interfere with Loran signal reception and accuracy of fixes.

Everyone has had the experience of trying to tune in a distant AM radio station, especially during periods of high electrical disturbance, such as in a thunderstorm, only to have the signal drowned out by interfering static and crackling noise. The effect of such electrical disturbances is seen in poor reception of a Loran signal which may cause unstable readings and cycle slip.

Some degree of electrical background interference is always present, which accounts for part of the decrease in signal reliability at greater distances. With the onset of thunderstorms and severe electrical activity, this range of reliable signal reception is lessened considerably.

Fig. 7.3 illustrates the extent of weather effects on Loran reception. It is a graph published in 1980 by Micrologic, a manu-

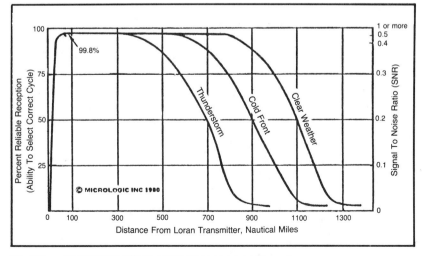

Fig. 7.3   Approximate Effects of Weather on Loran Reception
Graph courtesy of Micrologic, Chatsworth,CA

facturer of Loran receivers. It depicts the signal to noise ratio and percentage of reliable reception in relationship to distance and weather.

As the graph illustrates, the range for good signal reliability may be further reduced by hundreds of miles with the coming of cold fronts and thunderstorms. Beyond this range in these conditions, it is likely that erratic readouts will affect the accuracy of the plotted position. (Note that in all cases, the signal to noise ratio drops with increased distance.) A signal to noise ratio of 0.2, or expressed ratio 1:5 will give a 50% reliability, while a signal to noise ratio of 0.5 (or 1:2) will give a 95% reliability.

The onset of rain showers, wet fog, and sometimes even snow flurries, may also cause some interference at long ranges. Known as precipitation static, which generates electrical noise which will mask the signal, its effect is that of reducing signal strength and causing cycle slip as the receiver moves further into the signal pulse for tracking. Depending on the position in relation to the hyperbolic grid (gradient) this may cause position errors of a mile or more.

The possibility of this type of interference may be most disturbing to Loran users. For it is when visibility is reduced by fog, rain, or snow that that extra security from Loran is needed the most. Note, however, that in all these cases of atmospheric or weather disturbances affecting readout, it also depends on how far away from the transmitters the receiver is located. If it is relatively close to a transmitter, say 400-500 miles, usually reliable readouts can continue to be expected even while experiencing most atmospheric disturbances. Loran-C still provides a very high degree of accuracy - even when these conditions occur: i.e., precipitation static doesn't occur every time there is fog. But the possibility of this type of interference exists, and the operator should be on the lookout for inaccurate readings. Again, it's just common sense to not rely on any single technique or tool in navigation - regardless of the conditions.

2. External man-made interference. Other sources of interference come from high voltage power transmission lines, industrial sources or transmitters which radiate energy near the 100 kHz frequency. Electrical noise competes with, and may obscure, the Loran signal, making it difficult for the receiver to lock on and track the signal. An illustration of this type of interference is seen in an alert which was given in the *Radionavigation Bulletin No. 14* issued May, 1984. According to the bulletin, reports along the U.S. Eastern seaboard, from Mayport, FL to Portland, ME indicated interference in receiving signals from both the Northeast U.S. 9960 and Southeast U.S. 7980 Chains. After some investigation, the source of this new interference was found to be a U.S. Navy transmitter located near Norfolk, VA. Actually the transmitter had been in operation for sometime, but had changed its transmitting frequency to 77 kHz, which is close enough to the 100 kHz Loran band to cause interference. Since the U.S. Navy indicated that operation was going to continue at this frequency, the alert suggested that Loran users experiencing difficulty in tracking these chains should have their receiver's notch filters adjusted to reduce this level of interference.

External noise of this nature can do anything from preventing reliable signal tracking to producing wild, erratic readings and cycle slip - all of which affect the accuracy of plotted fixes. Noise interference can be detected either by an alarm if the receiver is so equipped, or by a low SNR (signal to noise ratio). Notch filters can be used to compensate for this kind of interference. (See Chap. Three).

Some man-made noise is so great that it is impossible to screen out with notch filters. The receiver then, in an effort to obtain a stronger signal may move further into the pulse where there is more power and experience cycle slip so that readouts are off by increments of 10 microseconds. This, of course, will affect the accuracy of the plotted position. The receiver can be allowed to track in this cycle if the amount of the error is known and mathematically added or subtracted to each subsequent reading. Or, by using the cycle step procedure for the receiver, it can be manually put back on the correct cycle and put in the lock or track mode. It is even possible to assist the receiver in overcoming noise interference by purposely making the receiver track further into the pulse by using cycle stepping. If left to track in this cycle, each reading will have to be mathematically compensated for or fixes will reflect the error.

3. Shipboard noise interference. On board noise which may originate with a boat's engine or auxillary electrical equipment may compromise receiver operation and accuracy. With the almost endless list of electronic gear that is now available to the boating community; motors on various pumps, blowers, digital instruments such as windspeed indicators, knot-logs, fluorescent lights, it is important to know that they are all potential sources of electrical interference in a Loran receiver.

The results of this type of interference are that the receiver may not be able to acquire or hold signals, or that it will experience cycle slip. Low SNR values indicate that any readouts which are obtained are unreliable and are symptoms of noise. On board generated interference usually involves locating the offending piece of equipment and installing filters on it. (See Chap. 3 Noise Supression Techniques).

Land Propagation Errors (ASF)

It is always interesting to talk with someone who is just beginning to use Loran. They usually try it out at the dock at their marina slip and find it puts them ½ mile inland. They then complain and wonder about the alleged 200 foot accuracy. They even often feel that something is wrong with their brand new set.

The problem, of course, is very likely due to signal retardation as the Loran radio waves pass over differing terrains. Only when radio waves travel through space is there no retardation of the signal, and then the speed is the same as the speed of light: 186,000 miles/second. On passing through any medium (ex. the earth's atmosphere), radio waves are slowed down. This speed is further affected by the terrain over which they travel: land will slow them down more than water. (The retardation over water is called the Secondary Factor; the retardation over land is called the Additional Secondary Factor or ASF because it is in addition to that which is caused by an only sea-water path.) The situation is further complicated by the fact that not all types of land will slow down radio waves the same: they travel at different speeds over the prairies as opposed to over mountainous areas.

The Loran system, which is based on predicted time delays between receiving radio signals from two different stations, depends on accurate measurement of these time delays. The predictions are made on the assumption that the radio waves are traveling over an all sea-water path at a fixed speed. This, obviously, is not always true, as many stations are based inland or the signals must travel over some interfering land mass to reach a particular body of water. As a result, signals may not be received at the exact time they are predicted to be. The resulting position errors may vary anywhere from a few hundred feet to better than a mile - so it is without a doubt that ASF is the single greatest factor which affects the accuracy of a Loran fix.

It is ASF which causes a fix to be 1300 yards off from actual position at the San Francisco Entrance Channel. It is ASF that can throw a boat 2000 yards off an approach to Corpus Christi, Texas. It is ASF that may cause a miss of the North Entrance to Cape Cod Canal by 600 yards. There are literally very few areas within the

CCZ that are not affected at least to some degree by ASF and, because of this, it has become the Achilles Heel in Loran-C navigation.

Not only does the amount of ASF vary from one area to the next, but it even varies within a given locality according to which secondaries are being tracked. A good example of this is seen in landlocked Lake Superior which is covered by the 8970 Great Lakes Chain. This chain has its master at Dana, IN, and three secondaries: W at Malone, FL; X at Seneca, NY; and Y at Baudette, MN (See Fig. 7.4). It stands to reason that those signals received from the W secondary in Florida would exhibit a greater land propagation error than those received from the other two secondaries because the W radio waves must travel a greater distance over land terrain. This is quickly verified by looking at the ASF

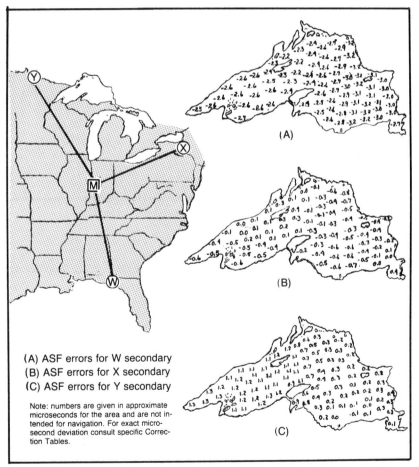

(A) ASF errors for W secondary
(B) ASF errors for X secondary
(C) ASF errors for Y secondary

Note: numbers are given in approximate microseconds for the area and are not intended for navigation. For exact microsecond deviation consult specific Correction Tables.

Fig. 7.4   ASF Values For Different Secondaries Of The 8970 Great Lakes Chain

Correction Tables for the region, where it is found that the ASF errors for the W secondary vary from -2.0 to -3.3 microseconds. It is also reasonable to infer that the ASF corrections for the X and Y secondaries, which are located closer to Lake Superior, provide smaller ASF corrections.

Since a microsecond is such a small unit of measured time, it may seem insignificant to make a correction of just a few microseconds. A second look at gradients, the distance each microsecond is worth, will point out the fallacy in that thinking.

Keeping in mind that the gradients do change depending on location within the hyperbolic grid, a rough equivalent of 0.1 microsecond to equal 45 meters, or a little less than 150 feet can be used. Deviations that are only ± 0.1 to ± 0.5 microseconds are too trivial to be concerned with. For example, in Lake Superior, where the deviations are usually less than 1 microsecond, especially in the Eastern half - sailors don't even bother to correct for it. In fact, for those who cruise the area, many don't even know what is meant by land propagation errors. However, if the cruising area is one in which the ASF errors are on the order of 2-4 microseconds, such as in some of the areas off Nova Scotia, that produces errors that are on the order of 10 times greater or more. As an illustration, cruising in the coastal waters off Halifax can be used. According to observed corrections published by the Canadian Coast Guard (See Fig. 7.5), if the X secondary from the 5930 Canadian East Coast Chain were used there could be position errors that are off in excess of 3 microseconds. This is the equivalent of 1350 meters, or almost ¾ nm - an error which must certainly be considered in this fog prone area.

Correcting for ASF

Probably the only good thing about ASF is that it is constant for a given area. Another plus for Loran users is that the error can be measured either by theoretical propagation delays or from actual observed data. With this information, it is possible to correct for the error and obtain the accuracy for which the Loran system is reputed. There are a number of ways to do this which are outlined in Fig. 7.6.

1. One of the easiest ways to deal with ASF is to ignore it and navigate entirely with waypoints which are derived from previous Loran readouts - either TDs or Lat/Lon. Both the original reading and present receiver data will still contain the error, but if it is a repeat visit, for example to the entrance to an anchorage, and those

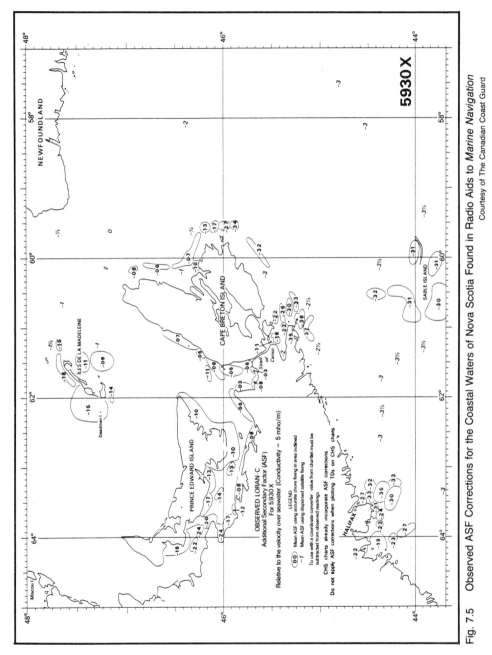

Fig. 7.5   Observed ASF Corrections for the Coastal Waters of Nova Scotia Found in *Radio Aids to Marine Navigation*
Courtesy of The Canadian Coast Guard

coordinates were retained, they can be used for future return. If plotted on a chart, the coordinates could put the position on land, but it doesn't matter as long as it is known that these are the coordinates that originally gave the entrance. The disadvantage in using this method is in that there has to be a first time. The area

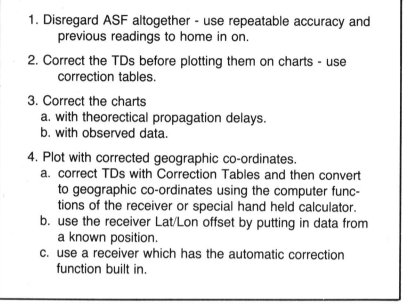

1. Disregard ASF altogether - use repeatable accuracy and previous readings to home in on.

2. Correct the TDs before plotting them on charts - use correction tables.

3. Correct the charts
   a. with theorectical propagation delays.
   b. with observed data.

4. Plot with corrected geographic co-ordinates.
   a. correct TDs with Correction Tables and then convert to geographic co-ordinates using the computer functions of the receiver or special hand held calculator.
   b. use the receiver Lat/Lon offset by putting in data from a known position.
   c. use a receiver which has the automatic correction function built in.

Fig. 7.6   Ways of Compensating For ASF

has to be visited and the navigation "toughed out" when geographic position may be different from plotted position.

It is important to note that many receiver functions are not affected by ASF. Those functions which are "relative" or depend on comparing one position with another, such as distance run and speed over ground, will still be accurate. Even if the position for point A is geographically wrong because of ASF, the position for point B will also be in error - by the same amount and in the same direction. In other words, the errors will cancel each other out and distance between the two points will be the same as if there were no error.

2. In the early days of Loran, before the charts were updated with theoretical propagation delays, the only viable way of dealing with ASF was to correct the TDs themselves before plotting a fix. This was done by using Correction Tables published for each chain by the DMAHTC. Since most charts now are updated with corrected lattices derived from at least theoretical propagation delays, this method of dealing with ASF is little used.

3. The Coast Guard, along with the Defense Mapping Agency and National Ocean Survey, is involved in an extensive program to update Loran charts with lattices corrected for ASF. At this volume's publication most of the charts have been compensated for

ASF with theoretical calculations of propagation delays which has greatly improved the accuracy of plotted fixes. There are, however, still some areas where ASF deviations are outside of acceptable parameters - namely ¼ mile accuracy. Then it is only with observed data obtained in field testing that the lattices may be corrected to meet existing standards. At this time there are only a few areas where the charts reflect corrections from actual observations, but over the years as the data comes in, more and more charts will be upgraded.

4. Some skippers respond to the ASF problem by saying, "I don't have to worry about it - I do all my chart work and navigating in Lat/Lon." Somehow Lat/Lon readouts carry an air of authority which is not justifiable. It is important to note that ASF doesn't somehow magically disappear, just because TDs aren't being used. The reason why Lat/Lon coordinates are no more accurate than TDs is that the Lat/Lon coordinates are computed internally by the receiver from received TDs. If TDs contain an ASF error, so will their Lat/Lon counterparts - unless the latter have been corrected for the error. There are a number of ways in which these corrections can be made.

One of the most common ways of correcting Lat/Lon derivatives for ASF is to manually correct the incoming TDs by using the government Correction Tables and then using the computer functions of the receiver to convert the corrected TDs to corrected Lat/Lon readings. This technique is demonstrated in Chapter Four. It is also possible to do this with a specially programmed hand held calculator.

Another common way to correct Lat/Lon readings for ASF, is to manually program in the error and then the receiver will automatically correct each subsequent reading. This is a particularly valuable technique because the ASF is fairly constant for a given area. There are two different ways this can be done. One is to program in the correct Lat/Lon taken from some known charted position, such as a dock, a buoy, etc. Another way is to program in the actual error. The error may be one computed from a known actual position, or it may be one the receiver computed and which was recorded at an earlier date for the area - one of the benefits of good record keeping. Because the error is constant for a given area, once known, it can be used again and again when returning to that location.

NOTE - A word of **caution** when navigating with corrected geographic coordinates or with the receiver in a corrected mode. When using the homing capabilities of the receiver to return to a previous waypoint, it is important to clear out the Lat/Lon offset - if it were not used the first time. If the first time at a particular position the operation was in a straight uncorrected Lat/Lon mode, and then an attempt is made to return to that position with a correction factor programmed in, the original position will not be reached.

The final way of correcting Lat/Lon coordinates for ASF is to have a receiver that does this automatically without any manual input. To do this a very complicated model of the surface conductivity of a particular area is programmed into the receiver's permanent memory. This is supplemented with literally thousands of field observations at known locations. The receiver then automatically computes the correction for the land path delays.

For years there were only a few Loran manufacturers who offered this option of automatic correction for ASF. Then in the mid 1980's, there was a revolution in the Loran industry that was second only to the big change seen a few years prior in switching from TD only receivers to those with Lat/Lon capabilities. Many more manufacturers began offering Loran receivers with the automatic ASF correcting function, and at a price that was a fraction of what the feature had been in earlier models.

Summary

In some cases, the accuracy of a fix will depend on whether it is plotted with TDs or with Lat/Lon coordinates.

A TD fix that is plotted on a Loran chart with a corrected lattice will be more accurate than an uncorrected Lat/Lon reading plotted on a conventional chart. This is not to say that TDs are more accurate than Lat/Lon readings. They aren't - both contain the same ASF error. But if the TDs are plotted on charts on corrected Loran lattices the resulting fixes will be more accurate than those derived from uncorrected Lat/Lon coordinates.

If this doesn't appear to be true, try this exercise in an area which is known to have at least some ASF error. The first step is to plot a set of TD readings on a Loran chart with corrected overlay lines. Then the geographic coordinates should be plotted on the same chart. The difference in plotted position may be surprising. This was done in the author's home cruising grounds of the Apostle Islands in Western Lake Superior where the ASF error isn't very large. An example of these results is seen in Figure 7.7 where both TDs and Lat/Lon readings were taken at anchor. Using a corrected Loran chart, the TD fix was "right on", the Lat/Lon fix put the position a few tenths of a mile inland. The difference was still within ¼ mile accuracy, but the better fix is obvious.

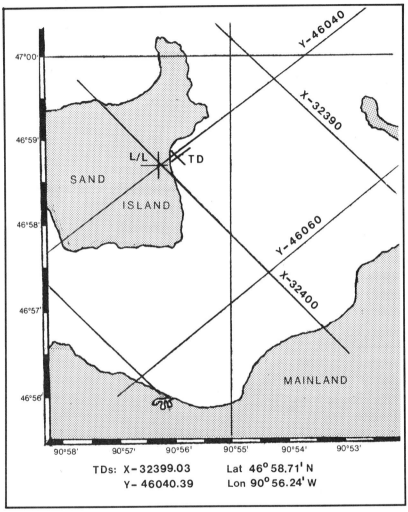

Fig. 7.7   Plotting A Fix With TDs & Lat/Lon

The Final Analysis: How Good is Loran-C?

After looking at all the different factors which could possibly affect the accuracy of a Loran fix, some may marvel that the system is able to deliver any degree of accuracy at all. Certainly there are limiting factors which can affect the system - as there are when using any other navigational tool. The material presented in this chapter is given primarily so that the Loran user is aware of what could affect the accuracy of a plotted fix - it helps to be aware of system limitations so it is known what to look for and trouble can be identified if it should appear. However, most of the time it will be found that Loran-C does live up to its reputation. Rarely are these factors going to be present to the point where Loran can't deliver according to the original intents of the system: ¼ mile accuracy, 95% of the time, within the CCZ. In fact, the Coast Guard boasts that Loran is far exceeding initial expectations - in most cases it produces better than ¼ mile accuracy. For continuous navigation, there is nothing at this time which can come even close to delivering what the Loran system has to offer. Loran-C does work - and it works well.

Yet, as many are finding out, how good Loran is depends a lot on the area being cruised. Because of this, when venturing into a new area for the first time, it would seem that the best approach would be to use Loran with caution (as with any other tool) and certainly not as the sole means for determining position or updating a running fix. Once an area is learned, and it is known if large ASF errors, or sources of strong interference are present, corrections can be made and Loran used with confidence in continued navigation. And the more Loran is used, the more there is an awareness of just what it can and cannot do. Like every tool, it has its limitations, but unlike so many other navigational aids, its uses are quite varied and almost endless - subject only to the applications of the imaginative skipper.

CHAPTER EIGHT

Navigating With Loran-C:
Practical Applications

A Personal Narrative

When we first got our Loran-C full function receiver, we were so impressed that there were times in which we foolishly thought it could replace all of our instruments except the depth sounder. For in addition to being able to plot our position, we now had such extras as knowing our true course and speed over the bottom. Quickly, we discovered how much easier it was to use the true course in our chart work and steering as opposed to manually adding or subtracting for magnetic variation and deviation with a compass course. We also found that the Loran speed over the bottom was usually more accurate than our knotmeter readout. By the same token, our dead reckoning was neglected, and often we fell behind on fixes, leaving everything up to the Loran and its instant readout of position. In those early days, we even had a saying: "The LC does everything except raise the sails." Then it happened.

We had been sailing along Lake Superior's South shore making our approach into the Whitefish Bay "bottleneck" where Superior empties into Lake Huron via the St. Mary's River. Everything had been going smoothly, when for no apparent reason, the Loran receiver started going haywire with flashing numbers, a sure indicator that it was not tracking accurately and was receiving spurious signals. Caught without an accurate fix (we had even become slack in recording data from the receiver), I realized that in just a few short weeks we had become so dependent on the Loran, that the prospect of going back to just dead reckoning and working angles with the hand bearing compass and RDF was enough to make me almost panic. The situation was further complicated with deteriorating visibility and with the big lake freighters all converging down that tight slot it became even more important that we know our position and keep an accurate running fix.

As I got to work with the dividers and parallel rules, I chided myself for becoming so lax - and vowed that never again would we be left dependent on only one method of navigation. The lesson was well-learned, and its moral was the realization that the Loran was not an "end all" in navigation - but only one of the many tools to be used with the other aids and techniques in navigation.

Use, of course, is the key to the effectiveness of any tool or technique - to use them everyday. A good example of this is illustrated by a fellow we met one summer in the North Channel of Lake Huron. His 45 foot power boat left nothing to be desired; it had everything. While chatting with him on one of the local town docks, the subject of Loran-C came up, and he remarked that he hardly ever used it - didn't have confidence in it. Now radar, that was another thing, he used it all the time. From his statements we can find a clue in the trust one places in a particular navigational aid: Loran-C, like any other tool, gains its place in our confidence only through constant use - in fair weather as well as foul. If you wait until that foggy day to turn on the Loran, you may find that not only do you lack confidence in the system, but also the "know how." Like anything else, Loran-C requires practice in order to develop proficiency. The more you work with Loran, the more you will realize that Loran-C can be much more than just position fixing.

Waypoint Navigation

After the basic function of position fixing, probably the most used feature of a Loran receiver is to program in a particular destination as a waypoint and determine ship's range and bearing from that point. From this, course deviation (cross track error), distance to go, time to go etc., are calculated.

A waypoint can be any position: the entrance to an anchorage, a particular buoy in a channel, a reef where fishing is good, or even a point out in the wide open waters where it may be desirable to change course. Waypoints can be determined either by lifting them directly from a chart or by using coordinates obtained from a previous visit. Which is used may make a difference in hitting the target on the other end. Because of land propagation errors (ASF), chart coordinates (Lat/Lon), may yield less than desirable accuracy, i.e., ship's position may not end up as planned. On the other hand, if the ASF for the area is known (perhaps from a previous visit to a nearby anchorage) it can be programmed into the receiver and improve the accuracy of arriving at specific chart coordinates.

If, for the waypoints, coordinates are used from a previous visit, there is the capability of homing in on these with that often reputed 50 foot accuracy. Therefore, whenever possible, previously observed and recorded coordinates should be used as opposed to chart coordinates to represent waypoints. Because of this, at a good reference point, such as outside an anchorage, the readings should be recorded or captured with the present position function of the receiver for use at a later date.

Waypoints can be programmed into a receiver in a number of ways. One is to enter them manually either as TDs or Lat/Lon coordinates. Some receivers will take both kinds of data; others will accept only the Lat/Lon derivatives. If the receiver is of the latter type, and for some reason or other only TDs are available for a particular waypoint, the computer function of the receiver may be used to convert the TDs to their Lat/Lon equivalents. The results can then be manually programmed into the receiver.

Another way of entering waypoints is to record them automatically with the present position function of the receiver as a particular point is being passed over. The coordinates are then logged in the receiver's memory and can be retrieved in order to return to that position. For additional hints on charting and record keeping in navigation, see Chapter Six and Fig. 6.13.

Using Loran as a Homing Device

In this day of Lat/Lon receivers most operators tend to disregard TDs. Certainly it is easier to understand a geographic fix than TDs. Yet, there are times when a TD fix will be more accurate than a Lat/Lon fix. And even with TDs alone, it is still possible to do manually most of what Lat/Lon receivers do automatically. For example, even if a receiver does not have the waypoint option, the same results can be achieved and the Loran can be used to assist in directing a vessel to a particular position by using it as a homing device. This technique is a valuable one to know, because it is possible to experience a receiver malfunction (as has happened) during which all functions except the ability to track TDs are lost.

To head for a waypoint with TDs alone, first the present position is plotted on the chart using TD coordinates. Then, with a protractor or parallel rules and dividers, the direction (course) and distance to the given position are determined. In effect, this is determining the range and bearing to the destination. This will provide the course to steer and bring the vessel in close to the desired position. Cross track error can also be manually calculated - see section on "Deviation from the Rhumb Line." As the destination is approached the TDs are noted for the desired position, either taken directly from the chart or from a previous visit. By watching the TDs on the receiver a pattern will be seen to emerge as they get larger or smaller as the "waypoint" is neared and the boat can be steered accordingly to home in on the desired position. Again, use of previously recorded TDs, as opposed to TDs from a chart to home in on will provide a greater degree of accuracy. If chart TDs are used, they should be those corrected for ASF by some means, such as programming in the ASF error if known.

Using the Loran to Check Other Instruments

Daily use of the Loran will lead to checking it against the other instruments. Particularly if other systems of navigation are being used, as they should be, similarities and differences will be noted between ship's instruments and the Loran. Even if the receiver is just the basic Loran which displays only TDs, by checking receiver position against dead reckoning it is possible to verify or discredit the accuracy of other instruments, such as the compass, the knotmeter, and distance log.

Compass

To check the compass all that is needed is to compare the compass course against the course established with TDs. For example, if it is a calm day and the course steered is a magnetic course of 95°, with the idea of getting a true course of 90° after adjusting for magnetic variation the compass can be checked. If plotting a series of TD readings to establish a running fix indicate an actual course of 83°, it shows the compass is off. (Note: the technique assumes there are no adverse currents or seas, as they could produce similar results.)

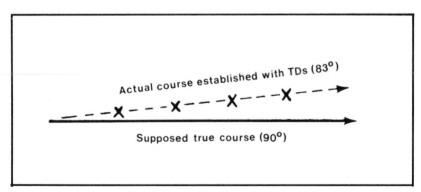

Fig. 8.1   Using TDs to Check Your Compass

This can be carried to its logical end; with care and calm conditions, the Loran can be used to swing the compass and a deviation card can be constructed. With a Lat/Lon receiver it is even easier, because all that needs to be done is to pit the magnetic compass against the true course of the receiver. The important thing is to remember to add or subtract for magnetic variation on the compass course, and a good idea of the accuracy of one of the most important ship's instruments can be obtained.

Knotmeter

Another instrument which can be checked with Loran is the knotmeter. To do this a calm day with no wind or running seas is needed.

With a Lat/Lon receiver the knotmeter can be checked by simply contrasting it with the "speed over ground" function of the receiver. But, because of the sensitivity of the Loran, the speed displayed will vary as the boat is bounced around and moved through the water. Thus, it is best to take a series of readings over certain time intervals and average them rather than to rely on a single reading. This method was used to solve a perplexing problem of years standing.

Knotmeter Readout in Knots	Loran Readout in Knots	Deviation in Knots
3.5	3.93	+0.43
4.0	4.61	+0.61
4.5	5.27	+0.77
5.0	5.85	+0.85
5.5	6.45	+0.95
6.0	6.82	+0.82

Fig. 8.2   Knotmeter Speed Vs. Loran Ground Speed

It had been puzzling for years that, when comparing notes with other sailors there was usually quite a discrepancy when it came to discussing boat speeds on a day's run. Coming into anchorage after an exhilerating sail of 7 knots would often result in being surpassed by another boat's reported 8 knots. Boats passed at 6 knots often reported doing 7! Occasionally sailors like to exaggerate when it comes to proclaiming winds, waves, speeds, etc., but these discrepancies were happening so often it became a concern. The knotmeter became suspect and dead reckoning confirmed the suspicions. The margin of error was larger than it was comfortable to admit. (See Fig. 8.2)

Initially, the Loran did show that there was a difference between the "speed over the ground" readout and the knotmeter, and that this difference varied depending on speed. But it was important to know exactly what these variances were so they could be used in future navigation. On a calm day the following data was collected. First, the boat was run with the knotmeter set at 3.5 knots, then 4.0, then 4.5, etc. Each speed was set for 15 minutes and readings from the Loran "speed over the ground" were tabulated approximately every 20 seconds. The Loran readings were averaged for each knotmeter speed and yielded data seen on fig.8.2.

These results allowed the construction of a graph (see Fig.8.3) and the suspicions were confirmed. The greater the boat speed the more the knotmeter was off. Even the apparent drop in the Loran speed and deviation at 6 knots can be explained, for towards the end of the experiment, the conditions changed and a bit of a headwind was experienced.

By using the Loran to check the knotmeter, it was realized that, in the efforts to put the knotmeter transducer in a protected place next to the keel, some interfering turbulence produced by the

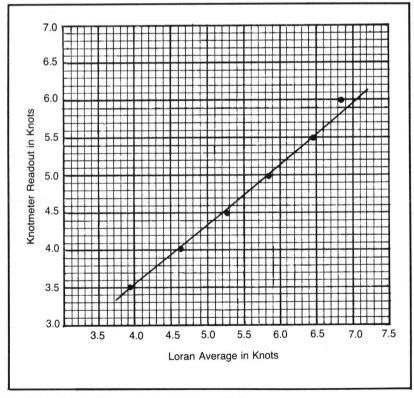

Fig. 8.3   Graph of Knotmeter Data Vs. Loran Data

keel was experienced as the speed increased. Now that the deviation data and graph are available, corrections can be made to knotmeter speed as needed for working future navigation problems. The line on the curve has been extended to get those deviations needed for speeds higher than 6 knots.

Since it is not known if the relationship is strictly a linear one the experiment should be done again at higher speeds. This, however, involves sailing instead of motoring - which usually means seas which may have enough interference from waves to call the results into question.

There is another way to check the knotmeter, using only TDs. This is particularly helpful for those who do not have receivers with the "speed over the ground" function. To do this the boat must be set to run at a specific speed, perhaps 6 knots. Then at various time intervals TD readings are taken so that positions can be established - and the distance run between them. In essence, this is doing the same thing manually that a full function receiver does automatically by establishing distance traveled between two points in a given length of time. (Note: the longer the time interval, the smaller the percentage of error will be, so time intervals should be of at least 30 minutes. Large scale charts with Loran overlay lines should be used as opposed to small scale charts because errors in establishing position with TDs will be smaller. In this particular example with boat speed set at 6 knots, TD readings are taken at 10:15 and 10:45 at points A and B respectively.

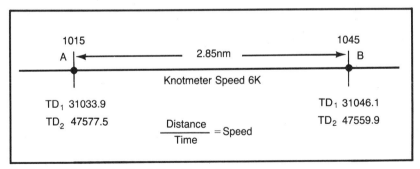

Fig. 8.4   Using TDs to Check Your Knotmeter

The fixes are plotted with these TDs and dividers are used to determine the distance between. In a half hour running time at 6 knots the distance should be 3 nautical miles, but if the distance measured is 2.85 nm, that is a deviation of 0.15 or 0.3 nm in one hour. The knotmeter is reading 0.3 knots too high and, according to the Loran distance made good the boat is moving at only 5.7

knots instead of 6. Possibly the knotmeter is off (it should be further checked on subsequent occasions), or there may be a current affecting it. In this case the information is valuable and can be fed into further navigation.

Distance Log

This same method can be used to check the distance log. All that is needed is to determine position at two points with the Loran, measure the distance between, and compare the results to the distance log. It is necessary to have calm conditions and no currents as the log depends on the water passing by the keel for its operation and this can be responsible for readings that are different from the actual distance over the bottom. By doing this on different occasions, for varying distances a good idea of the log's accuracy can be obtained. To determine the percentage error of the log the difference between the log readout and the distance determined by the Loran is divided by the log readout and then multiplied by 100. The result will be expressed as the percentage error of the log and can be used in further calculations.

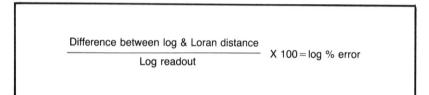

Fig. 8.5   Calculating Log % Error

This assumes that the distance determined by the Loran is correct. And, like anything else, repetition will do much to confirm the results.

The reason that these methods can be used to check instruments is that the Loran system is so incredibly accurate in establishing position. Distance made good can be determined with precision. Even if the readings contain propagation errors due to the varying speeds at which radio waves travel over land versus water (ASF), these will cancel each other out when the established positions are in the same area and are used only to determine distance.

Depth Sounder

To some extent the Loran can be used to do rough checks on the depth sounder. If the Loran puts position on the 24 foot contour line and the depth sounder is reading 45 feet - either the depth sounder is off or the Loran position is off. To do this the position fix must be very accurate (ASF accounted for etc.), and since it is not known that position is at exactly the same point where the depth reading was taken, a certain degree of variation is to be expected. Also, sometimes depth sounders have a way of giving inaccurate readings off different bottoms. But, with periodic checks on depths versus positions, it will help to determine the reliability of another important instrument.

Checking Other Navigational Techniques

Not only can the Loran receiver be used to check the accuracy of other shipboard instruments, but it can also be used to check various navigational techniques. Every skipper has experienced that uncertain feeling of wondering, when he has advanced a running fix, if he really is where he thinks he is: has he accounted for the set and drift of the current, did he allow for the leeway effects of the wind? Loran can help develop confidence in the ability to navigate with other tools and it can assist in identifying errors when things go amiss. The following are a few ways that Loran will help in improving various navigation techniques.

Dead Reckoning

Dead reckoning is still one of the best tools to be used in navigation, and it is always a good idea to use it independently, but simultaneously, when using Loran. If, for nothing else, it becomes a check on the Loran system itself for reassurance that the data being received is at least plausible and the results are realistic. For example, dead reckoning can help determine which side of the baseline position is on, or if there are errors from skywave interference or cycle slip.

The Loran also becomes a check on dead reckoning when the advancement of a running fix is checked against the plotted position from the Loran readout. It may be a pleasant surprise to discover that one's ability with this age-old method of determining position is better than anticipated. It can also help to identify errors, and when the two systems don't match up it is time to start rechecking. As a result Loran can help polish technique and gain confidence in the ability to use dead reckoning so that, without Loran, one can proceed with greater assurance in the accuracy of fixes.

Using an RDF

Many have tried taking a bearing off a radio beacon with an RDF (radio direction finder) and not been sure of reading the exact null. It is easy to be off by as much as 15°. By using Loran, position can be plotted and bearing manually determined with a protractor, or the coordinates of the beacon can be programmed as a waypoint to get its bearing from current position. In either case, knowing the bearing of the beacon can help improve technique to the point of more accurately identifying the RDF null.

Determining Distance Off

There are a number of ways to determine the distance off from an object. Some of the more modern ones are: bow and beam bearings, doubling the angle on the bow, and two bearings with a run between. By checking the results from these methods against a Loran fix, the Loran can assist in developing confidence and proficiency in a given technique.

This can even be carried one step further by using the Loran to help improve abilities in taking those bearings in the above techniques in the same way as checking bearings with an RDF. Gaining confidence in the ability to determine distance off and improving technique to take bearings will both be helpful for those times when the reliability of the Loran data is questionable.

Using a Sextant

For those who are just beginning to unravel the mysteries of navigating with a sextant, the Loran can be an invaluable tool for giving a known position against which to check a sextant fix. As skill develops the sextant navigator can begin to get a good idea of just how accurate his fixes are by comparing them with a Loran fix - a valuable piece of information to have when navigating outside an area where there is adequate Loran coverage.

Deviation from the Rhumb Line

Geometry states that the shortest distance between two points is a straight line. For most, this is the way they navigate, using dead reckoning to get from point A to point B. When there is a deviation from this line, because of strong winds or currents, it is going to take longer to get to the destination, whether it be rounding the next buoy in a race or that shoal where the fishing is great.

Simple plotting of TDs to establish a running fix will quickly tell if the shortest route is being taken. This is basically the same technique as used for checking the compass, except that now the deviation is corrected and the Loran will quickly tell when the boat is back on course. What is being done is computing cross track error much the same way a receiver with the automatic function accomplishes the same thing.

This technique was particularly helpful when a malfunction in the Loran receiver threw out the Lat/Lon capabilities and all those functions dependent on Lat/Lon. All that remained were TDs, and after becoming used to waypoint navigation and its advantages of range, bearing, cross track etc., subseqent navigation was initially at somewhat of a loss. But it was quickly discovered that even with TDs alone cross track error could be determined and corrected for. (See Fig. 8.6)

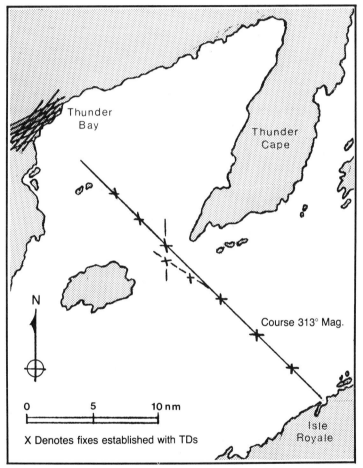

Fig. 8.6   Using Loran To Correct For Deviation From A Rhumb Line

An example of how this was used occurred on a day when a run was made from Isle Royale in Northern Lake Superior to Thunder Bay. Chart work had shown a course of 313° magnetic. As the boat neared the large headlands which guard the bay, some strong gusty winds off Thunder Cape were picked up and the Loran TDs showed it was being blown off course. A quick measure with a protractor showed a difference of 10° between the Loran course and the projected course of 313°. Further calculations showed that if a correction were made for this 10° by steering 323°, the run would be parallel to the intended course and not clear the small group of islands which lay ahead outside of Thunder Bay. Another quick calculation showed that sailing north for approximately 1.5 miles, the original course would be reached and then easing off to 323° would make good the intended course of 313°. For those who doubt the importance of these fine adjustments in navigation, a quick check with the racing circuit will show that many boats are now being equipped with Loran receivers as standard equipment.

Another adaptation of this technique is to use it to calculate set and drift due to currents or wave action. Once known, the information can be used for further navigation.

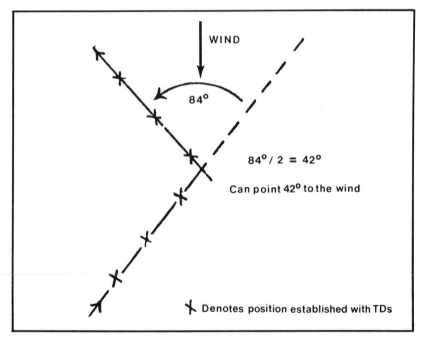

Fig. 8.7   Using Loran To Determine Windward Ability

Determining Windward Ability

Another use for the Loran is to determine a sailboat's efficiency in windward work. This had been done for years by using rough approximations with the compass. But, as the readings would fluctuate as the boat plunged through the waves and adjustments would have to be made for magnetic deviation on different points of the compass, it was often difficult to get an accurate appraisal of the boat's ability to point into the wind.

By using the Loran an alternate way was found to determine a boat's windward ability. All that is needed is to take TD readings (or Lat/Lon coordinates) for a number of fixes on each tack and plot them on a chart the same as a running fix. The line is then extended from the first tack so the angle can be measured between the tacks with a protractor and divided by two. This will tell how close one can sail to the wind close-hauled. It is interesting to do this for different wind strengths because, up to a certain point it is possible to sail closer to the wind when its strength increases. Whether racing or cruising, this type of information can be recalled at a future date in planning navigation strategies, i.e., how close to the wind can the boat be efficiently sailed. (See Fig. 8.7)

In Tacking: Using Loran to Know When To Come About

One of the ways in which Loran has been adapted to daily navigation is in tacking. For the majority of those who cruise on sailboats, dead reckoning is fine until beginning to tack, and then only by strict adherence to changing compass course and distance run can one be reasonably sure of position. Without a distance log and dependent only on time and a knotmeter to determine distance made good, the situation is further complicated as the speed will vary with the wind.

Because of this the Loran receiver has been found to be an invaluable tool in determining position when tacking. An extension of this is in using the Loran to determine when to come about to clear the next point or reach a particular destination. By determining position with the Loran and knowing windward ability, a few simple projections with the protractor or parallel rules will tell when it is time to change tacks. An example illustrates these techniques best.

On a weekend cruise the decision was made to leave the home cruising area of the Apostle Islands in Western Lake Superior and take the 30 mile run to visit a quaint little fishing village at Cornucopia, Wisconsin. It had been a good sail until the wind switched; and after 12 miles of beating, every one was tired of tacking and it was decided to not come about until it was certain that the harbor entrance could be made on the next tack. But how could that be determined?

With the Loran and a few simple calculations, the problem was quickly solved. (See Fig. 8.8) The first step, and the most important, was to determine position with the receiver (Point A). The course had been 290°, and by doubling the windward ability (previously determined to be approximately 45°), and then subtracting this from the course, the result was that a course of 200° could be made good on the next tack.

290° - 2(45°) = 200°

By projecting a course of 200° from the Loran established position at Point A, it could be seen that although Eagle Island would be cleared, and most probably its shoal to the SW, there was no way to clear the mainland point which lay to the east of the destination. Clearly, this tack had to be continued further before coming about. To determine how much further, the reciprocal of 200°, which is 20°, was used to determine the bearing from the harbor entrance. When this 20° bearing was plotted from the harbor to intersect with the 290° course, it could be seen that position had to be at

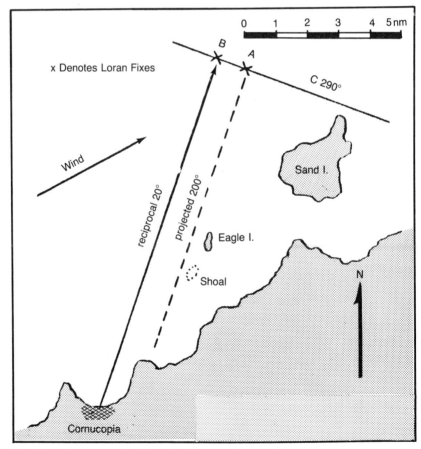

Fig. 8.8   Using Loran To Determine When to Change Tacks

Point B before changing tacks. Calculations could even tell that the present course should be maintained for approximately another 1.2 miles before tacking. The reason this could be done with reasonable confidence is the Loran system's ability to establish position with incredible accuracy.

It is doubtful if dead reckoning, no matter how diligent a running fix was kept, would have given this kind of precision. Once the above principle is understood there is a quicker way to determine when to come about in tacking by just using the Loran receiver and not going through all the chart work. All that is needed is to determine the destination (which point has to be cleared, harbor entrance etc.) as a way point and to enter it into the receiver. Next, the receiver heading on the present tack is noted, the angle of windward ability is doubled and added or subtracted from the present heading depending on which direction will be assumed on the next tack. Using the waypoint bearing function of the receiver, it is time to tack when the bearing to the waypoint is the same as the course determined for the next tack.

Using Loran To Avoid A Specific Object or Area: Running a Safety LOP

There is a particularly wicked, very large shoal in the Eastern end of Lake Superior. It lies approximately 3-4 nm offshore, covers more than a square mile and has areas of least depths of 4-8 feet. Unfortunately, there are no distinguishing landmarks or buoys in the area upon which to determine bearings. Furthermore, radio beacons are too remote for reliable position fixing. Therefore, it was only by diligent dead reckoning that one could determine the location of this shoal. For years the decision was simply to avoid this area by going miles out of the way. But, with Loran, a few techniques were quickly developed to simplify the problem.

Since travel was usually north or south in this section of the lake, the easiest solution was to establish a safety longitude LOP and make sure there was no crossing to the shoal side. Giving a margin of safety, it was known that staying east of 84°42.50' W was safe. A longitude like 84°42.00' was picked and then Loran was used to run either up or down that longitude. (See Fig. 8.9)

This worked fine until one occasion when tacking against a headwind and nearing the shoal area the course was not on a latitude or longitude line that could be followed, but one that was at an angle so the latitude/longitude were constantly changing. Giving a margin of safety, a safety LOP was drawn and a waypoint programmed in at the other end. Now the cross track function could be used to tell if the shoal were too close. Without the cross track function, the same thing could have been done with TDs by charting subsequent fixes to determine if there were a deviation from the rhumb line (See Deviation from Rhumb Line) which was now the safety LOP. The technique could even be used to run a TD LOP the same as a single latitude or longitude LOP, as long as the TD line angle and direction come close to the desired course.

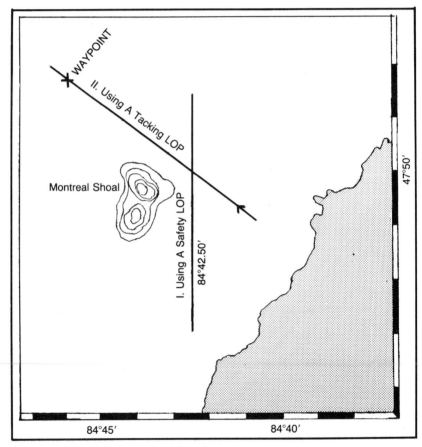

Fig. 8.9   Using Loran To Avoid A Specific Area

Navigating In Fringe Areas Of Loran-C Coverage: Extending Range

A quick look at Fig. 1.3 shows that Loran coverage is divided into two types: primary and secondary. The US Coastal Confluence Zone (CCZ) is very well served by primary coverage, but many favorite cruising areas, such as the Eastern Bahamas and the

Caribbean lie outside this zone, in the areas of secondary coverage. In primary coverage areas, groundwave signals are utilized, while reception in secondary areas is usually via skywaves. There are recorded incidents of receiving good groundwave fixes well out into the Atlantic and in other areas beyond those usually regarded as having primary coverage. Sometimes skywaves are also used in the far reaches of prime coverage areas, and it is in these fringe areas and secondary coverage areas where there often is difficulty in obtaining accurate tracking signals.

Signal strength is one of the main determinants of how far away groundwave signals can be reliably tracked. It varies with different transmitters because of varying power outputs. Basically, signal strength decreases in proportion to distance as it increases. As signals become weaker, it becomes more difficult for the receiver to lock onto the signal and, in particular, track the signal at the right cycle in the signal pulse. Quite often, the receiver will track further into the pulse where there is more power to compensate for reduced power in a weakened received signal. It is this phenomenon, which is called cycle slip, which throws time difference readings off and thus the accuracy of the plotted position.

The telltale signs of inaccuracies due to cycle slip are microsecond readings that are off by increments of 10 microseconds. To recognize cycle slip one needs to be working with TDs and have verification by an independent fix from some other method such as dead reckoning, being at a known spot, a buoy or some other known feature. It is more difficult to spot cycle slip when using Lat/Lon coordinates because even though an error will be shown when the fix is compared to a known position, it can't be known if the error is due to cycle slip or something else, because the distinguishing multiples of ten microsecond differences will be missing. If the correct TDs for a given position are not known (i.e. the work is with Lat/Lon and there is no chart with TD overlay lines) the computer functions of the receiver, if it is equipped with this function, can be used to convert a chart Lat/Lon reading at a known geographical position to its corresponding TDs. The computed TDs are then compared to the receiver TDs.

Once it is known that the receiver is experiencing cycle slip, and by how much, this amount can then be mathematically added or subtracted to subsequent readings. If a chart with Loran overlay lines is not available it may be possible to use the computer functions of the receiver to convert the corrected TD readings to their Lat/Lon equivalents.

With many receivers, it is possible to prevent cycle slip from occurring in fringe areas by disabling the automatic cycle selection mode and placing the receiver in a "lock" or "track" mode. It must be determined that the receiver is tracking the correct cycle by checking readouts against a known point of reference or the error will in fact be locked into all subsequent readings. The technique is particularly useful if position is first in an area of good coverage and it is known the cruise will go into an area of fringe coverage. By locking on to the correct cycle in an area of assured readout accuracy, it can be extended into the fringe area, for a receiver in the locked mode can reliably track the correct cycle even when the signal to noise ratio drops as low as 1:8 and 1:16.

There is another computerized trick to increase reception in fringe areas that is possible with some receivers. This is to purposely select tracking cycles that are further into the pulse to assist the receiver in pulling in a weak signal. This can be done for either the master or the secondary, or both. The technique, which is called cycle stepping, may or may not affect the time difference (TD) readouts. If just the master is cycle stepped, TDs will be less than they should be by increments of 10 microseconds (10 microseconds for each cycle stepped.) If just the secondary is cycle stepped, TDs will increase by increments of 10. These TDs can still be used if the error is known and added or subtracted accordingly. If both the master and the secondary are cycle stepped and the tracking point is moved the same number of cycles into each pulse, the errors will cancel each other out and the TDs will read exactly as if there were no cycle stepping. In this case, the receiver may still flash a warning that it is experiencing cycle slip, even though the readings may be used without correction.

Although cycle stepping will usually allow considerable extension of the receiving range from a distant transmitter, there is a danger in using this technique. This is because moving deeper into the pulse increases the chance of picking up skywaves instead. Fortunately, most receivers are equipped with warning signals or alarms that indicate when skywaves are being tracked as opposed to groundwaves. Some receivers will even automatically reject skywaves as long as they can obtain good groundwave readings.

Using Loran-C With Skywaves

In fringe areas, skywaves may be all that a Loran receiver is able to track. TDs taken from skywaves will be different from those taken from groundwaves, reflecting an error that is due to longer propagation time to the ionosphere and back. Yet, it is possible to correct for the error and then use skywaves in continued navigation.

There are a number of different ways in identifying whether skywaves are being tracked or not. One, of course, is being at a known position and noting that it is not the same position as given by the Loran readout, a prime warning. Unfortunately, the difference in skywave transmissions may vary so there isn't the characteristic 10 microsecond differences seen with cycle slip. Other indicators may be signal strength or signal to noise ratio numbers which are much higher than would be expected for a groundwave signal in that area. Some receivers will flash some kind of warning or give an alarm to indicate that skywaves are being used instead of groundwaves. In other receivers the condition may be indicated by flashing or unstable numbers.

Once it is known that skywaves are being tracked, the magnitude of the error needs to be determined by comparing receiver position with a known position established by some other means. When the error is known a correction can be fed into the receiver in the same way as a correction for ASF error using the Lat/Lon offset. Navigation can then continue with the Loran, even though skywaves are being tracked instead of groundwaves. The accuracy, however, will probably not be as good. A common term used to describe skywave accuracy is that fixes can be obtained which have the potential of "sextant accuracy." (See Fig 8.9B).

One of the biggest disadvantages of using skywaves for navigation is that the time it takes skywaves to reach a given locality is not always consistent. This is because conditions are continually changing in the ionosphere which make the reflecting layers vary in their distance from earth. (See Chap.2) This will affect the TD readouts, as TDs are a measure of the time it takes the signal to travel a given distance. If the distance changes, so will the TDs. Especially on a two or three day passage, traveling both day and night, drastic changes in TD readouts will be seen as the ionosphere layers move further away from the earth at night. Therefore, even though skywaves are used for continued navigation, it is important to verify fixes by some other means whenever possible. One of the best ways to do this is with a SAT NAV fix.

Using Loran-C With SAT NAV

The question can be legitimately asked: "If you have SAT NAV, what do you need Loran for?" To answer this, it is necessary to look briefly at the strengths and weaknesses of both systems.

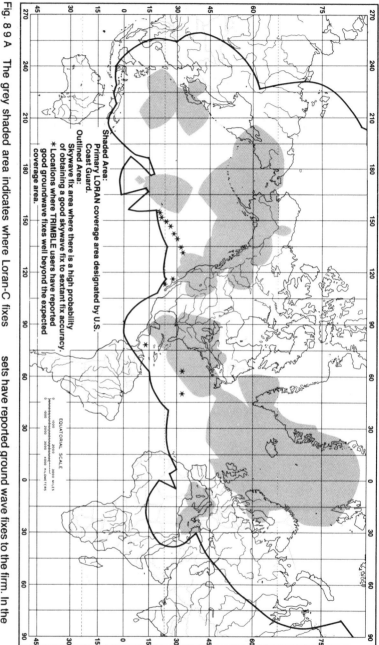

Fig. 8 9 A The grey shaded area indicates where Loran-C fixes with ground waves can be expected at least 95% of the time. It is also possible at times to obtain ground wave fixes well beyond the shaded area. For example, the asterisks indicate areas where users of Trimble Loran-C sets have reported ground wave fixes to the firm. In the much larger area outlined on the map there is a high probability of obtaining good skywave fixes most of the time. Skywave fixes have the potential of sextant accuracy.

Shaded Area:
Primary LORAN coverage area designated by U.S. Coast Guard.
Outlined Area:
Skywave fix area where there is a high probability of obtaining a good skywave fix to sextant fix accuracy.
★ Locations where TRIMBLE users have reported good groundwave fixes well beyond the expected coverage area.

EQUATORIAL SCALE

Map courtesy of Trimble Navigation

One of the most significant advantages in using Loran is that it can be used for continuous navigation. There is no waiting around for a fix - it is always there whenever needed.A spin-off of this, is that accuracy in waypoint navigation and related functions is usually good. One of the main disadvantages in using Loran is that ASF errors are almost always present and need to be corrected for in precise navigation. Another disadvantage is that Loran can't be used everywhere; there are many areas in the world where even fringe Loran coverage is not available - the Southern Hemisphere in particular. (See 8.9A)

SAT NAV, on the other hand, provides world wide coverage - there isn't anywhere that a satellite can't be received if one waits long enough. SAT NAV also isn't plagued with inconsistencies caused by land propagation errors, and as a result, SAT NAV fixes are incredibly accurate. But the biggest disadvantage with SAT NAV is that there isn't continuous navigation between fixes except by dead reckoning. To do this, there are three options.

Dead reckoning can be done in the usual manner by advancing a SAT NAV fix with course and distance made good by computing speed X elapsed time. Another option is that, with many SAT NAV receivers, speed and heading can be manually programed into the unit and then it will electronically dead reckon between passes. The disadvantage is that speed may not always be consistent (especially with vessels under sail) and there must be a correction for each change in course, no matter how slight. These problems can be overcome somewhat, in that with many SAT NAV receivers it is possible to get an interface with the knotmeter and a compass which is installed for this specific purpose. Then the receiver will automatically dead reckon electronically between satellite passes without manual input. The exact position is recalculated with each subsequent satellite fix. There still may be errors however, the magnitude of which increases as lapsed time increases. These dead reckoning errors will be further reflected in waypoint navigation and related functions such as range and bearing to a given location.

Satellite passes may vary from 30 to 90 minutes - but it may be much longer than that between accurate fixes. This is because the receiver may have to reject a pass because its angle of elevation is unacceptable or the receiver isn't able to lock on long enough to get a fix. Thus it can be as long as 7 or 8 hours between accurate fixes with the SAT NAV system.

By using Loran and SAT NAV together one has the best of both worlds. SAT NAV becomes an excellent means by which to verify a position fix from Loran and, by comparing the two, calculate the error for ASF. The error is then programmed into the Loran receiver and is used for continued navigation between satellite passes. In the same manner, errors caused by cycle slip and sky-waves can be determined by pitting the Loran readout against a SAT NAV fix. This is especially useful when navigating in those remote areas where all there is to work with in Loran is skywaves. By updating the Loran every few hours with a SAT NAV fix, even inconsistencies in skywave propagation can be determined and corrected for. In this way, SAT NAV becomes a very important complementing tool in extending the range of a Loran receiver. The Loran receiver, meanwhile, provides continuous navigation between satellite passes. The integrated use of both systems in these situations is so valuable, that at present there is at least one manufacturer which offers a SAT NAV interface with its Loran receiver and there are others on the way with this option.

Using Loran With Other Navigational Aids and One TD

So far all of the applications of Loran discussed in this chapter assume the ability to track a master station and at least two secondaries. There may be times, however, that for one reason or another, only one set of station pairs can be tracked. Perhaps the distance is too great to pick up the other secondary or it is temporarily off the air for repairs.

This happened a few years back when one of the stations, in the only chain available, was shut down for two hours each day for servicing. Without that second TD LOP a fix could not be determined nor could a simple latitude or longitude reading be determined as the receiver is dependent on both TD LOPs to convert to Lat/Lon. Without Lat/Lon, there were none of the other nice extras such as range, bearing, course, speed over the ground, etc. All of these functions are dependent on the receiver establishing position, which it can't do without those two LOPs. All that was left was that single TD to work with. Many boaters in the area gave up in disgust and simply turned their sets off. It finally took a tight situation to force a realization of what can be done with just a single TD.

To begin with it is important to look at that single LOP. As with any line of position it tells a lot of things. Naturally, it tells that position is somewhere along that line. But perhaps even more important, it tells where the position is not. This can be useful in avoiding a particular obstruction, shoal etc.

For example, a trip may include powering along a shoreline on a true course of 30°. The chart shows there is a shoal in the area and it is important to know that it is going to be missed. All there is to work with is a single master-secondary pair and the one TD readout which is 46134.5. A quick plot on the chart shows that position is somewhere on that LOP and, as long as the present course of 30° is maintained, the shoal area will be avoided. (See Fig. 8.10)

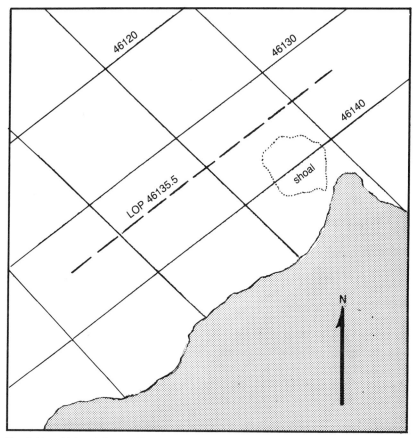

Fig. 8.10   Using A Single TD To Know Where You Are Not.

The TD LOP is just like any other LOP, and if it is crossed by a second LOP - even one derived from another navigational aid or technique (hand bearing compass, RDF), position will be established. The general rules of crossing angles apply here as elsewhere - larger crossing angles mean more accurate fixes by reducing the circle of expected position where one may actually be. (See Chap. 2) A third LOP, if it is available, will reduce this area of possible position even further, by forming the familiar "cocked hat" or triangle from the three LOPs. Taking these factors into consideration, there are a number of different ways in which a single

TD can be used to establish position by using it in conjunction with other navigational aids. The following are but a few examples to illustrate that the application of this concept is subject only to the ingenuity of the individual sailor.

Using a single TD and the depth sounder. There may be times when knowing the depth can help in identifying just what the position is on a single TD LOP. This can be especially useful if it is known that position is on a particular contour line and it can be crossed with the single TD.

An illustration of this idea could be a situation in which a boat is cruising in reduced visibility and the depth sounder reads 19 feet. The Loran gives the TD LOP as 32314.1, so it is known that position is somewhere along that line. By "crossing" this LOP with the depth sounder reading, the possible position has been narrowed down considerably.

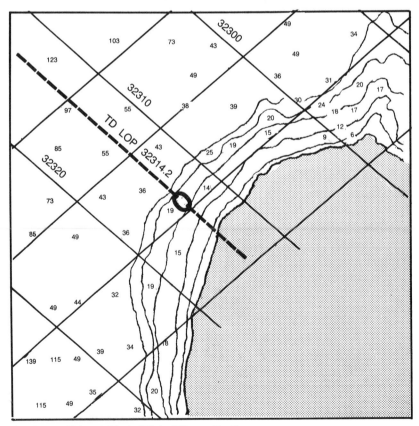

Fig. 8.11　Using A Single TD And Known Depth

Using a single TD and a bearing from a known object. Another way of determining position with only one TD is to cross it with a bearing taken from a known object with a handbearing compass. In the example shown (Fig. 8.12), it is possible to get a bearing off the beacon on Big Bay Point of 170°T after correcting for magnetic variation. At the same time the Loran readout for the single master-secondary pair is 31806.4. The position is somewhere along each LOP. Where they cross is the fix. In this particular case some caution is required in accepting the fix because the crossing angle between the two LOPs is so small - 24°.

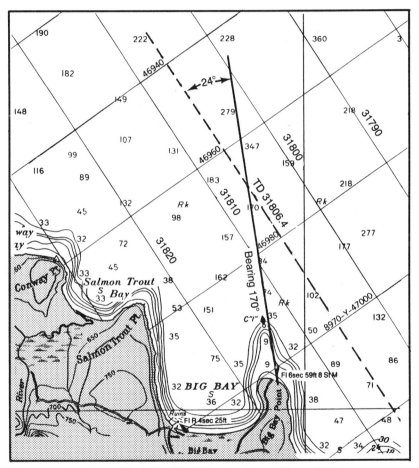

Fig. 8.12   Crossing a Single TD With A Bearing From A Known Object

If it is also possible to take a bearing off the flashing red beacon at the Big Bay Harbor entrance, not only would the crossing angle be larger, but there would be a third LOP to substantiate the fix.

The above technique can also be used by taking a bearing from a radiobeacon with an RDF and crossing it with the single TD. This is particularly useful in those areas where one beacon is all that can be picked up and a second LOP is needed to determine the fix. The technique can even be used by taking tangent bearings off the end of a point or an island and crossing them with the TD LOP. See Fig. 8.13

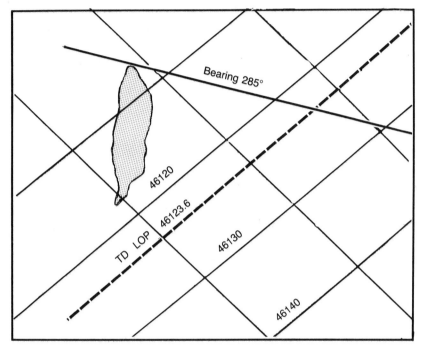

Fig. 8.13   Crossing A Single TD With A Tangent Bearing

Using a single TD with a range. A similar technique to the above, is to line up position with a set of range markers and cross that with the single TD. Again, this works only if the angle between the TD and the range extension is sufficiently large. As the two LOPs approach each other in the same direction, accuracy of position is lessened considerably. Even if there are two TDs, using a range (along with other aids), gives that additional LOP to confirm position. (See Fig. 8.14)

More often than not, an official navigation range may not be in the area where it is needed. But the technique can still be used if a range can be established by lining up any two charted objects. These should be conspicuous landmarks such as tall buildings, stacks, radio towers, etc. If their positions are marked on the chart, they may be used to establish a range. Even a natural range, such as lining up two islands or the end of a point with an island, can be used for this purpose. The established range gives a line of position which can be crossed with the single TD to give a fix. For example, a trip may include cruising to the south of a small island and a prominent headland can be seen in the distance. When the two line up there is a range which can be crossed with a single TD LOP to establish position. (See Fig. 8.15)

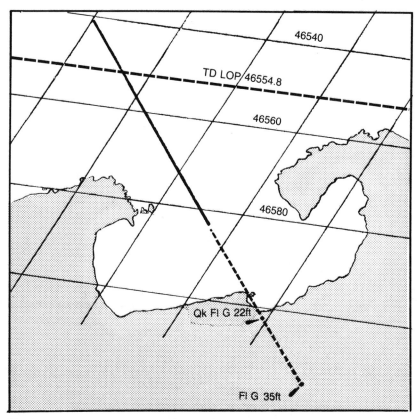

Fig. 8.14   Using A Range With a Single TD

Advancing a fix with just a single TD LOP. Sometimes it is possible to experience intermittent coverage from a particular Loran station. There may be a very low signal to noise ratio observed with one of the secondaries so there is uncertainty about the fix coordinates produced - yet the other secondary is still giving good strong numbers. It may be then prudent to switch to using only that TD which is certain. As an illustration, a vessel is on a course of 45°T and at 0815 there is a good solid fix with a Lat/Lon readout of 47°32.25'N and 87°48.81'. Sometime during the next

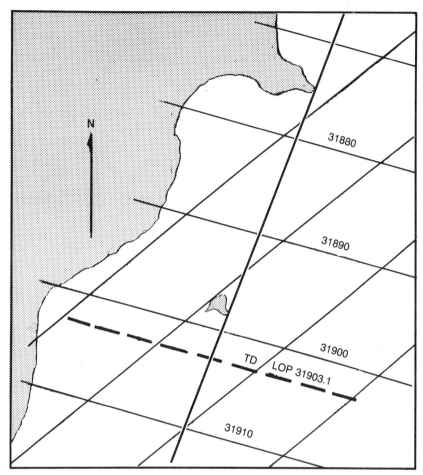

Fig. 8.15   Lining Up A Natural Range To Be Used With A Single TD

hour the ability to track the Y secondary is lost, but the X secondary continues to give good numbers. Without two TD LOPs, a Lat/Lon fix is no longer available, but it is possible to switch to just that single TD and, using a course of 45° advance the fix from one hour ago. Even though the receiver is tracking only one station pair, it will be a fairly reliable fix. Note that in this situation , the technique works only because the X secondary has a fairly large crossing angle to the advance line of the fix. Had the situation been reversed and all there was to work with was the Y secondary, position reliability would be extremely low because of the small crossing angle between the Y secondary LOPs and the course.(See Fig.8.16)

Advancing a single TD LOP. A single TD LOP can be advanced in exactly the same way as a running fix is in dead reckon-

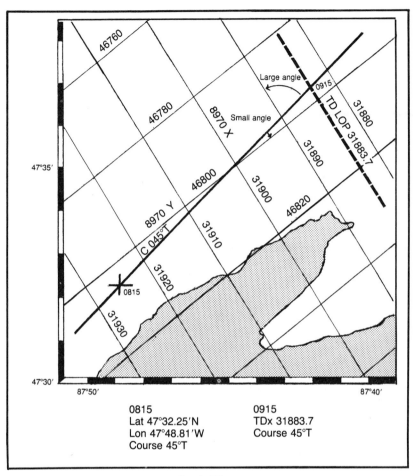

Fig. 8.16   Advancing A Fix With A Single TD

0815	0915
Lat 47°32.25′N	TDx 31883.7
Lon 47°48.81′W	Course 45°T
Course 45°T	

ing, by computing distance made good as a product of speed and elapsed time. To find the exact position on the advanced LOP a second LOP, determined from some other navigational aid, is needed. The technique is useful if the situation is such that there is an inability to obtain a TD LOP and another LOP from a different source at the same time.

For example, a cruise includes navigating in a fringe area of Loran reception and only one master-secondary pair can be tracked. The course is 17°T and the vessel is traveling at 6 knots. At 1030 a single TD reading of 32945.5 is recorded. At this point there is no other information available to determine position on this TD line, but it is recorded anyway. Sometime in the next 10 minutes the master is lost also, so now even this station pair cannot be tracked. At 1100 Guano Rock is spotted and a handbearing compass determines its bearing as 320°T. (See Fig. 8.17). Position can now be determined by advancing the single TD in the following way:

Step 1. The 1030 TD is plotted in the area being cruised.

Step 2. An extended line is drawn to indicate the course of 17° anywhere on the 1030 TD LOP. Three nm are marked off with dividers on the course line. (Distance made good in ½ hour = speed or 6 k times ½ hour or 3 nm.)

Step 3. At the 3nm point on the course line, a second LOP is drawn which is parallel to the 1030 line of position - position is somewhere on this line. (Note - it is not known what the TD reading for this line is - nor is it necessary).

Step 4. The bearing of Guano Rock is used to determine position on this second LOP by drawing the reciprocal of 320° or 140° from the rock.

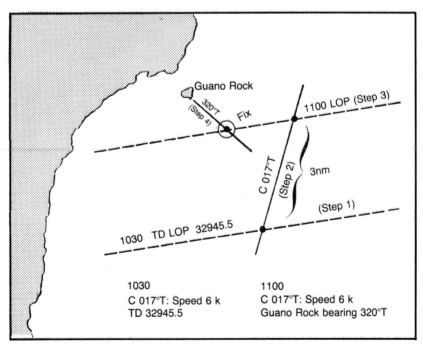

Fig. 8.17 Advancing A Single TD LOP

Position is now known even though the Loran receiver has not been working for the past 20 minutes.

The beauty of this technique is that Loran can be used to be establish position even after it is no longer tracking any signals. Note that in this particular situation, the two LOPs (the Loran LOP and the bearing LOP) were not even obtained at the same time. Upon first receiving the Loran LOP there was nothing around to help in establishing position on it. But by the advancement of this line it could be used later when a second LOP became available. It also points out the need for good record keeping. If that 1030 TD hadn't been recorded, it couldn't have been advanced later on when it was needed.

Using a single TD with radar. Radar is but another tool in the navigator's arsenal, and it too can be used in conjunction with Loran. This can be shown with an example of cruising in a situation where visibility has been reduced considerably by fog. On radar, the Sand Point daymarker is picked up as it has a radar reflector mounted on top. It is found that the marker is 4.3 nm away. Position is somewhere on a circle of position (COP) with a radius of 4.3 nm from the daymarker. (See Fig. 8.18) But there is also the single TD reading of 43281.1 and it is known that position is somewhere along this LOP. Where the two LOPs cross is ship's position - taken from two independent navigational aids.

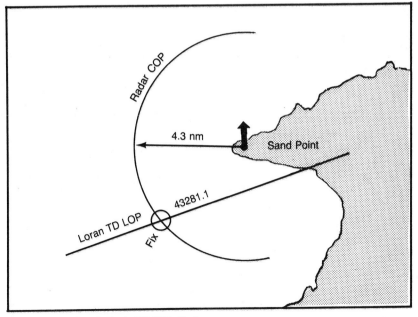

Fig. 8.18   Using A Single TD With Radar

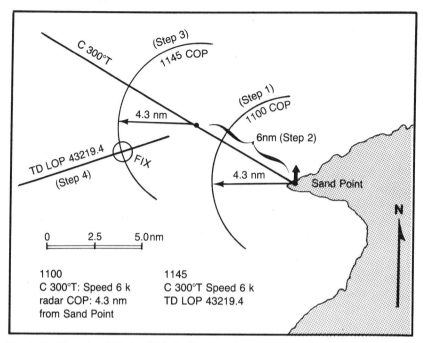

Fig. 8.19 Advancing A Radar COP To Be Plotted With A Loran TD LOP

A radar COP can be advanced in the same manner as a TD LOP. This is a useful technique for those times when information is not available from each system at the same time. The important thing to remember about advancing a radar COP is that it is the center point which is advanced the distance made good and then the COP radius is added to that. An example best depicts how these different techniques can be used to adapt to individual circumstances.

Using the same situation as shown in Fig. 8.18, but because of fog, and having only one TD to work with, the run is primarily done by radar. In fact, when the radar reading was taken which showed 4.3 nm from the daymarker, it was accepted that position was somewhere along the radar COP and no Loran reading was taken. Since it was noted that the radar COP was established at 1100, cruising continued on a course of 300°T at a speed of 8 knots. After 45 minutes running time there is reason to believe that the radar is giving spurious readings and it is necessary to get a more accurate determination of position. A TD reading of 43219.4 is recorded and plotted with an advance of the 1100 radar COP in the following manner:

Step 1. The 1100 radar COP is charted with the Sand Point daymarker as the center and a radius of 4.3 nm. Position at 1100 was somewhere along this COP.

Step 2. The center point of the radar COP is advanced 6nm (distance traveled at 8 k in 45 min.) on a projected course of 300°. It should be noted that this is not a line of position - all that is being done is moving the center of the COP according to direction and distance traveled.

Step 3. A new COP is charted, with a radius of 4.3 nm from the new center point. Ship's position at 1145 is somewhere on this advanced COP.

Step 4. The 1145 TD LOP is entered on the chart. Position should be very close to where the TD LOP and advanced radar COP cross.

(See Fig. 8.19)

Using the Loran Receiver As a Computer

There are a number of ways in which many Loran receivers can be used to assist in solving navigation problems. Whether it is to know the range and bearing to the next destination, the range and bearing between any two points in the world (regardless of current position), or the total distance between a series of course changes, a Loran receiver can supply ready answers by using its computer functions. This becomes a particularly useful function when a receiver is having trouble in locking on to any signal at all. In fact, it is possible to use the receiver as a computer when position is well outside of any coverage area or the antenna to the receiver isn't even hooked up. To do this, a receiver usually must have Lat/Lon capabilities and related functions.

Two point range and bearing. If the geographic coordinates of any specific point are known, these can be entered into the receiver along with the coordinates of any other point and range and bearing between the two can be computed. Even if the two points are in another part of the world, distances will be computed. The information can be useful in cruise planning, particularly if one destination is being debated over another.

A very useful application of two point range and bearing can be made when the receiver is no longer receiving any signals. By using present position (as determined by some other means such as a sextant fix, RDF, etc.) as one of the entered points, range and bearing to a given destination can then be determined even though the receiver is not tracking a signal.

Waypoint rolling. Since two point range and bearing is strictly a straight line distance, it may be necessary to carry the technique a step further and program in a series of points to accommodate course changes and roll through them as in waypoint rolling. Distances and direction can then be recorded for each leg of a cruise and stored for use when needed. In this way dead reckoning positions and cruise directions can be computed to follow later when the string is actually being run through, even though this information can't be obtained by the receiver's actually tracking and giving position.

Long distance or great circle planning. Many receivers have the ability to compute great circle routes between positions with large distances between each other and then break them down into smaller equal segments by waypoints. The initial Lat/Lon can be programmed in along with the destination Lat/Lon and the receiver will break up the distance between the two into a series of intermediate waypoints equally spaced along the great circle route. The waypoints can be rolled through to determine the range and bearing between each.

Filling in missing data. As presented in other sections of this book, there may be times in which the computer functions of a Loran receiver may be used to fill in missing information. Whether it is converting from TDs to Lat/Lon derivatives or vice versa, there may be times in which one is available and the other is needed. For example, the TDs for outside an anchorage have been given by a friend, but the receiver will accept only Lat/Lon coordinates for waypoint input. Perhaps it is necessary to know the TDs for a specific geographic location so cycle slip can be checked. It may be that the cruising area is covered by more than 1 chain and it is desirable to convert the TDs in one chain to the TDs in another chain for a given location. There are many situations such as these in which the receiver can be used to compute information needed for further navigation.

A look at the total Loran picture today shows that, within a few short decades Loran-C has become one of the greatest aids in the history of marine navigation. It is no accident that it has been eagerly embraced by commercial and recreational navigators alike. Especially when it is used along with other navigational aids, its applications in navigational problems seem almost endless. Whether it is homing in on a previous fix, calculating set and drift of currents, or checking on other instruments and navigational techniques - use of Loran-C is getting to be a lot more than just position fixing.

CHAPTER NINE

What's New In Loran
An Update on Product Technology

Recent years have seen a number of improvements and trends in the manufacturing of Loran receivers. In fact, the changes in receiver technology in the past decade have far surpassed those developments in all prior years. This is largely due to the development of microprocessors and the advent of microcomputers. In just a few short years the electronics industry has produced a number of product innovations in Loran receivers, and it has done this at a fraction of the cost of past receivers.

Getting More For Less

It is certainly surprising to see Loran receivers listing at well below $500. In some instances there are models which cost even less than a VHF receiver. Without a doubt, price reduction has been the greatest benefit in receiver technology toward the end of the 1980's and early 1990's. Some of the reasons for lower prices have been the spin-offs in the electronics industry. Not only is it possible to get more information on a single microchip, but chips now cost considerably less.

Micrologic's most inexpensive receiver. Note absence of alpha-numeric keys, 100 waypoints, three notch filters. Still has all the "bells and whistles" of Waypoint Navigation.

Another factor which has helped to drive prices down has been the increased demand for, and resulting sales of, receivers. As more and more potential users jump on the Loran bandwagon, manufacturers can afford to drop the cost of receivers. To illustrate this dramatic increase in the use of Loran, one has only to look at the Coast Guard projections which conservatively estimated the user community at 500,000 by the year 1990. Yet, by the early 1990's the user community approached and passed 1,000,000 users.

Not only are the prices much lower, but what is available today for the Loran dollar far exceeds purchase options of just a few years back. The "bells and whistles" of the 1980's top of the line receivers have now become commonplace on the receivers of the 1990's. While at times it may be difficult to filter through all the alternatives which are now available, there are some definite trends which have emerged in product technology, both in receiver design and performance options.

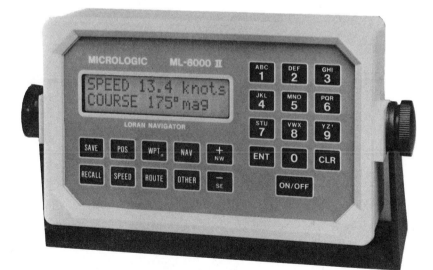

An example of "Thin Packaging". Alpha numeric touch key pad. Totally waterproof, 250 waypoints, 6 preset notch filters, can be connected to up to four Remote Control Displays. Micrologic's "Top of the Line" receiver.

Receiver Design

Receiver Housing

A definite trend in the design of Loran receivers is packing more into smaller boxes. Receivers which can be held in the palm of a hand are now commonplace. "Thin packaging" is a trend with some manufacturers in which the depth of the unit is only a couple of inches. There is also a trend with a number of manufacturers towards making their receivers water resistant and even gas tight.

Another way of reducing size is to split the unit into a two part system so that the main processing unit can be tucked in an out-of-the-way locker and the smaller control head is mounted in the navstation. This is a particularly nice feature for those with small navstations, or ones that are already overcrowded with electronics.

Micrologics "Top of the Line" ML8000-11 put into a hand-held portable. Waterproof, 250 waypoints/waypoint navigation Alpha-numeric keys, fullfunction backup. Operation options: 12 Volt, 110 Volt, N1-Cad Battery (rechargable).

Portable Lorans

A natural application of smaller housing lends itself to the development of the portable Loran. These units can run off either the ship's 12 volt electrical system or a battery pack, which makes them a nice backup in case of a power failure with the ship's main electrical system. Because they have their own self-contained telescoping antenna, another advantage with portable Lorans is that they have no complicated installation procedures. It is even possible to transform some regular receivers into portable units by attaching an optional battery pack and telescoping antenna.

One common use for the portable Loran is a second unit in the cockpit. Some manufacturers even include a simple bracket for mounting on a cockpit bulkhead. Because portables are often constructed with waterproof housing, a natural application is to use them for dinghy exploring, reef diving or returning to a favorite fishing hole. They can also be taken home for practice or to enter waypoints, cruise routes, etc. ahead of time. Another application is to include one in your gear if you're going on a charter in an area which has Loran coverage.

Advertised as "The World's First Hand-held Loran". Micrologic puts their most inexpensive full function Loran into a hand-held portable, the "Sport Nav". Includes all features of their Voyager. Operates on 6 AA Alkaline batteries with @ 24 hours of use.

Data Display

In spite of the trend towards smaller housing units, a reverse trend is seen in the size of the screen for the data display. Whereas models in the mid 1980's had one or two display lines, today it is not uncommon to have four or more lines in a screen display, which is appropriately called a page. Gone are the days when a navigator had to switch continuously from one function to another to obtain information.

In addition to simple Lat/Lon position, each page contains a wealth of information with options such as range and bearing to the next waypoint, actual speed and course over the ground to the waypoint, cross track error and time to go. One of the reasons for having larger displays with more information is that receivers are performing more functions which, likewise, yield more information. For example, it is now possible to do such exotic things as get adjustable speed and course averaging, call up functions which check and diagnose different aspects of signal quality.

A few receivers use vacuum florescent displays (LED) which are a little harder to read in daylight. However, there is an increasing tendency to employ adjustable backlit multipart dot matrix Super Twist LCD displays. Another trend is to present information in larger numbers which can be read easily from the cockpit. A number of manufacturers are also using different means of graphic portrayal of cross track error.

Keypads

Today, most Loran receivers are using sealed membrane touch pads, part of the trend in making receivers more water resistant. Probably the most recent advance in keypads has been the incorporation of alpha numeric keys. It used to be that the operator could enter only numerical data, such as TD's, Lat/Lon, waypoint numbers, etc. Now, with many receivers, it is possible to enter letters and full words to give waypoints personal names. In some cases one can even enter full messages, such as a personalized identification message at power-up: "Welcome aboard RENEGADE of Newport".

The keyboarding of these messages, however, can be a little tedious. For example, the letters "A", "B", and "C" may be assigned to the same key which also displays the numeral one, a system similar to that used with touch telephones. To get the letter "C", the operator has to push this #1 key three separate times in the letter mode. So message entry in Loran receivers has yet to approach the ease of operation of other computers.

Remotes

Another area in which Loran receiver design has become more sophisticated is in the use of remote units. A remote is a secondary receiver which is run off the main unit and stationed at another site, such as in the cockpit or on a flying bridge. It used to be that these remotes had no input, but would only perform as a repeater displaying a few functions such as range and bearing to a waypoint and cross track error. Now many manufacturers are offering full function remotes which can access all the information from the main unit. With some it is even possible to display a completely different set of information on the remote than is present on the main unit screen. In some systems, the main receiver is capable of driving more than one remote head, again with different readouts on each.

Some remotes are so sophisticated that they can actually accept input data independently of the main unit creating a multi-unit system. For example, waypoints and present position data can be entered directly on the remote. It is even possible to calculate navigation problems separately from the main drive unit. Thus, it is possible for a skipper to compute the course to the waypoint in use with a remote in the cockpit, while the navigator calculates waypoints in a completely different sail plan in the nav-station down below, all on the same Loran system.

Notch Filters

A final improvement in receiver architecture in recent years has been the addition of more notch filters. Seven or eight are not uncommon, and manufacturers are turning more to automatic notch filters. It used to be that notch filters had to be tuned at the factory for a particular area. In the case of an extended cruise which covered thousands of miles, it used to be necessary to send the Loran receiver in for retuning. With most contemporary receivers, this is no longer necessary.

Another spin-off from modern technology, the secret with notch filters is in the software programming, which no longer is that difficult. Unless cruising in one of the known trouble spot areas, such as the Annapolis area, it is no longer necessary to have a Loran with specially set notch filters.

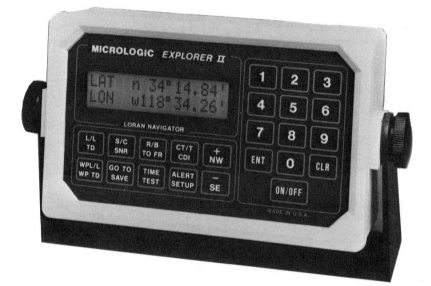

More "thin packaging", but notice the absence of alpha-numeric keys. Waterproof, 100 waypoints, four preset notch filters. Still has all "bells and whistles" of WP navigation. Micrologic's "Mid-Line" receiver.

Performance Options

User Friendly

In spite of the fact that there is a trend towards sophistication in what receivers can do, there is a definite tendency for receivers and accompanying instructions to become more user friendly. This is accomplished in a number of ways.

The first is in the receiver itself. Not only does keyboard labeling make more sense, but the tendency to assign multiple related functions to individual keys is often accompanied by the use of plain language helpful prompts. Sequencing commands to access specific functions has also been simplified. Many receivers are so user friendly that it is possible to sit down and start operating them to get basic functions without a users' manual. Some units even have built in learning programs which are designed to take the novice through a series of waypoint entries and navigation exercises.

Another way in which the receiver performance options have become more user friendly is seen in the manuals themselves. Manuals are no longer written in the confusing language of engineers and computer programmers. Today's manuals are written with laymen terminology and in logical, easy to understand steps. Now there are also commercially prepared video tapes which explain the use of Loran and the operation of many of the major models from different manufacturers.

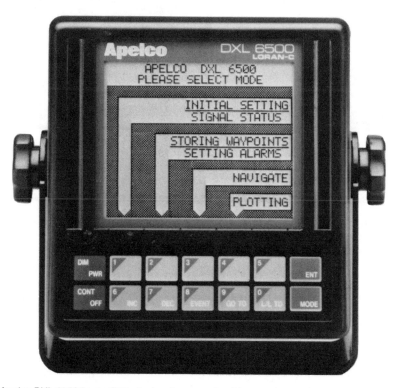

Apelco DXL 6500 Loran-C Navigator. An example of the trend towards more user-friendly menu driven programming.

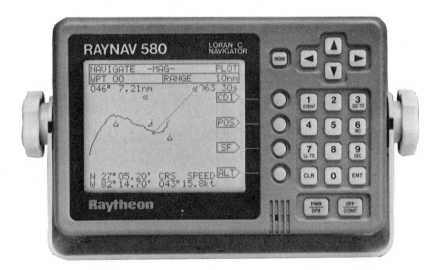

Raytheon's RAYNAV 580 Loran/Plotter simplifies navigation with on-screen self-prompting menus to guide users through its operating functions, and a built-in plotter to take the guesswork out of route planning.

Waypoints

One area which has seen the greatest change from receivers of the mid 1980's is the inclusion of more waypoints. Where ten, or even up to fifty waypoints used to be common, now one hundred seems to be the minimum and many manufacturers boast of units which can store two hundred or even 250 waypoints. Another trend is to provide the performance option of waypoint sequencing, i.e., the ability of the unit to switch automatically to the next waypoint once a waypoint is achieved. This function used to be found on only more expensive receivers, but today most manufacturers offer waypoint sequencing, sometimes with as many as up to forty waypoints.

A logical extension of waypoint sequencing is to organize waypoints into routes which can be called up and used repeatedly. The number of available routes has also increased, and with some receivers it is possible to have as many as nine different routes, each with twenty five waypoints in its memory.

Lat/Lon Readouts

In the early 1980's, just as Loran was beginning to "catch on" for the recreational user, most Loran receivers gave position only in the form of TDs. Lat/Lon readouts and were found in only top-of-the-line expensive receivers. This meant, of course, that position could be determined only through the use of specially prepared Loran charts which were printed with the TD overlay lines.

Today, virtually every Loran manufactured provides position readouts in Lat/Lon as well as TDs. In fact, the far majority of Loran skippers do all of their chart work in Lat/Lon on traditional charts. True, there are a few diehards who still work with only TDs, arguing their fixes are more accurate—which, depending on the receiver formula used for Lat/Lon conversion and the ability to correct for ASF, may prove them correct. However, TDs are still important for their usefulness when trouble shooting problems with Loran use.

Automatic Correction For ASF

A distinct trend in performance options has been the filtering down of functions which used to be available only with more expensive receivers to medium and even low price units. This has been especially true with the inclusion of automatic correction for land propagation errors or ASF. Now, most major brands of Loran receivers have the ability to correct for ASF in one form or another. However, it is important to note that not all receivers make this correction with the same degree of accuracy.

The secret again is in the programming of the software which, in recent years, price reduction has made accessible to even low priced receivers. The problem is to enter a mathematical model which contains the ASF corrections for each separate area-no small task. Some manufacturers have been very meticulous in the inclusion of highly complex models. Others have condensed the model by averaging or interpolating between readings—at a great reduction in production cost. While there is nothing wrong with this practice (in the majority of areas the corrections will be sufficient), it should be noted that even if a manufacturer advertises a unit with automatic ASF correction, there are differences between receivers in performing this function. Therefore, it is still prudent to periodically match up receiver position with a known position and in some instances override automatic ASF correction with manual input.

Interfacing With Other Instruments

By far the most exciting advances which are taking place in Loran technology are in the area of interfacing. Actually, interfacing with other instruments is not all that new and for years, the most common interfaces with Loran have been with autopilots and track plotters.

In order for a Loran receiver to be able to interface with another instrument it must have a special port, such as NMEA 81 or NMEA 83 built into the unit. In the early 1980's when interfacing first began to become popular, the marine industry came to the conclusion that if marine electronics made by different manufacturers were to be compatible, it was necessary to produce common serial ports. The letters "NMEA" stand for the National Marine Electronics Association. The numbers "80", "83" etc. refer to the year in which these ports were introduced.

Today, some of the most common interface combinations are to interface Loran with either radar or existing satellite systems. In the case of radar there are a number of manufacturers and different options to choose from. The most basic option is having the Loran information readout on the radar screen, an advantage which means there is only one screen to observe. Typical displayed information in addition to Loran position (both

Lat/Lon and TDs) is also ship's heading and speed over the ground all against the radar backdrop which shows ship's position in relation to surrounding land masses.

One of the more sophisticated integrated options with radar provides four different operating modes. In one of these it is possible to simply select a Loran waypoint by moving a cursor within the given radar range in use. The waypoint is then identified with a dotted circle along with a dotted course line from your position to the waypoint and a data readout of range and bearing. As the waypoint is approached and the ship's radar heading line and the cursor merge, there is an excellent graphic display of crosstrack error, all in relation to surrounding land masses.

Recent years have also seen the integration of Loran with satellite systems: Sat Nav and now GPS. From the beginning, the merging of Sat Nav and Loran made sense. Loran could be used to establish position between Sat. Nav fixes; the high degree of accuracy of a Sat Nav fix could be used to identify and measure a correction factor for Loran ASF. Today there are a number of manufacturers who offer the option of Sat Nav integration and in at least one instance it is possible to cross manufacturing lines: using the Loran from one manufacturer and the Sat Nav from another.

Because of the delays in the deployment of fully operational GPS, the early 1990's provided intermittent two dimensional position fixing for the maritime user. Thus, Loran enhancement between fixes became a viable option. At least a couple of manufacturers offered a GPS interface. One provided a triple combination of Loran/GPS/dead reckoning computer with the unit automatically choosing which mode provides the best fix.

One of the more interesting applications of integration is the combining of Loran with a fish finder. Once again, it is possible to have both systems in the same box or in separate integrated units. A favorite for fishermen, it shows position on the water and what is below at the same time. By using the present position function of recording waypoints, it is possible to geographically register where the fish are biting or where a promising bottom contour is found. Some self-contained units even come with an option of a flux gate compass sensor which allows use of the display as an accurate digital compass. Other units incorporate a track plotter which portrays a visual display of previous positions so that a return to a favorite "hot" spot is possible.

The culmination of integration is not just with one or two units but the merging of all ship's electronics into one integrated system. One innovative manufacturer provides separate modules of Loran, Sat Nav, radar, electronic flux gate compass and Loran controlled autopilot integrated into a single display on the radar screen. Everything is controlled by a single microprocessor and modular construction provides for a remote control keyboard and separate control panel. With an eye to the future, the system has been designed with four expansion slots to accommodate future capability with other electronic instrumentation. The beauty of this system is that it can be purchased as a complete package or as stand alone units which are added according to individual requirements.

Video Plotters/Electronic Charts

One of the hottest items with integration is the combining of Loran with electronic charts. Use of Loran with track plotters which record a ship's position in real time has been commonplace for many years. The ultimate extension of this is to superimpose Loran position on electronic charts as displayed on some kind of video plotter.

In a decided trend towards the end of the 1980's, most major Loran manufacturers either developed their own video plotters or contracted with other manufacturers to produce plotters that can be interfaced with their units. Basically, the technique involves digitizing navigational charts, projecting them on some form of display screen and then interfacing with Loran (Sat Nav or GPS) so the ship's position is pinpointed on the chart.

Depending on the manufacturer, the type of display unit varies. In some cases a self-contained dedicated unit is produced which involves no actual interfacing, but is a single unit housing both Loran and electronic chart functions. In others, the electronic chart system consisting of a display screen, program software and chart models is in a separate box which is then integrated with a Loran receiver in a similar manner to which Loran is integrated with radar. In a couple of instances the application program software and chart cartridges can be fed into a regular computer such as a Macintosh, IBM, or IBM compatible, which is then integrated with the Loran receiver. There are even a couple of systems which are designed to be used with a seven or nine inch color AC/DC television screen. Screen display varies from monochrome green, varying shades of monochrome gray to full color. Whichever method is used, the resulting effect is that navigational calculations and Loran functions are superimposed on the electronic chart display.

Probably one of the most important differences in various systems is in the resolution of chart graphics. Some systems have gone to great expense in digitizing actual NOAA charts, which display all marked navigation aids such as buoys, lights, depth lines and shore landmarks. Others have used the technique of interpolation so the electronic chart is just an approximation of the real thing. These charts still display position in graphic relation to surrounding land masses; however, the resolution when zooming down to large scale display is severely distorted as shorelines are represented as abrupt jagged lines which bear little resemblance to actual contours. The difference in system resolution is closely related to cost, with the higher technology tied to a higher price tag. Prices for electronic chart systems can range anywhere from $2,000 to five times that amount.

Depending on the system, charts are stored either on disk or individual cartridges, which can contain one or a given number of charts for a specific area. The number of individual charts per disk/cartridge varies depending on memory. Most systems come with one complimentary disk/cartridge for an area of choice. Additional disks/cartridges cost anywhere from just under $100 to approximately $300.

Functions include all the usual Loran functions that come with waypoint navigation, route planning etc., plus a number of extras. One of these is the extraordinary capability of changing the size of the chart/area displayed, or, in essence, the scale of the chart. Thus, it is possible to have a small scale view of a large area and then zoom in for precise navigation with a large scale blow-up of a particular sector. Each screen constantly updates all aspects of boat performance: SOG, COG, range, bearing etc., regardless of which scale is being used. Available ranges/scales vary with different systems. For example one offers scale functions from five to one hundred while another provides zooming capabilities from ½ to 4,000 nm.

One of the decided advantages of using Loran with electronic charts is that waypoints can be automatically downloaded to the Loran via a cursor using arrow keys or a trackball/mouse without entering any specific data. Another feature with some systems is that of authorship. In otherwords, if there should be an unmarked shoal or obstruction it can be entered onto the chart and it will be saved. Favorite anchorages, marinas, etc. can also be entered. A number of systems provide user friendly on-screen Help menus. One manufacturer even offers a computerized cruising guide which lists marinas, yacht clubs, fuel and repair facilities along with a data base with information on Rules of the Road, safety, and tides and currents. One advantage of displaying electronic charts with integrated computer systems is that, in some instances, a printer can even print individual charts, logs, way point rosters etc.

In this age of high technology, hardly a few months go by that there isn't some new electronic device or application to add to the navigational arsenal. The trends have been established, and as the last decade of this century is closed there will be more, better, smaller, and all for less.

New Loran Chains:
Closing the Mid-Continental Gap

Although the Loran system was primarily designed as a maritime navigation aid, the 1980's saw increased use of the system by the aviation community. A major impetus in this use occurred when the Federal Administration (FAA) made the decision to allow Loran-C as an authorized aid to enroute navigation and non-precision approaches. This means that pilots are now able to fly directly from one point to another and avoid flying along crowded air routes. In non-precision approaches, Loran-C use allows the pilot to fly within a minimum distance and altitude from a certified airport giving access to approximately 4,000 additional airports, access which usually would not be permitted in conditions of reduced visibility.

Unfortunately, because of the location of Loran stations to serve the maritime community, coverage has been limited to areas adjacent to the coastal waters of the United States and Canada. To meet the increased demand for Loran use within the interior of the country, in 1985 the FAA and the United States Coast Guard (USCC) signed an agreement to close this "mid-continental gap" between coverage by coastal chains and extend Loran coverage in the Central U.S.

The FAA provided $36.5 million from the National Airspace System Plan for the project, called the Mid-Continent Expansion Project (MEP). It also acquired the land for the new stations, while the Coast Guard was given the responsibility for the construction and operation of the new chains. By dual rating some of the stations in existing chains and adding just four new stations (two of which are also dual rated), two completely new chains have been added to the Loran system.

Previous stations which have been dual rated to accommodate the new chains are located at Raymondville, TX; Grangeville, LA; Searchlight, NV; Baudette, MN; and Williams Lake, B.C. The new stations are located at Havre, MT; Gillette, WY; Boise City,

OK; and Las Cruces, NM. All of the new stations, except Boise City, have solid state 400 kW transmitters: Boise City uses an 800 kW transmitter. They are each manned by a four or five person crew to maintain transmitting equipment, and are controlled by the remote operating system in an unattended mode. Under this system operational control and data transfer are accomplished remotely from the control site. The station at Malone, FL (master in Southeast US Chain/W secondary in Great Lakes Chain) is used to control all five secondaries in SOCUS. The station at Middletown, CA (X secondary in the US West Coast Chain) controls the three secondaries in NOCUS.

The new chains are called the North Central U.S. Chain (NOCUS) and the South Central U.S. Chain (SOCUS). The group repetition rates for these chains are 82,900 microseconds (GRI 8290) for NOCUS and 96,100 microseconds (GRI 9610) for SOCUS.

The NOCUS Chain became operational in late December 1990. It consists of a master and three secondaries. The master station is located at one of the new sites, Havre, MT. Of the three secondaries, the X secondary is also located at a new site, Gillette, WY. The remaining two secondaries have been dual rated from previous chains: the W secondary is at Baudette, MN which also serves as the Y secondary for the 8970 Great Lakes Chain; the Y secondary is at Williams Lake, B.C. which is also the master for the 5990 Canadian West Coast Chain. Monitor stations are located at Great Falls, MT; Grand Junction, CO; Bismark, ND and Whidbey Is, WA. (See figure I A.)

Coverage for the NOCUS Chain extends well into the heart of Canada, serving the lower latitudes of British Columbia, Alberta, Saskatchewan, and Manitoba. Coverage within the United States is provided for those states in the northwest and midwest sectors extending from Puget Sound in the West to Lake Superior in the East.

The SOCUS Chain became operational in April, 1991, and was dedicated on May 14, 1991. It bears special mention because it represents a milestone in Loran navigation by being the first chain to have five secondaries. Its master is one of the new stations located at Boise City, OK, which also doubles as a new Z secondary in the 8970 Great Lakes Chain. Two of the secondaries are also new stations: V at Gillette, WY, which is also the X secondary for NOCUS, and X, which is located at Las Cruces, NM. The

Figure I A
GRI 8290 NOCUS

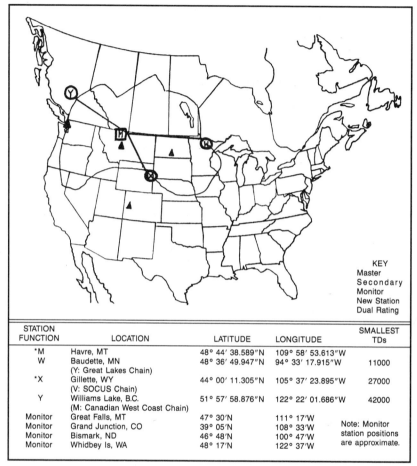

STATION FUNCTION	LOCATION	LATITUDE	LONGITUDE	SMALLEST TDs
*M	Havre, MT	48° 44′ 38.589″N	109° 58′ 53.613″W	
W	Baudette, MN (Y: Great Lakes Chain)	48° 36′ 49.947″N	94° 33′ 17.915″W	11000
*X	Gillette, WY (V: SOCUS Chain)	44° 00′ 11.305″N	105° 37′ 23.895″W	27000
Y	Williams Lake, B.C. (M: Canadian West Coast Chain)	51° 57′ 58.876″N	122° 22′ 01.686″W	42000
Monitor	Great Falls, MT	47° 30′N	111° 17′W	Note: Monitor station positions are approximate.
Monitor	Grand Junction, CO	39° 05′N	108° 33′W	
Monitor	Bismark, ND	46° 48′N	100° 47′W	
Monitor	Whidbey Is, WA	48° 17′N	122° 37′W	

remaining three stations have been dual rated from pre-existing chains: W at Searchlight, NV, which is also the Y secondary for the 9940 US West Coast Chain; Y at Ramondville, TX; and Z, which is located at Grangeville, LA. These last two stations also serve as the X and W secondaries respectively in the 7980 Southeast US Chain. Monitor stations are located at New Orleans, LA; Little Rock, AR; Midland, TX; Grand Junction, CO and Bismark, ND. (See Figure I B.)

Coverage is in the large central portion of the United States extending beyond Texas into Mexico and the Gulf of Mexico. Coverage has also been expanded in the Great Lakes Chain with the addition of the new Z secondary at Boise City, OK.

241

(See Figure I C.) Another part of the expansion project increased coverage of the Gulf of Alaska Chain by dual rating one of the stations (Port Clarence) in the North Pacific Chain. For the total picture of Loran-C coverage in the continental United States and Canada in the 1990's. (See figure I D..)

A big question now facing Loran users is whether their receivers will be able to pick up the transmissions from these new stations or not. Most manufacturers of Loran receivers are now including software to access these new stations and chains. Some of the more sophisticated receivers manufactured before 1991 have the memory and capability of having access information programmed into them either by the user or by the factory. Most

Figure I B
GRI 9610 SOCUS

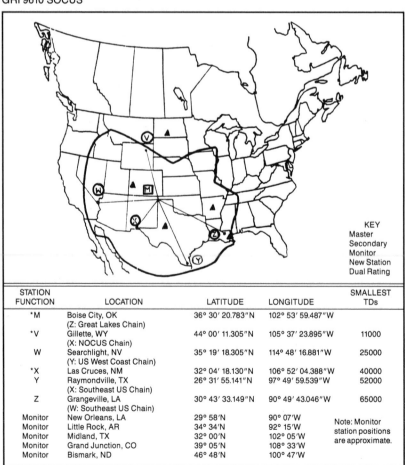

STATION FUNCTION	LOCATION	LATITUDE	LONGITUDE	SMALLEST TDs
*M	Boise City, OK (Z: Great Lakes Chain)	36° 30′ 20.783″N	102° 53′ 59.487″W	
*V	Gillette, WY (X: NOCUS Chain)	44° 00′ 11.305″N	105° 37′ 23.895″W	11000
W	Searchlight, NV (Y: US West Coast Chain)	35° 19′ 18.305″N	114° 48′ 16.881″W	25000
*X	Las Cruces, NM	32° 04′ 18.130″N	106° 52′ 04.388″W	40000
Y	Raymondville, TX (X: Southeast US Chain)	26° 31′ 55.141″N	97° 49′ 59.539″W	52000
Z	Grangeville, LA (W: Southeast US Chain)	30° 43′ 33.149″N	90° 49′ 43.046″W	65000
Monitor	New Orleans, LA	29° 58′N	90° 07′W	Note: Monitor station positions are approximate.
Monitor	Little Rock, AR	34° 34′N	92° 15′W	
Monitor	Midland, TX	32° 00′N	102° 05′W	
Monitor	Grand Junction, CO	39° 05′N	108° 33′W	
Monitor	Bismark, ND	46° 48′N	100° 47′W	

early models of receivers going back to the mid 1980's and earlier do not have this capability. Since this varies with the different models and manufacturers, the user's best recourse is to contact the specific manufacturer of his receiver.

Figure I C
GRI 8970 Great Lakes Chain (Expanded)

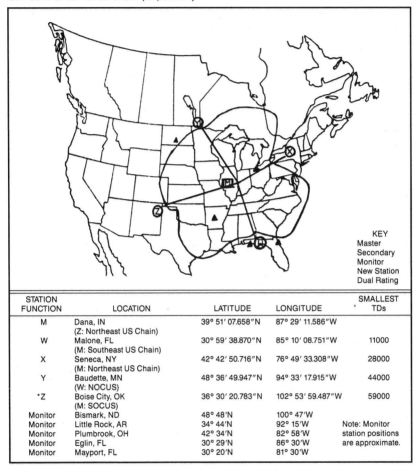

KEY
Master
Secondary
Monitor
New Station
Dual Rating

STATION FUNCTION	LOCATION	LATITUDE	LONGITUDE	SMALLEST ' TDs
M	Dana, IN (Z: Northeast US Chain)	39° 51' 07.658"N	87° 29' 11.586"W	
W	Malone, FL (M: Southeast US Chain)	30° 59' 38.870"N	85° 10' 08.751"W	11000
X	Seneca, NY (M: Northeast US Chain)	42° 42' 50.716"N	76° 49' 33.308"W	28000
Y	Baudette, MN (W: NOCUS)	48° 36' 49.947"N	94° 33' 17.915"W	44000
*Z	Boise City, OK (M: SOCUS)	36° 30' 20.783"N	102° 53' 59.487"W	59000
Monitor	Bismark, ND	48° 48'N	100° 47'W	
Monitor	Little Rock, AR	34° 44'N	92° 15'W	Note: Monitor
Monitor	Plumbrook, OH	42° 34'N	82° 58'W	station positions
Monitor	Eglin, FL	30° 29'N	86° 30'W	are approximate.
Monitor	Mayport, FL	30° 20'N	81° 30'W	

Figure I D
LORAN-C Coverage in the Contiguous US & Canada in the 1990s

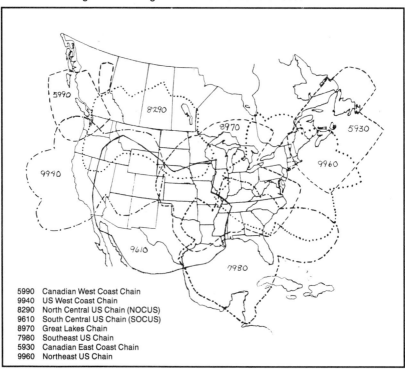

5990	Canadian West Coast Chain
9940	US West Coast Chain
8290	North Central US Chain (NOCUS)
9610	South Central US Chain (SOCUS)
8970	Great Lakes Chain
7980	Southeast US Chain
5930	Canadian East Coast Chain
9960	Northeast US Chain

Radionavigation:
A Look to the Future

Heading into the 1990's there is a bright new navigational star on the horizon. Hardly a month goes by without some new information about this new nav-aid appearing in the periodicals. With the inherent potential of pinpoint position fixing as never before possible, many are saying it will be the end all in radionavigation, making all other systems obsolete. This new navigational wonder, a satellite based system: NAVSTAR GPS.

Sat Nav

Actually, navigating with radio signals transmitted from satellites is not all that new. In the early 1960's, the U.S. Navy established the Transit system to help position its nuclear submarines. More commonly called Sat Nav, this system consists of a constellation of four or five satellites which circle the earth in the low (640 miles) polar orbits. The basic principle of the system is inherently different from Loran-C. With Loran, radio signals from three different stations (one master and two secondaries) are needed to establish a fix, whereas only one satellite is needed to establish a fix with Sat Nav.

The basic principle of Sat Nav is that a receiver determines range/distance from the satellite by measuring the change in signal frequency (Doppler Shift) in two minute intervals as the satellite moves in orbit towards or away from ship's position. At the same time, the satellite transmits messages of its exact position as a function of time. These two pieces of information, range and satellite position, produce an LOP for that two minute period. Subsequent time periods produce additional LOPs which are crossed to produce a very accurate fix.

One of the main disadvantages in using Sat Nav is that the system is not continuous. There are often long periods of time between satellite passes so that some means of continued navigation between fixes must be provided. Another disadvantage is the time element required to determine a satellite fix. A typical satellite pass may consist of a twelve to fifteen minute period during which five or six LOPs are determined. During this time, vessel speed and heading must be accurately entered into the receiver or proportionate errors will result. Because of these disadvantages, and the fact that Sat Nav produces only two-dimensional fixes, the military is putting all of its navigational eggs in the GPS basket.

GPS

GPS (Global Positioning System) evolved in the 1980's as the military's answer to a worldwide continuous positioning fixing system. Although use of Loran-C has been most eagerly embraced by the maritime; and now those in aviation communities, its main disadvantage is that it isn't worldwide and is limited to those areas where there are Loran stations. As a terrestrial based system, this means that there are large segments in the world, i.e. oceans, where there is no Loran coverage. Sat Nav satisfies the requirement for worldwide coverage, but falls short in that it can't deliver continuous coverage. GPS provides the best of both worlds.

GPS is a satellite based system which is designed to deliver highly accurate fixing, velocity and time information. It consists of a constellation of twenty one operational satellites and three orbiting spares which are placed in very high orbits (10,800 nm). GPS differs from Sat Nav in that more than one satellite is required to determine a fix: three satellites for two dimensional position fixing, and four satellites for three dimensional position fixing. It also differs from Sat Nav in that satellite range is determined by actual transmission time as opposed to measuring Doppler Shift. One similarity of the two systems is that exact satellite position must be known to determine a fix. In both cases this is periodically updated by computations from ground stations.

Although GPS will not become fully functional until all satellites are in position (approximately mid 1993), there is a great concern among users of other systems (Loran-C & Sat Nav) as to the future status of these systems. Federal agencies which are responsible for the development and maintenance of these federally funded systems are also taking a hard look at the future. Basically, these agencies are the Department of Defense (DOD) and the Department of Transportation (DOT).

The FRP

To address the concerns of overlap and redundancy of existing and future radionavigation systems, the DOD and DOT, in a joint effort, produced a Federal Radionavigation plan in 1980 which is updated biennially. Commonly called the FRP, the plan sets forth the support policy of federally funded radionavigation systems for the remainder of this century and into the early part of the next. A major goal of the plan is to select a mix of "common-use civil/military systems which meets diverse user requirements for accuracy, reliability, availability, integrity, coverage, operational utility, and cost; provides adequate capability for future growth; and eliminates unnecessary duplication of services".

The impetus for the development of the FRP has been the introduction of GPS, which is expected to have an impact on other radionavigation systems, at least in the light of military use. According to the FRP, the military requirement for other systems will be phased out as GPS becomes fully operational. This does not mean, however, that just because the military no longer has use for a system that it will be terminated. A good case in point is Loran-C. Although the military requirement for Loran-C will end December 31, 1994, the FRP states that "the Loran-C system serving the continental U.S., Alaska and coastal areas with the exception of Hawaii will remain part of the radionavigation mix into the next century".

The picture for Sat Nav is not nearly so bright. In fact it is clearly an interim system and the FRP bluntly states the "DOD requirement for Transit will terminate and system operation will be discontinued in December 1996". Actually this date has given Transit a few years of reprieve as it was originally scheduled to be shut down in 1992. This is because the Space Shuttle Disaster in January of 1986 set back the launch schedule of GPS satellites a number of years until an alternative deployment vehicle could be found. Interestingly, in the early 1990's Sat Nav coverage reached an all time high with thirteen satellites (seven operational and six spares) as all available satellites were deployed for the final years of system use.

The Future of Loran-C

Within the continental United States, Loran-C is alive and well, and its continued existence is assured well into the next century. A look to the development of two new mid-continental chains in the early 1990's and the increased use by the aviation community substantiates this fact.

Outside of the United States, the Coast Guard has already begun phasing out its operation and control of overseas stations. In many cases, control is being taken over by the host country so that system operation remains intact. A good example of this is the takeover of the old Commando Lion Chain by Korea. Likewise, there have been discussions between the US and Japan for the latter to assume similar operations in that country.

It is also important to note that in many areas of the world, countries are actually in the process of either expanding present Loran systems or implementing Loran as their official radionavigation system. For example, Canada is studying the prospect of expanding present coverage. It is also in the process of upgrading old tube transmitters to solid state units to increase signal availability. Mexican and South American governments, such as those serving Venezuela, Brazil and Chile, have entered into various degrees of dialogue aimed towards the implementation of Loran, especially in aviation enhancement programs.

In light of deteriorating DECCA stations, many European countries have been looking to expanding/establishing Loran as the navigational norm in European waters. For example, in 1990, the United Kingdom declared DECCA replacement by Loran-C. Pending negotiations, other European countries are expected to expand existing Loran coverage. Further to the east, India has decided to replace DECCA chains in certain key harbors with Loran and there is the possibility that Loran will be extended into Bangladesh.

GPS/Loran-C Interoperability

One of the most exciting possibilities for the future of radionavigation is the merging of GPS and Loran-C into an integrated hybrid system. In Public Law 100-223, the Secretary of Transportation has been directed to study the feasibility of the interchange of GPS and Loran-C data. Under this law, the FAA has also been directed to establish minimum standards for a sole means navigation system. Thus, much of the impetus for the possibility of an integrated system comes from the aviation community.

Use of the Loran-C in aviation has provided the advantage of non-precision approaches in virtually every airport in the US. Not only has this eased the demands on the current VOR/DME system, but Loran provides the ability to free pilots to fly to any point in the National Air Space as opposed to being limited to those airways between known VOR installations. However, use of Loran-C is not without its limitations. ASF errors, poor crossing angles in some ares, season change of signal strength/timing, sky-wave distortions, and possible station shutdown for repairs or failure, all contribute to the fact that Loran-C by itself is not relia- ble enough to meet sole means navigational criteria.

Although GPS is predicted to provide high reliability and availability, it too is not without its deficiencies. Any number of factors can affect accuracy of fixes: ionospheric error, clock bias between satellite and receiver clocks, incorrect satellite position input, receiver errors due to electrical noise, satellite shut-down/control by the government in times of national emergency. A very hot issue in the GPS community is the degradation of sys-tem potential accuracies through the implementation of Selec-tive Availability. With these types of errors, either natural or induced, GPS by itself may not meet requirements and lack value as a civilian sole means navigation utility.

A distinct answer to these problems of providing highly accurate position fixing capabilities to the non-military commu-nity may be in interoperable GPS/Loran-C navigation. In the early 1990's, there was at least one major manufacturer (Trimble) who put both systems in the same box.

There are a number of ways to utilize interoperable GPS/Loran-C, but two seem to stand out as having the greatest potential. One of these is to combine the pseudorange measure-ments of GPS and Loran so that a large number of range meas-urements are provided which will detect and cancel out errors from any source. The combination will probably provide enough reliable data in such a manner that could satisfy sole navigation means requirements.

The other possibility of integration is to use the Loran com-munications channel to broadcast GPS signal adjustments (differential GPS). Using Loran to communicate information has been done before and used by the Navy in such a manner for years. Problems with this concept involve addition of support facilities (ground monitors), addition of new communications network and questions about the ability of Loran to handle GPS data requirements.

A look to the mid-90's and beyond shows the potential users of GPS/Loran-C interoperability far exceed those of just the avia-tion and maritime communities. Emergency medical personnel, law enforcement officers, carriers of hazardous materials, wild-life management and forestry workers, truckers, taxi drivers and even the average driver will all have a use for the new utility. The applications are endless for anyone who requires reliable, efficient and precise position fixing.